LEARNING RESOURCES CENTER

MONTGOMERY COUNTY COMMUNITY COLLEGE

Cognitio Ad Futurum

1964

BLUE BELL, PENNSYLVANIA

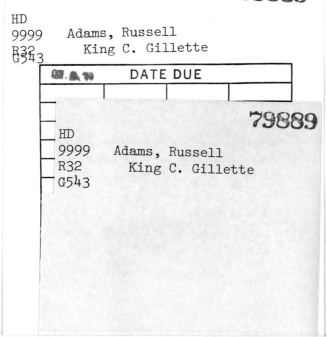

Also by Russell B. Adams, Jr.

The Boston Money Tree

King C. Gillette

King C Gillette

His favorite photograph, taken in 1907

King C. Gillette

The Man and His Wonderful Shaving Device

by Russell B. Adams, Jr.

Little, Brown and Company   *Boston*   *Toronto*

FIRST EDITION

T 11/78

The passage from *Babbitt* by Sinclair Lewis, appearing on page 113, is reprinted with the permission of Harcourt Brace Jovanovich, Incorporated.

Library of Congress Cataloging in Publication Data

Adams, Russell B.
  King C. Gillette, the man and his wonderful shaving device.

  Includes bibliographical references and index.
  1. Gillette, King Camp, 1855–1932. 2. Gillette Company—History. 3. Businessmen—United States—Biography. I. Title.
HD9999.R32G543   338.7′68′850924 [B]   78–15749
ISBN 0–316–00937–7

Designed by Chris Benders

Published simultaneously in Canada
by Little, Brown & Company (Canada) Limited

PRINTED IN THE UNITED STATES OF AMERICA

For my mother and father

Preface

THE GILLETTE COMPANY, beginning with the first safety razor with disposable blades, has been part of daily life in America and much of the rest of the world for more than three-quarters of a century. Are there any adults who do not know of Blue Blades, or who would fail to recognize the face and signature of King C. Gillette? Is there anyone who has not heard of Right Guard, Toni, Foamy, Earth Born, or Paper Mate? Indeed, it is a tribute of sorts to the range and universality of the company's wares that some of them, marketed under different names, are bought and used by consumers who have little or no inkling of the Gillette connection.

Even among corporate giants, Gillette is a substantial company, employing some thirty-five thousand people — ten thousand of them in the United States. At the close of 1977 the Boston-based company posted annual sales of more than $1.5 billion, and its total assets came to $1.2 billion. On *Fortune*'s standard list of the five hundred largest American industrial corporations, Gillette ranked a comfortable enough 150.

Such eminence has not come by accident, nor has it come purely by shrewd and calculated design. Like nearly all institutions, Gillette has confronted setback and miscalculation along with triumph, but it has generally managed to rise above adversity and continue on its successful way. In times of rapid change Gillette has proved capable of change, too, and has prevailed perhaps as frequently as it has merely endured. Little more can be asked of any commercial enterprise.

And like a number of other institutions, Gillette is built around a dream spun in the mind of a single, determined individual, who in this case must surely rank among the most fascinating — and in the end, as one of the most enigmatic — figures to emerge from the social and industrial ferment of nineteenth-century America. This is his biography, and the story of the widely diversified international corporation that carries his name and remains grounded on ever more sophisticated versions of his original invention.

Without the complete cooperation of Gillette officials and the free access to company records that went with it, this book could not have been written. From the outset, however, those few Gillette executives directly concerned with the project agreed to impose no constraints on content, emphasis, or interpretation. At no time was this agreement breached, and greatly to the credit of Chairman Colman M. Mockler, Jr., retired Chairman Vincent C. Ziegler, and David A. Fausch, vice-president for corporate public relations, they believed their company strong enough to undergo the full and honest examination that the author and the publisher believe this book to be.

R.B.A., Jr.

Contents

Illustrations

Except as otherwise noted, all illustrations are courtesy of The Gillette Company.

King C. Gillette

1

I Have Got It

"Such a man does not enter upon a hopeless struggle"

WALKING THE NARROW, sweeping ribbon of Nantasket Beach in the summer of 1895, King Camp Gillette had every reason to believe he was about to begin the realization of his life's mission, one that would forever mark him as a great benefactor of mankind. It was, perhaps, a quixotic ambition for a forty-year-old traveling salesman and amateur inventor who was supporting his wife and young son on a salary of $2,000 a year, but Gillette had set lofty goals for himself, goals beyond the imaginings of most men. His aim, in fact, was nothing less than a lasting cure for the social and economic ills of his age, the achievement of earthly paradise.

Now, almost miraculously, his bold vision seemed clearly in view. In New York and Boston and Baltimore, in Los Angeles and San Francisco and Seattle, and in the great midwestern cities in between, small but determined groups of men and women were gathering to discuss Gillette's plan for a new social order that would fulfill man's ancient yearnings for utopia. Gillette, awaiting the inevitable sum-

mons to leadership from his growing ranks of followers, had come
with his family to the small summer resort of Kenberma, on a penin-
sula just south of Boston. The man of destiny, hailed by one of his
disciples as an American Bismarck, would need to be well rested
before assuming the awesome duties that surely lay ahead.

Gillette's rapid rise from relative obscurity had begun quietly
enough, with the appearance in late 1894 of a book which he
called *The Human Drift*. Grandly dedicated "to all mankind," this
manifesto explained Gillette's theory that competition, the very cor-
nerstone of the American way of life, is in fact the source of all evils.
Get rid of grasping competition, Gillette said, and injustice, poverty,
and crime will wither away, allowing humanity to move joyfully into
a sunlit state of permanent grace from which no fall is possible.

Such thoughts were common enough coinage among the hardy
bands of populists, socialists, communists, and utopian reformers that
flourished in the latter days of the nineteenth century, but Gillette
had taken them a step further and conceived what he saw as a practical solution "whereby the people might gradually absorb and eventually come into complete possession of the world and its wealth."
Outlined in painstaking detail, his plan called for a giant corporation,
owned by the people as stockholders, which would in time acquire
the assets of all the industries of the world. Such popular ownership,
he reasoned, would eradicate competition of any kind, and men and
women would then be free to devote their lives — save for a five-year
period when they would gladly labor for the commonweal — to the
pursuit of culture, leisure, and the arts. In the United States, at least,
this idyll would take place in a gargantuan city where upwards of
sixty million people would live in row after row of glass-domed,
circular apartment towers. All in the name of efficiency, this metropolis would be located near Niagara Falls, whose waters would be
harnessed to produce electrical power for the vast industries required
to support the huge population center.

Like all messianic thinkers, Gillette was utterly convinced that an
eager and grateful world would, on first hearing, embrace the universal truths he believed he had discovered. For the time was nigh: "We
are rapidly nearing the most critical period in the history of this
country," Gillette wrote, adding that the next twenty years would
witness either disaster or the triumph of reason. But even Gillette,

secure in his righteousness, was probably not prepared for the reception granted his book by the influential (in zanier radical-reformist quarters, at least) weekly magazine *Twentieth Century*, which waged a tireless campaign against wealth and privilege and called for public ownership of all major industries. "Our postal service," wrote one contributor, "is a standing illustration of the economy and efficiency with which the people, even under adverse circumstances, can conduct a great enterprise."

Quite simply, the editors of *Twentieth Century* believed that *The Human Drift* was the most important book of the decade, if not of the entire century. By March, just four months after its publication, the book was advertised in a five-volume combination package that included George Bernard Shaw's *Fabian Essays*, Edward Bellamy's already-classic *Looking Backward*, and works of the less remembered reformers Ignatius Donnelly and Laurence Gronlund. Then in April, *Twentieth Century* announced that it had gone beyond mere propagandizing for Gillette's cause and had actually formed a company that would be the nucleus of the all-embracing corporation described in *The Human Drift*. Called the Twentieth Century Company, its president was none other than King C. Gillette, and readers were urged to buy stock at five dollars per share. When all was in readiness, they were told, when an initial seed capital of $30,000 had been raised, Gillette would be prepared to "devote all his time and best efforts" to the affairs of this nascent world concern.

Meanwhile, some members of the radical community were distressed that the normally cynical editors of *Twentieth Century* had put so much trust in Gillette. Who is this King C. Gillette, anyway, they asked, and why should self-respecting radicals believe in him and his scheme? Indeed, the editors replied, it was more their wont to embrace principles rather than men, and "there must be some extraordinary reason why people so little given to hero worship as we are, should say to any man, 'Do thou lead and we will gladly follow.' " The answer, they said, could be found in Gillette himself, described as being "in the prime of his manhood. He is of commanding appearance, standing fully six feet high, and would attract attention anywhere. A man of affairs, always accustomed to deal with large business interests, his success as a leader of an industrial movement would not be questioned by anyone who had ever met him. . . .

Prudence, tact, foresight and a clear understanding of the situation are all qualities that he possesses, but such a man does not enter upon a hopeless struggle. We need him, and need him badly, but it is for you to say how soon we shall have him." The message was clear: here was a man well fitted for greatness, if only reformers would produce the funds to get his enterprise under way.

Such was the high praise running through Gillette's mind as he walked the beach at Kenberma that summer, but something else was on his mind, too, something far less cosmic but no less pressing to a man of his temperament. For even as Twentieth Century clubs from coast to coast were poring over *The Human Drift* and subjecting it to doting exegesis, even as he was being sung in some circles as the greatest social thinker of the age, King C. Gillette had come up with yet another idea. One early spring morning while in the midst of shaving, his face well slathered with warm soap, he had conceived the disposable razor blade.

"I can set my own razor and shave myself perfectly well"

History does not tell us when men first began to shave. But it is likely that facial hair has been removed in one way or another for at least as long as man imposed upon man to create the inequities that galvanized King C. Gillette into action as a social reformer. Prehistoric cave drawings frequently depict men who, if not clean-shaven by modern standards, are clearly beardless, their whiskers most probably scraped away with clamshells or sharpened animal teeth. Later, as primitive man learned to put an edge on flint implements, flint became the preferred means of whisker removal, though the common practice of stretching a beard across a log and then hacking it off with a flint ax does not seem like much of an advance over scraping the face with a well-honed wolf's fang. In time, flint technology advanced to a point where it was possible to fashion a serviceable razor from the stone, though it is certain that no one used such an implement every day — the face would have needed some time to heal before the next operation.

It may well be asked just why prehistoric man went to any great and painful lengths to remove hair from his face. Indeed, the same question might be asked of men in any age, as George Bernard Shaw can attest. "I was about five at the time," said Shaw, "and I was standing at my father's knees whilst he was shaving. I said to him, 'Daddy, why do you shave?' He looked at me in silence, for a full minute, before throwing the razor out of the window, saying, 'Why the hell do I?' He never did again." In any event, it is not known what motivated the earliest scrapers and shavers. In the absence of mirrors or even of any clearly defined standards of beauty, mere vanity can probably be ruled out. It may be that beards, to the extent that they appeared as men grew older, were associated with aging and death, and were removed as a talisman against mortality. Or perhaps ill-kempt beards simply got in the way when the wearer was drinking and eating, or provided a bothersome nesting place for vermin. Barring some great anthropological breakthrough, we will probably never learn what drove our first human forebears to do away with their beards.

We know a bit more about the shaving customs of ancient Egyptians and other inhabitants of their fertile quarter of the world. In the earliest known Egyptian dynasties, some seven thousand years ago, men shaved both their faces and their heads, probably with flint razors. The reason was practical enough in those times of no-holds-barred, close-in combat: a smooth head and face deprived an enemy of a handhold to grip while gouging at his victim with a jagged dagger or hacking him with an ax. To be spared such a fate, thoughtful males of the time would gladly submit to close shaves with even the crudest flint razor, just so long as it was wielded by a friend. Later, as Egyptians mastered the art of metal smelting, copper razors were widely used, replaced in time with even keener bronze blades that were occasionally entombed with their owners. These razors were of three basic types, none bearing much resemblance to their latter-day counterparts. One was shaped like a broad, curving knife blade, not unlike a crescent; another had the appearance (and the basic shaving characteristics, no doubt) of a hatchet or meat cleaver. What was probably the most sophisticated model featured a circular blade held by a handle extending at right angles from the center.

Other early civilizations, too, produced razors of various types. At Knossos, on Crete, archaeologists have unearthed long-bladed razors similar in shape to the familiar straight razor still favored by modern barbers, and in both Crete and Italy, a tongue-shaped blade was widely used about 1200 B.C. Digs in Germany and Sicily have yielded blades that seem to have been equipped with sheathlike handles into which the blade could be folded for safe storage. And by the time iron appeared on the metal-working scene, it was possible to fashion blades that did their work considerably more efficiently than their predecessors of copper and bronze, not to mention flint.

The steady advance of civilization altered men's attitudes toward beards just as surely as it changed the implements used to remove or groom them. As random passages of arms became less frequent, it was feasible to cultivate facial hair rather than merely cut it off for safety's sake. In some cultures the full beard was a sign of masculinity, as well as a handy way to separate men from mere boys, and, at a distance, from women. The ancient Assyrians pictured their gods with beards cut squarely at the end, a style that was emulated by high-society citizens. Babylonians made much of their luxurious full beards, and considered no oath binding unless sworn on the whiskers; among Egyptians, the smooth face remained a badge of high caste, but pharaohs occasionally affected godlike airs by strapping artificial beards of gold or silver wire on their chins. Even Egyptian queens sometimes resorted to this divinely inspired device.

The Greeks and the Romans wore beards through much of their early history, believing them to be marks of wisdom as well as of maturity. But Alexander the Great put an end to his own beard wearing in the fourth century B.C., and all but the most stubborn Greek philosophers soon followed suit. Some said that Alexander removed his beard to better display his handsome profile, but he himself explained that it was to set an example for his soldiers, whose faces he ordered smoothed to deny enemies a deadly grip in battle. Inspired by the victorious Greeks' example, Syrians and Persians were not long in taking off their own beards, perhaps in the hope that this would change their fortunes in war.

The earliest Romans prized their beards as tokens of manhood and well-being, but by about 300 B.C. they were doing as the Greeks did and were shaving themselves. According to Pliny the Elder it was not until around 200 B.C. that Rome got its first daily shaver in the person of Scipio Africanus (his other claim to fame was that he conquered Hannibal). As shaving spread throughout Rome and the empire, beards became the mark of slaves, servants, and barbarians, and Roman officers frequently took along their favorite barbers to keep their jowls smoothed during campaigns in the distant provinces. Finally, in the second century A.D., beards made something of a comeback when the emperor Hadrian grew one to mask battle scars and an unsightly wart. Lesser mortals seeking to curry imperial favor followed Hadrian's lead, and it presumably became somewhat more difficult to distinguish noble Romans from the raffish barbarians who were sweeping down from northern Europe. Even at that, clean cheeks were still more common than beards, and it was not until the collapse of Rome that beard wearing spread throughout the Western world. The hirsute Franks, Goths, and Vandals, after all, had overrun once-mighty but generally beardless Rome, a fact which many must have seen as evidence of the beard's moral superiority.

For the next several centuries, most men remained bearded, possibly because they had at last decided that vanity and fashion were foolish reasons to submit to the crude shaving implements of the day. Later, as crusaders marched off to free the Holy Land from the cursed infidels, medieval metallurgists greatly improved the quality of steel available for armaments, and these higher-grade alloys soon found their way into razors as well as broadswords. Keener edges made shaving relatively more comfortable, and thus more popular; the smooth-cheeked swain became the beau ideal of ballad and story. Beards still had their day, however, and were frequently ushered both in and out of fashion by pace-setting kings whose subjects were eager to ape the royal example. Early in the sixteenth century, Francis I of France sprouted whiskers while recuperating from a head wound; not to be outdone by his Continental rival, Henry VIII of England did likewise, and beards were soon *de rigueur* for the well-turned-out Frenchman or Briton.

Elizabethan gallants carried beard wearing to absurd extremes, sometimes dyeing, starching, and curling their whiskers into such fanciful shapes that special boxes were designed for keeping the beards unruffled while their owners slept. But this was the beard's last great fling for some time to come, and with the introduction in the seventeenth century of voluminous wigs for men, competitive arrays of facial hair dwindled and then disappeared. By 1661, Thomas Fuller was describing beards as "ornamental excrement," hardly the sort of thing to be sported by a respectable man — though a discreet Vandyke or a slim mustache was still within fashionable bounds.

With the demise of the beard came the rise of the razor, if not of the daily shave. For even during the heydays of beardlessness, few men had followed the lead of Scipio Africanus and submitted to the daily services of a barber. In the smoothest-cheeked times of the Middle Ages, a man was considered well groomed if he shaved twice a week; when an Elizabethan edict barred beards on law students at Lincoln's Inn in London, a beard was defined as more than a fortnight's growth. Five o'clock shadow was a curse yet undreamed of, and most men agreed with the old Russian proverb "It is easier to bear a child once a year than to shave every day."

Another proverb, variants of which were current in nearly every nation of Europe, had it that "barbers learn to shave by shaving fools." And customers of even the most accomplished barbers must have had a pronounced streak of foolhardiness or masochism to put up with the bloodletting that so often attended barbershop shaves of the seventeenth and eighteenth centuries. The alternative, of course, was self-shaving, and those who mastered the art could count it as a signal blessing that they were able to avoid the ministrations of their neighborhood barber. Others, not quite so skillful, tried alternate means. Samuel Pepys, for one, found it "very easy, speedy, and cleanly" to remove his beard by rubbing it away with a pumice stone, the same technique that had been used centuries before by Roman legionaries. This must have required a certain amount of fortitude, a quality in which Pepys was surely not lacking — he thought nothing of quaffing a breakfast of hot beer laced with wormwood.

In time, Pepys abandoned pumice and learned the intricacies of the straight razor, an accomplishment that pleased him mightily for its saving of both time and money, not to mention blood. It was a comfortable feeling to be freshly shaved, Pepys found, noting on one occasion after shearing off a week's worth of stubble: "Lord! how ugly I was yesterday and how fine today." Another time, planning to work at home, Pepys went down to his study unshaven, but soon found that "without being shaved I am not fully awake nor ready to settle to business." This was, perhaps, one of the first recorded testimonials for the daily shave.

In America, Benjamin Franklin was a notable self-shaver — none of the signers of the Declaration of Independence wore beards, by the way — and once wrote: "I reckon it among my felicities that I can set my own razor and shave myself perfectly well: in which I have a daily pleasure, and avoid the uneasiness one is sometimes obliged to suffer from the dirty fingers or bad breath of a slovenly barber." Indeed, it was felicitous to shave oneself, though the more patrician George Washington was kept clean-shaven by a servant who was presumably more kempt than the average barber of the time.

The eighteenth century was the most beardless era in the history of Western man, but such fashion is nothing if not changeable. With the passage of the stylized wig — it had at last been deemed a bit of French frippery — men were once more wearing their own shorter hair and finding that a bit of a mustache or beard added character to the male face. Slowly at first, then with increasing speed, men happily put aside their razors and began sprouting luxuriant growths of whiskers. In the United States, at least, this trend was ratified when President-elect Abraham Lincoln began cultivating the famous beard that would make him the first — though surely not the last — bewhiskered occupant of the White House. Beards became even more popular during the Civil War, when officers and men alike found it more comfortable to grow beards than to shave under field conditions. ("Come out o' that bunch o' ha'r! I know you're in thar! I can see your ears a-workin'!" said Southern soldiers to newly bearded comrades.) By the end of the war — which was both won and lost by bearded commanders — men sported bewildering bristles of mustaches, beards, goatees, and side-whiskers of every description. A fashion analyst of the day would have had ample reason to surmise that the beard had made a long-lasting comeback from more than a century and a half of eclipse.

It would have been a bad guess. After about a score of years when a clean-shaven man seemed almost an oddity, beards slowly fell out of favor. No one really knows why — it just seems to have been one of those mysterious vagaries of fashion, an inexplicable tide in the affairs of men. Not that beards were no longer worn. Far from it. Older men, particularly those who had sprouted martial whiskers during Civil War service, frequently maintained these grizzling remnants of dashing youth. But younger men, possibly out of rebellion against their elders, shied away from beards. As callow youths they might raise a few chin whiskers, just to assure the world and themselves that they had it in them to do so, but with maturity they chose to remain relatively clean-shaven, or at most to hold their facial adornment to a tasteful mustache. By the early 1880's, and certainly by 1890, the majority of American men were beardless, though daily shaving was still an elusive ideal. Indeed, many men who might have wanted to indulge in a daily shave were prevented from doing so because of the expense involved in having a barber perform the task, and because shaving at home remained almost as onerous as it had been throughout history.

For the nineteenth century, despite its momentous strides in transportation, communications, and manufacturing, had not yet been able to produce a razor that was much different from the earliest Bronze Age models. True enough, the steel forged in the great razor and cutlery towns of Sheffield, England, and Solingen, Germany — which together supplied most of the world's razors — was many cuts above the copper and bronze smelted in antiquity, and a marked improvement over the medieval armorers' finest steel. But the blades remained basically the same, and so did the method of application. After lathering up his face to moisten the whiskers and make them softer and easier to cut, the user put a highly sharpened two- or three-inch blade to his face — he hoped at a not too rakish angle — and proceeded to scrape away his growth of beard. Even in the steadiest of hands, it was a problematic job; for the clumsy, shaving became a fearful business, and it is small wonder that those who lacked the skill for self-shaving or the cash for barbering would generally shave only twice a week or so.

Numerous attempts had been made to improve upon the traditional straight razor. As early as 1762, a French cutler devised a protective guard for clamping over a conventional razor; theoretically, this would prevent major gashes, though enough of the blade was left exposed so that the careless or inept shaver could still break considerable skin. Similar devices followed in the early nineteenth century, but they all suffered from this same deficiency. Later, so-called safety razors — little more, really, than short sections of a conventional straight razor blade clamped or clipped, hoelike, to a handle — appeared, often to the hosannas of grateful users. One satisfied customer was Oliver Wendell Holmes, who tried out a Star safety razor (patented in 1876 by the brothers Frederick and Otto Kampfe of Brooklyn, New York) on a trip to Europe in 1886. Shaving, he noted later, is never a delightful process, and it is an even more unpleasant duty on shipboard. But with his safety razor, Holmes said, shaving "could be performed with almost reckless boldness, as one cannot cut himself, and in fact had become a pleasant amusement instead of an irksome task."

The *Scientific American*, commenting in 1893 on the "well-known" Fox safety razor, was a bit more guarded in its praise, claiming only that "it is an exceedingly rare thing for one to cut one's self while shaving" with it. Perhaps so, but one surely risked nicking oneself when removing the blade from its handle, placing it into a special patented holder, and then moving it rapidly back and forth on a heavy leather strop before inserting it once more in the ready-to-shave position. For the cutting edges of these earliest safety razors required the same meticulous care and treatment demanded by straight razors, those forbidding instruments that were not infrequently handed down from father to son. The blades needed stropping before each use, and in time they required expert honing in the hands of a cutler. These new implements were, in short, merely slight variations on the straight-razor theme, and the user paid in time and aggravation for their somewhat dubious safety features. Nor were the blades particularly economical.

Like the Fox, the Star brand featured a patented stropping device for keeping its dollar-apiece blades in trim before disposal or between trips to the grinding wheel. Like the Fox, too, the Star had its relatively small corps of faithful and satisfied users — most shavers, from habit or a disinclination to fiddle with the smaller safety-razor blades, stuck with the old tried-if-not-true straight razor — but the traveling salesman–inventor–social reformer King C. Gillette was not among them. As curious about new mechanical devices as he was about economic affairs, Gillette had tried the Star and found it wanting. And just as he had determined to reshape the way men lived in relation to property and to each other, he set out also on a less ambitious mission to revolutionize the way men shaved.

It was almost as if Karl Marx had paused between *The Communist Manifesto* and *Das Kapital* to develop a dissolving toothbrush or a collapsible comb — but then, Gillette had a far more pragmatic imagination than Marx, and was able at one and the same time to entertain visions of communism and to practice the despised antithesis of competitive capitalism. Years later, he would explain this apparent contradiction by observing that one must take the world as it is, even while plumping for sweeping alteration. "The man who," he said, "under our present system, did not invest his capital to yield him a secure and comfortable income, would be a fool indeed." And King Camp Gillette was far too much the quintessentially practical American idealist to let himself be taken for a fool.

"But how many things are there like corks, pins, and needles?"

Chicago in the 1860's was already Carl Sandburg's brash and brawling hog butcher, toolmaker, wheat emporium, and national freight handler. Hallmarked by towering grain elevators and sprawling stockyards, served by fifteen railroads that made it the central marketplace of the entire Middle West, it typified the expansive spirit of nineteenth-century industrial America. Chicago's byword was efficiency, and its pork packers often bragged that they found some use for every part of a pig but the squeal.

King C. Gillette arrived at this great temple of untrammeled free enterprise at the impressionable age of four, when his father, George Wolcott Gillette — a sometime postmaster, weekly-newspaper editor, and inventive tinkerer — moved with his wife and children to Chicago from Fond du Lac, Wisconsin, where young King was born on January 5, 1855. His royal first name honored a Judge King who was a friend of George Gillette's.

The Gillette family could trace its American origins to Nathan Gillet, one of two brothers who arrived in Massachusetts on board the ship *Mary and John* in 1630. These Gillets were sons of the Reverend William Gillet (sometimes spelled Gylet) of Chaffcombe, Somerset, England, whose French Huguenot forebears had apparently fled to Britain from their native Bergerac, in the ancient southern duchy of Guienne, not long after the great massacre of Saint Bartholomew's Day in 1572. As late as 1851, when he bought the small house in Fond du Lac where King Gillette was born, George Gillette was still spelling his name Gillet; he turned to the more familiar form not long afterward, as had numerous other descendants of the prolific *Mary and John* Gillets.

King Camp Gillette's mother, the former Fanny Lemira Camp, also sprang from early Colonial stock, and the pre-Revolutionary Camp house still stands in Salisbury, Connecticut. Members of both families had moved steadily to the West, where Fanny Camp distinguished herself early by being the first white child born in Ann Arbor, Michigan. It had been at nearby Marshall that she met and married George Gillette, not long after her graduation from Albion Seminary.

Possibly because of a serene and even disposition, Fanny Camp Gillette was to enjoy a prolonged and vital old age — during much of which she was known respectfully as Madame Gillette — and died at the age of ninety-eight. According to her youngest and sole surviving child, King, she often used to say that "if she had her life to live over again, she would ask for little change." He would also say that he never knew her to speak a cross word or to say anything unkind. Even so, Madame Gillette was a stern disciplinarian, always in control of her household, and if she could often find excuses for mistakes made by others, she looked for near perfection from her own offspring. It was probably under her influence that King Gillette developed his lifelong belief in efficiency, and his hatred for wasting time.

With his older brothers, George and Mott, King attended public schools in Chicago through the 1860's, while their father worked as a patent agent, promoted a new kind of shingle-making machine, and launched a couple of wholesale hardware businesses. Lest they be idle, the Gillette boys were encouraged to work with their hands, to figure out how things work and how they might be made to work better. It was a busy, self-sufficient family, described later by King Gillette as "knit together by close bonds of affection and mutual interest." Indeed, the Gillettes were so independent and self-sufficient that it would become a durable family trait seldom to socialize, almost never to give parties except for close kinfolk. More than a century later, Mott Gillette's son George would observe of his grandparents' household that "they would gather in the sitting room and talk about old times and themselves."

Sometimes, too, they would talk about Mrs. Gillette's pet project, which she managed to pursue even with three sons and two daughters to raise. Brought up in easy circumstances despite frontier beginnings — her father had been a hotelkeeper, and the Camp family lived in the hotel — she had been surprised and embarrassed after her marriage to find how ignorant she was of even routine cooking and domestic chores. To spare other women the same plight, she began collecting and compiling recipes and household hints, with the idea that she might put them all together in a book someday. She would test each recipe on her own family, and afterward they would discuss the dish and then vote on whether it should appear in the projected cookbook. Willing to try anything, she once prepared a dinner of rattlesnake meat; almost unanimously, the Gillettes cast their ballots against its inclusion.

The Gillette family's mechanical and stove-top experiments aside, it was a heady decade in Chicago. There was the excitement of the Civil War years, there was the growth of great new industries and the rise toward fortune and almost universal fame of men with names like McCormick, Pullman, and Armour. There was the emergence, too, of a strong labor-union movement, spurred in part by the immigration to Chicago of European-born workers with radical notions about the relationship between labor and capital. Strikers — and strikebreakers — were seen frequently on the streets, and newspapers were filled with reports of labor strife. Other staple items in the press of the day included tales of rising crime rates and of the poverty that seemed always to come in the train of industrialization, and of men who stood above it all, the grain speculators who made fortunes by manipulating wheat prices and driving up the cost of bread. In retaliation, many workers set up cooperative enterprises, most of them for distribution of goods, but some for actual production. Chicago was a great manufacturing center, but it was also a center of radical political activity — by 1870, it ranked second only to New York as a hotbed of American socialism.

Much of Chicago was swept away by the disastrous fire of October, 1871, which ravaged some 2,100 acres, killed nearly 300 people, and destroyed 17,500 of the city's largely wooden buildings. Most telling of all for a commercial and industrial center, the flames wiped out property worth some $200 million. One of the losers — nearly all he had was swept away — was George W. Gillette, and though Chicago's leaders vowed that a new and greater metropolis would soon rise from the ashes of the old, Gillette eventually decided to pull up stakes and move once more to a city of greater opportunity. He did not, however, choose the burgeoning West; instead he packed himself and his family off to New York, where he set up with his two oldest sons in the hardware-supply business. Seventeen-year-old King, meanwhile, had gone into the same line of work, but on his own. With an independence of spirit that he would display through most of his life, he took a job clerking for the wholesale hardware house of Seeberger & Breakey in Chicago. With two years of experience under his belt, he signed on in a similar spot with a New York company, then job-hopped again, this time to a Kansas City firm that promoted him, at the age of twenty-one, to traveling salesman. He was now a private in that great army of drummers who traveled their territories by rail, in Pullmans when they were prosperous, by coach when times were hard.

But there was something that set Gillette apart from his fellow travelers. He didn't sell hardware just to make a living — he genuinely enjoyed tinkering with metal products, and soon had some patents to prove it. In 1879 he patented a combination bushing and valve for water taps, and four years later took out a patent for a much refined version of the device, setting up with his brother George a short-lived Gillette Tap Valve & Faucet Company to exploit it. In early 1889, he and George were granted patents for two types of conduits for electrical cables. But none of these could really be called a major invention, and Gillette gained little profit from them. Much later, he would say of his early inventions that they "made money for others, but seldom for myself, for I was unfortunately situated not having much time and little money with which to promote my inventions or place them on the market." In short, he had to work for a living, and was always on the go, rattling from city to city peddling his various wares.

Apparently, Gillette was a star salesman, several cuts above the crowd. In the late 1880's, the firm of Enoch Morgan had enough faith in him to send him to London to sell the popular household scouring powder Sapolio, whose talented advertising manager, Artemas Ward (no kin to the humorist of similar name), had made the product a household word. From Ward, Gillette learned much about the value of continuous, hard-hitting advertising, and years later, after a complacent Sapolio had been outadvertised by the rival Bon Ami, Gillette would observe knowingly to an associate that "Sapolio is as dead as a salt mackerel."

His London-Sapolio sojourn ended, Gillette returned to the United States in 1889, and the following year married Atlanta Ella Gaines, called Lantie, the daughter of a prosperous Ohio oilman. In 1891 he joined the Baltimore Seal Company as sales representative in New York and New England. His wife was pregnant now with their first — and only — child, and it was time to start thinking of settling down and spending more time at home. Even so, Gillette was on the road a good deal, and went frequently to company headquarters. When he did so, instead of putting up at a hotel he stayed with the president, William Painter, either in town or at Painter's summer place in nearby Pikesville.

Like Gillette, Painter was an inventor; unlike Gillette, he had made money from his inventions, one of which was a soft-rubber valve that had made it possible to use pumping equipment to empty urban cesspools and privy pits in the days before widespread sewerage. Baltimore Seal's major product was a rubber stopper, extracted with a metal loop, that was widely used by brewers and soft-drink bottlers. Not long after Gillette went with the company, Painter developed an improved stopper consisting of a cork-lined tin cap that was crimped tightly over a bottle top. It did so well that Baltimore Seal changed its name to Crown Cork & Seal Company, and Painter's invention was soon standard throughout the bottling industry. In a single year, it brought the inventor more than $350,000 in royalties.

As kindred inventive spirits, Gillette and Painter struck up a close personal as well as business relationship, and their conversations frequently turned to the development of useful and novel products. Salesman that he was, Gillette could talk a good game, but it was Painter, the proven and prosperous innovator, who spoke from really hard experience. And one day, he said something that would always stick in Gillette's mind.

"King," said Painter, "you are always thinking and inventing something. Why don't you try to think of something like the Crown Cork which, when once used, is thrown away, and the customer keeps coming back for more — and with every additional customer you get, you are building a foundation of profit." It was easy enough to dispense such advice, Gillette replied, "but how many things are there like corks, pins, and needles?" Painter looked at Gillette thoughtfully. "You don't know," he said. "It is not probable that you ever will find anything that is like the Crown Cork, but it won't do any harm to think about it."

Gillette did think about it. Indeed, he confessed later that Painter's words became an obsession with him, though he was at the same time obsessed with more than mere mechanical invention.

"One corporate body, with one corporate brain"

Saint Paul saw the light on the road to Damascus; King Camp Gillette's glittering vision had come in a Scranton, Pennsylvania, hotel room not long after his return from London. It was a dreary, blustery morning, and rain fell in such torrents that even the conscientious Gillette decided to stay in and skip his sales calls. As he sat at the window watching the passing scene, he noted the growing confusion of streetcars, wagons, and water-logged pedestrians stalled by a disabled grocery wagon. Never given to idle observation, Gillette began mulling over ways that such bedlam might be avoided, and as he described it later, he "became absorbed, oblivious to my surroundings and weather conditions." In quick succession, he imagined all the ultimate destinations of the foodstuffs borne by the broken wagon, then backtracked to the sources of the goods, tracing spices to the Orient and coffee to the plantations of Brazil. Until that moment, he would recall, he had always looked upon the world's industries and their various instruments of production as separate entities, but now, inspired by that lowly grocery truck, "came the thought that is destined to change man's conception of industry — THE THOUGHT — *Industry as a whole is one vast operative mechanism. Included in it are the governments of every country, and our combined system of social, political and industrial economy.*"

Some men might have been satisfied to tuck such an insight away in the recesses of their minds with scarcely a second thought. Gillette, characteristically enough, was moved to action. Social and economic problems had interested him since his youthful days in Chicago, and having now visualized the whole world as a gigantic machine, he determined to become the master mechanic who would put the wheezingly inefficient works in proper running order. It was no small task since it involved, as he later said, "the displacement of governments and the amalgamation of all the people in the world into one corporate body, with one corporate brain." But first, the people would have to be shown the way to redemption, and the way to do that was with a book.

By modern standards, Gillette was not an educated man, though it is well to remember that a high school graduate of his time was in many respects as well educated as the average college graduate of a century later. But he was an avid reader, and was no doubt familiar with some of the socialist and populist journals that thrived in the last quarter of the nineteenth century. It is likely, too, that he had read much of the utopian literature of the period, including Edward Bellamy's *Looking Backward*, published just the year before Gillette's revelation in Scranton. In this imaginative novel, the hero wakens from a hypnotic sleep to find himself in the year 2000. The world as he knew it has been totally transformed — capitalism, competition, and war have been abolished, and with them have gone poverty, crime, injustice, and all the other assorted ills that plagued the nineteenth century and will in all probability continue into the twenty-first century as well.

Bellamy, like so many romantic utopians, had been long on descriptions of his perfect society, but short on explanations of how it came to be. No less a romantic, Gillette was also considerably more practical than the average visionary, and he determined that his book would be a step-by-step guide to a brave new world that others had merely dreamed of.

In deciding to become an author, Gillette may have been influenced by his mother's example. For she had at last, after some thirty-five years of collecting and testing recipes, put all her material into a book on which she collaborated with a former White House steward, Hugo Zieman. Called *The White House Cookbook*, it appeared in 1887, and was an instant best-seller (revised and updated, it has been reprinted several times, most recently in 1976). As was the mode in those days, the book contained tips on fashions and household chores along with directions for whipping up palatable meals; among other things, it advised that "the beard should be kept well trimmed and well combed." As for mustaches, "they should be neat and not overlarge. A mustache à l'Empereur is absurd and smacks of the fop." To help keep razors in good cutting trim, Madame Gillette suggested that shavers wet their heavy leather strops with a touch of sweet oil and then dust the surface lightly with flour of emery.

In any event, Gillette found time to put his plans on paper. By the summer of 1894 — much of which he spent with his family on the beach at Kenberma, where he shared a cottage with his good friend and bottle-cap customer Ward B. Holloway — he had finished his book, which he titled *The Human Drift* to underscore his belief that the natural human tendency is toward ever greater centralization. With a financial assist from Holloway, Gillette published his book in December, and arranged for national distribution through the Humboldt Publishing Company of New York, which just happened to be the publisher also of the populist *Twentieth Century*. Like his mother, Gillette was an author now — though of an entirely different kind — and he settled back to await public reaction to his work. Meanwhile, there were plenty of other things to occupy his thoughts.

"I have got it; our fortune is made"

Nearly a generation later, after his photograph and signature had been printed on so many hundreds of millions of razor-blade wrappers that much of the world took him for a mythical figure, the mere construct of artistic imagination, King C. Gillette graphically described the lightning flash of inspiration that illuminated his crowning invention. "On one particular morning when I started to shave," he wrote, "I found my razor dull, and it was not only dull but it was beyond the point of successful stropping and it needed honing, for which it must be taken to a barber or to a cutler. As I stood there with the razor in my hand, my eyes resting on it as lightly as a bird settling down on its nest — the Gillette razor was born. I saw it all in a moment, and in that same moment many unvoiced questions were asked and answered more with the rapidity of a dream than by the slow process of reasoning." That very day, according to Gillette, he rushed to a downtown Boston hardware store and bought steel ribbon, some pieces of brass, files, and a small vise, and set to work making a model of his brainchild. To his wife, who was visiting relatives back home in Ohio, Gillette wrote, with supreme confidence, "I have got it; our fortune is made."

This fetching account has become gospel in the annals of American innovation, and is fully in accord with popular notions of the mysterious workings of inventive genius. (It is also strikingly similar to Gillette's earlier description of the mental process that led to his world corporation scheme.) But like so many recollections given in the prosperous tranquillity of success, it is a bit fanciful, a kind of telescoped metaphor of actuality. For the true genesis of Gillette's razor involved the same plodding trial and error, leavened with luck and an occasional twinkle of insight, that underlies most inventions, both great and small.

Gillette had taken William Painter's advice to heart, and spent long hours mulling over lists of everyday items that might be improved upon, preferably with a throwaway substitute. It was a good way to pass the time while on selling trips, riding on Pullmans or overnighting in sparsely furnished commercial hotels. Possibly to give himself more time for concentration — and certainly to minimize the risk of gashing himself while shaving with a straight razor in a swaying railway lavatory — Gillette had bought a Star safety razor. It may well be that he was able, while scraping away with his Star, to let his mind wander to invention, but he had used the razor for some time before his thoughts focused on possibilities for improving on it. Then one day in the spring of 1895 — appropriately enough, while he was shaving — the idea popped almost idly into his mind. As Gillette explained somewhat laconically in connection with a patent suit in the early 1900's, "the thought occurred to me that no radical improvements had been made in razors, especially in razor blades, for several centuries, and it flashed through my mind that if by any possibility razor blades could be constructed and made cheap enough to do away with honing and stropping and permit the user to replace dull blades by new ones, such improvements would be highly important in that art."

Contrary to his own romanticized account, Gillette did not rush headlong to a hardware store to buy materials and tools. Instead, as most successful inventors have done, he began a methodical study of the products already available in the field. And the more he thought about it, he said later, "the more deeply I was impressed by the idea that safety razors as previously made and then on the market, did not differ materially from the old-style ordinary razors as respects the blade," which in both safety and straight razors consisted of a heavy, V-shaped piece of steel sharpened on one side. But all that was really necessary, Gillette decided, was a keen cutting edge, which could be placed on both sides of a wafer-thin piece of steel so inexpensive that the shaver could merely discard it when it grew dull.

In retrospect, it seems a simple enough idea, and Gillette himself, addressing a convention of Gillette Safety Razor Company salesmen long afterward, conceded that in many respects his razor blade "does not appeal to the average mind as being a great invention." On the other hand, he said, "there has never issued from the patent offices of the world, any article of invention to meet an individual need, which has equaled or approached the Gillette razor in its saving of time over the system it has displaced." Whether it was social reform or safety razors, King C. Gillette always believed in his product.

At the time of his first glimmering of invention, Gillette had recently moved from New York to Boston, where much of his business was centered. With his wife and son in Ohio — three-year-old King Gaines Gillette, nicknamed Kingie but called Babe by his father, was recuperating from minor surgery on swollen neck glands — Gillette had ample time to spend on his thin-bladed razor idea, and he proceeded to make scores of drawings of possible designs. Some were similar to the familiar style that finally evolved, though many of these models were envisioned with a small, lather-catching basket beneath the blade edge. Others showed a holder much like a conventional straight razor, built to accommodate a detachable, disposable blade. Gillette was living at the time in an apartment at 64 Westland Avenue, on the fringes of the fashionable Back Bay, and was a frequent caller at the nearby home of Ward Holloway, eastern manager of the Rochester Brewing Company and an important customer of Crown Cork & Seal. But Gillette seldom discussed bottle-top business while on these visits with the Holloways. Easily given to obsessions, he was obsessed now with safety razors, and could talk of little else. Young Margaret Holloway was living with her uncle at the time, and recalled later that Gillette "described the razor to me and to anyone who would listen to him. He was very enthusiastic."

He was still enthusiastic later in the summer, when he went with his family — including his mother-in-law — to spend the season at Kenberma, once again in a cottage shared with the Holloways. He made more sketches, refining his designs and explaining his novel throwaway concept to Holloway. Once, Holloway confessed that the whole thing might be easier to grasp if he could see a model, and Gillette obligingly whittled a crude wooden razor from a scrap of lumber picked up next door, where carpenters were building a new cottage. But it wasn't really the razor that was important, Gillette explained. The key to the whole idea was the blade, which would be so cheap that it could be used a few times and then thrown away.

All the while, Gillette the practical inventor coexisted with Gillette the utopian dreamer, and *Twentieth Century* reported to its readers in late August that King C. Gillette, titular president of the ambitious Twentieth Century Company, was putting the finishing touches on the corporation's prospectus. But even in the absence of this final document, the company was already in being, and had acquired — in a fittingly cashless transaction — the assets of the Humboldt Publishing Company. Investors were not exactly stampeding to buy shares in the Twentieth Century Company, but enough money was trickling in to keep the dream alive. The directors had decided that the company's first line of business would be insurance, thereby providing a profitable base for the world corporation preached by Gillette.

But something had happened to the leader's enthusiasm; if it had not been blunted by the razor idea, it had at least been divided and diluted. In late October the faithful were informed that "personal matters have occupied the attention of Mr. Gillette, our president, to the exclusion of everything else and we have every reason to know that he regrets this much more than any one else." The editors added reassuringly, "Our readers will have the pleasure of hearing from him soon, and no doubt, with telling effect."

Gillette's personal matters, of course, concerned his razor. Back from the beach at Kenberma, he had bought tools and materials, and by October he had turned out his first metal model. It was a crude affair, equipped with a somewhat ponderous lather catcher, and it failed miserably when Gillette gave it a try with a carefully sharpened thin steel blade. But Gillette was now utterly convinced that his idea was workable, and determined that nothing would stand in the way of its ultimate success.

At the same time, though, he kept the faith in his utopian vision, and in November, when readers of *Twentieth Century* heard from him again, he explained airily why he had remained aloof from some of the criticism that had been aimed at his program. He had kept silent, he said, "not from lack of courage to back up my convictions, but because the basic ideas advanced were beyond argument." For those who had questioned the breathtaking size of his projected city, he had only ill-disguised scorn: "I am willing to admit," he said, "that the idea of a central metropolis is in advance of this generation, and for this reason may not appeal to the average mind." And Gillette had scant patience for the limitations of the average mind. He was, after all, a full-fledged utopian thinker, one of a type described by Joyce Oramel Hertzler in *The History of Utopian Thought* as those who "stand out in their respective times almost without exception as men of intellectual originality and constructive imagination." They are further characterized, she added, by their "great inspiration and intense enthusiasm, their belief in their ideal." Put another way, they are fanatics.

Successful inventors often share many of the same qualities, seeing things from a different perspective than most people — those of average minds — and refusing to listen to arguments against their ideas. As both utopian and inventor, Gillette was blessed with two sources of the single-minded drive that would move him in the years to come; in the bargain, he had his practical streak to fall back on.

2

A New Razor

"Well, Gillette, how's the razor?"

IN THE FALL OF 1901, more than six years after King Gillette had carved out a rough wooden model to show Ward Holloway what he had in mind, the American Safety Razor Company was organized and incorporated under the laws of the state of Maine. Even as fledgling operations go, it wasn't much of a company. There were no offices or factory, no full-time employees, and only the barest minimum of funds; the three founding officers and directors all had other occupations that kept them busy. Gillette himself, the president and idea man, was away much of the time, out on the road selling bottle caps for Crown Cork & Seal. It almost seemed that the company's main advantage was that the founders had a firm idea of what business they were getting into, which they described in their certificate of organization as "razors, razor blades, and appurtenances." At least there could be no arguments about that. But the whole thing was still nothing more than an idea, an idea that appeared almost as farfetched as it had been when Gillette first came up with it in 1895. And the bare-bones corporation of 1901 had come only after years of bitterly frustrating struggle.

Until an invention has been transformed into a working model — indeed, until it has been thrown upon the iron-fisted mercies of the marketplace — it is an intangible, a gossamer in the mind of a dreamer. This had been particularly true of Gillette's razor blade. Not only was his first model a dismal disappointment, but the whole conception was diametrically opposed to the conventional wisdom that the ideal razor blade should be an expensive article that would last a lifetime with proper stropping, honing, and care. Now came King C. Gillette, an affable traveling salesman with a mind filled with exotic economic notions, to say that blades should be made of cheap sheet steel and thrown away after a couple of shaves. People who knew better — cutlers, metallurgists, and the like — told him that it couldn't be done, and the kindest thing that could be said of Gillette's idea was that it was laughable, as chimerical as his plan for a world corporation. "Well, Gillette," his friends would chuckle when they met him on the street, "how's the razor?" Years later, Gillette himself would concede that only blissful ignorance carried him through. "If I had been technically trained," he said, "I would have quit or probably never would have begun."

Once started, however, he went on with dogged determination. He approached numerous cutlers and machinists in the Boston area, and in his travels for Crown Cork & Seal he took the idea to experts in New York and Newark as well. Metallurgists at the Massachusetts Institute of Technology were consulted, too, but the answer was always the same: it is simply impossible to put a sharp edge on sheet steel. Prospective financial backers also had a stock reply: no. Only his old friend and inventive mentor William Painter, enfeebled with age in Baltimore, seemed to grasp the potential of Gillette's idea. "King," he said when he saw a model razor, "it looks like a real invention with great possibilities. I am sorry I cannot join you in its development, but my health will not permit it. But whatever you do, don't let it get away from you." A fanatic's zeal is usually self-sustaining, but Gillette was surely encouraged by the faith of the man who had first nudged him down the road that led to the razor blade.

Meanwhile, the high hopes fired by *The Human Drift* had cooled considerably. Much of the radical community got back into the political mainstream and boarded William Jennings Bryan's Populist bandwagon, and as the presidential campaign of 1896 drew near, interest in the Twentieth Century Company faded away. The insurance scheme never came to anything, and for a time there was talk of beginning the company's operations with a department store. But by the summer of 1896, with its chief architect's thoughts on sheet-steel razor blades, the notion of the Twentieth Century Company as savior was gradually put to rest; within two years *Twentieth Century* magazine was dead, too. The radical weekly had failed even to survive into the century that had inspired its name, thereby more than living up to its motto, "Always ahead of the times."

If he was disappointed at the apparent failure of his grand economic scheme, Gillette didn't show it, and he reentered the radical lists in the summer of 1897 with a thirty-two-page pamphlet urging a government employment law complete with a guaranteed minimum wage. "Let us reason together," Gillette wrote, and proceeded to cudgel readers with explanations of how his plan would solve most of the nation's pressing problems. Titled *The Ballot Box*, the thin booklet was peppered with boldface epigrams of the sort frequently carried through the streets on signboards by disheveled, mumbling men. Sample: "Brains were given a man to use. If he does not use them someone else will." By most standard definitions, the inventor of the disposable razor blade had become, if he was not already, a political and economic crackpot.

There is no evidence, though, that he ever let this curious condition interfere with his business career. Throughout his life, in fact, he seemed able to keep the two sides of his character neatly pigeonholed, never allowing one to interfere with the other. Engaged in commerce and industry, he was King C. Gillette, an inventive man of affairs who did not discuss his exotic brand of politics even with members of his own family — most of whom, it seems, regarded their kinsman's utopian dream as an unfathomable eccentricity to be tolerated but not talked about. Pushing for his sweeping social reforms, he was still King C. Gillette, but this Gillette billed himself as the noted advocate of world corporation, with only the barest mention of his more practical industrial pursuits.

At about the time he was readying the final draft of *The Ballot Box* for the printer, Gillette was making a second model of his razor and blade. The razor was more streamlined than the first — the cumbersome lather basket had been dispensed with — and Gillette had taken special care to temper and sharpen a number of blades to a keen edge. But the blades would hold neither shape nor sharpness, and were utterly useless for shaving. Finally, sometime in the summer of 1899, Gillette turned to Steven Porter, a Boston machinist with a shop on Atlantic Avenue along the waterfront — and possibly with a sense of humor, too. With Gillette's drawings and close supervision, Porter turned out three razors, and for the last one he made several blades. And then one morning fully four years after he had first had the idea, King Gillette lathered up his face and shaved with the world's first throwaway razor blade. At long last, success was in view.

Still, there remained more hurdles to clear, not least among them the matter of patent protection. And even Gillette himself, positive as he was of his invention's unique utility, nursed nagging doubts about its patentability. A year or two before, mailing some hastily scribbled drawings and descriptions of the razor idea to a Boston patent attorney, J. Steuart Rusk, Gillette had hedged on his usually supreme confidence by noting that the enclosed material when properly refined could "go far toward making the patent a good one *if allowed* [emphasis added]." Now, set to apply for a patent, Gillette received uncomfortable confirmation of his lingering uncertainties. A Washington colleague of Rusk's, who had been asked to do some preliminary checking at the patent office, reported back that in the opinion of one of the assistant patent examiners "no invention would be involved in making razors in the proposed manner." Once more, a supposed expert had told Gillette that he was on the wrong track. But once more, too, the inventive salesman put doubt behind him and moved firmly ahead, convinced that men of scant imagination were simply not capable of understanding what he had in mind. Days later, on August 11, 1899, he filed for his first patent on the device he had conceived four summers before, calling it in his application something "new in the art of razor manufacture and use."

It proved to be just that, but even after shaving himself successfully with a prototype blade and applying for patent protection, Gillette was still a long way from the marketplace. To get there, he needed to establish a company to make razors and blades; to do that he needed to raise money. But he had had no luck at all in finding backers for his seemingly comical scheme. Ward Holloway, who had already staked Gillette for publication of *The Human Drift*, had doubts about the razor, as did John Joyce, Holloway's partner in the highly successful Harvard Brewing Company. Gillette knew Joyce well — he was a major customer for Crown Cork's bottle caps — and under normal circumstances this wealthy Irish immigrant who had put together a fortune in utilities, breweries, and miscellaneous investments might have been a prime candidate for the role of financial angel. Unfortunately, Joyce was already playing angel to the New Era Carbonator Company, which Gillette was promoting on behalf of a friend who had developed equipment for making carbonated beverages. Holloway, too, was involved in this venture, which was turning out to be considerably more costly — and less successful — than he and Joyce had been led to believe. They were sticking with it, though, and Joyce was lending considerable sums to cover the hard-pressed Gillette's share of the investment. Supersalesman though he was, Gillette lacked the gall under these circumstances to give Joyce a strong pitch for the razor.

Gillette also tried the idea out on his father and older brothers, Mott and George, but they were a bit skeptical, too. They had seen enough of King's ill-starred inventions, both mechanical and sociological, and weren't about to do more with this one than wish him well. Besides, they had sufficient problems with their own affairs — including, coincidentally enough, the Gillette Clipping Machine Company, which made power-driven clippers for grooming horses. King Gillette had also lent a hand to this family enterprise, and it is said that while in London he managed to sell the machines to Queen Victoria's stable-keepers at Windsor Castle. Even so, the older Gillettes probably knew more about cutting edges than their younger son and brother did, and the whole idea of a sheet-steel razor blade seemed impractical, and hardly a prudent investment.

After all, Gillette's laboriously handmade blade was one thing, but turning out the thousands and possibly millions of blades needed to make the idea a commercial success would require automatic machinery that simply did not exist. And ingenious though he was, the design of such equipment was beyond Gillette's powers — if indeed it was even possible. Gillette would need quite a bit more than a clever idea before anyone would bet money on it, and the only solution seemed to be to find someone with solid mechanical abilities to complement Gillette's conceptual gifts. In five years, Gillette had not found such a man, but his fortunes were about to change. Indeed, he was about to meet someone whom he would later describe as "by luck or providential design . . . the only man in the world who could have perfected the razor."

"The blade was rather stiff for the handle"

One evening in the early part of 1900, William Emery Nickerson stopped by the Brookline home of his friend and sometime business associate Henry Sachs, a Boston stockbroker and manufacturer. With Sachs was one of his neighbors, Edward J. Stewart. On Crown Cork & Seal business, King Gillette had frequently called at Stewart's soft-drink bottling plant, and when the two men struck up a friendship, Gillette told Stewart about his razor. Stewart had agreed to see what he could do to promote the idea; so far, though, he had been unsuccessful. Sachs, in fact, had grown so tired of hearing Stewart talk about disposable blades that he had asked Nickerson to look over the scheme, certain that he would pronounce it a mirage. Nickerson, who had been trained as a chemist at the Massachusetts Institute of Technology, was a highly imaginative tinkerer and inventor who had once developed a light-bulb manufacturing process that even Thomas Edison had said was impossible. He seemed to have ideal credentials for passing fair and impartial judgment on King Gillette's long-simmering idea.

Nickerson listened patiently to what Stewart had to say, and then inspected a model razor. In time, Nickerson would devise the machinery to turn the model into mass-produced commercial reality, but he was not impressed at this first introduction. "The blade was rather stiff for the handle, which was of too-light construction," he explained later, "and it was not easy to see in that model the vast possibilities which lay concealed in it. I examined it critically at the time, failed to see anything in it and quickly dropped it out of mind."

Nickerson was hardly lacking in creative imagination. His considerable accomplishments as an innovator and inventor, in fact, surpassed even Gillette's. Born in Provincetown, Massachusetts, in 1853 — his family had lived on Cape Cod since shortly after the first Pilgrim settlement at Plymouth — Nickerson had quite early shown an avid curiosity about how things work. As a young boy, he mastered all the intricate knots in an authoritative book on the subject, and severely burned himself while experimenting with marsh gas collected from a neighborhood pond.

His thesis at MIT was on tannic acid, and when he got his degree in 1876 Nickerson was almost immediately hired by an association of leather tanners to investigate ways to improve methods of extracting the essential tanning compound from tree bark. After visiting a number of tanneries, the young Nickerson decided that the main shortcoming in the process was that the bark was not ground finely enough, and set out to fashion a machine that would do a better job. It was his first patent, and when he found that no one could make the special saws he needed for less than two dollars each, he designed his own saws that could be made for just thirty-six cents.

Nickerson may have been a clever inventor, but he was no businessman. He turned the domestic rights to his invention over to an established machinery company and failed miserably in his attempt to interest Europeans in the process. He returned to his native land from an abortive overseas selling trip in 1879 as a steerage passenger, stepping ashore like any foreign immigrant seeking his fortune in the New World. It was a bitter experience for this proud Cape Codder who took such great stock in his American ancestry, and he vowed that someday he would make up for it.

Back at home, Nickerson set up as an analytical chemist, and in the spring of 1881 he went south with a college classmate who was dredging gold in a northern Georgia river. Nickerson was impressed with what he saw, and took a lease on several miles of the Etowah River. With barges, a steam shovel, and pumps, he plied this watery El Dorado for nearly a year, but costs always exceeded the value of the gold he found. He sold the steam shovel and tried his hand for six months or so at less costly placer mining along riverbank hillsides. This, too, was a failure, but Nickerson was not yet ready to give up on the South. For a time he tried operating a sawmill, then a planing mill, and when those two enterprises faltered, too, he determined at last to go back to Massachusetts.

After his five-year absence, Boston hardly seemed a city of opportunity until Nickerson read of an elevator crash that had killed and injured several passengers. "Within twenty-four hours," he recalled later, "I had pictured to myself a safety attachment for elevators and then, as a matter of course, there was no rest until I had started in to make all elevators safe." It was a brand of tenacious resolve that King C. Gillette would surely have applauded, and for which he would one day be grateful.

In a rented room, Nickerson set up a cheap lathe and a drill press, and quickly turned out and sold several of his safety devices. Soon he was almost obsessed with elevators, and over the next several years he patented a number of other improvements. They were all ingenious inventions, some of them way ahead of their time, but Nickerson characteristically lost money on them. Soon enough, though, he was on to something new.

In the fall of 1889, Nickerson was approached by Jacob Heilborn, a Boston shoe wholesaler and industrial promoter who headed a syndicate for funding a pump to exhaust the air from incandescent light bulbs. The device was all that survived from an antic scheme to build a flying machine — fourteen years before the Wright brothers' epic flight — that would reach the North Pole. Heilborn, hearing later of the pump, had seen its possibilities in the lighting field, and when it failed to perform as hoped, a patent attorney suggested that he seek out Nickerson's advice. Heilborn made a strong impression on the Yankee inventor, and after listening to him for a half hour or so, Nickerson said, "Mr. Heilborn, you are either a very fine fellow or a damned good actor." Heilborn replied that he hoped he was the former, but Nickerson judged that he was both.

Nickerson agreed to see what he could do with the pump idea, and at the first glimmer of success he joined with Heilborn and a group of investors — including Heilborn's brother-in-law, Henry Sachs — to form the Beacon Vacuum Pump and Electrical Company. After many false starts, Beacon finally began turning out light bulbs. But in early 1893, the powerful Edison Company sued the company for infringing Edison's patents on all-glass bulbs; after a brief hearing, a judge upheld the Edison claim and Beacon was out of business almost before it had started.

Accustomed as he was to adversity, Nickerson was not totally discouraged. Mindful that his company was barred only from making hermetically sealed all-glass bulbs with wires melted into the crimped base, he determined to try another way. Thomas Edison himself had once said that there *was* no other way, and that his own success had come only after he had accepted the fact. But Nickerson didn't know about all this. "Being in blissful ignorance of it," he said later, "I went to work to try and do the impossible." Within just a few weeks, Nickerson had succeeded where Edison had failed, and Beacon was back in business with a line of bulbs whose bases were sealed by a special plug. To improve performance, Nickerson also designed a small glass part that expert glassblowers said was entirely impractical and unworkable. "The thorough-going inventor," Nickerson mused calmly, "has occasionally to do things that those skilled in the art believe cannot be done."

Ingenious as it was, the plugged bulb was admittedly inferior to the Edison article, and Nickerson had intended it only as a means of keeping Beacon alive until the basic Edison patent expired in 1895. Edison, however, had other plans. On the day the patent ran out, the price of Edison Company bulbs was slashed from thirty cents to fourteen cents, less than what it cost Beacon to make its bulbs. At the same time, Edison electric companies throughout the country announced that they would supply their customers with free bulbs. It was all over for the Beacon Vacuum Pump and Electrical Company.

Happily for Nickerson, a friend had been tinkering with an automatic weighing machine for the food industry, and in the waning days of the light-bulb enterprise Nickerson had taken an interest in the idea. When Beacon's business went down the drain, Nickerson turned his full time to the weighing-machine problem, and soon had his apparatus all but perfected. By the end of 1895, as King Gillette was just beginning to make the rounds with his first crude razor model, Nickerson and a few associates organized the New England Weighing Machine Company, and installed their first equipment at Chase & Sanborn's Boston coffee-packing plant. The machinery worked well enough, automatically doling out the proper weight of coffee into cans on a conveyor belt, but it had cost far more than Nickerson could reasonably charge. In the hole once more, he had to bring in fresh investors, in the process losing control of the company. But he did not lose sight of the fact that he was the brains behind the whole venture. Once, while in Minneapolis sweating out installation of one of his units in a large flour mill, he received from his Boston headquarters a letter berating him for his failure to keep management posted on his progress. Nickerson replied testily that he would stand for no such nagging. "If I cannot be allowed to work in peace," he said, "I won't work at all and will let the whole business go to the dogs, where it will go if I drop it."

Nickerson didn't drop it, and business went on apace. It was so good, in fact, that in late 1900 New England Weighing Machine bought out a competitive division of Pratt and Whitney. Unfortunately for Nickerson, this meant a corporate reorganization (a name change, too: New England was dropped from the corporate title) and the arrival on the scene of New York investors who decided to move the whole operation to Jersey City. Old-line New Englander that he was, Nickerson refused to make the switch, and accepted instead an agreement to spend every Thursday troubleshooting in Jersey City in exchange for an annual salary of $2,500.

Once again, Nickerson had taken the germ of an idea and transformed it almost single-handedly into a commercial reality. Once again, too, he had seen his labors exploited by others — his business sense was no match for his considerable mechanical gifts. Later, looking back at his record of success coupled with disappointment, Nickerson would regard it with equanimity as a training period, a time when he was "accumulating knowledge and experience to make the solution of the Gillette problem possible."

"No man can set a limit to it"

If Nickerson had not been impressed when he saw the model of King Gillette's razor and blade in early 1900, his opinion was unchanged when he examined it again a year later. This time it was in the hands of Jacob Heilborn, at whose urging Nickerson had gone into the pump and light-bulb business a dozen years before. Like Nickerson, Heilborn had been introduced to the Gillette idea by the enthusiastic soft-drink bottler Edward Stewart; unlike Nickerson, Heilborn had liked what he saw, and believed that it could be commercially developed. When Heilborn met with the inventor in the first part of 1901, Gillette told him of his problems in finding backers, and assured him that the only thing needed for commercial success was a practical man, experienced with machinery, who could devote considerable time and attention to perfecting the blade and razor.

Heilborn had thought immediately of Nickerson, who more than once had shown his ability to do what others said was impossible. And now that Nickerson was cutting back on his involvement with the weighing-machine venture, he would have plenty of time to spend on a new project such as the razor. But Nickerson was unmoved. An accomplished straight-razor shaver, he was unfamiliar with the safety razors of the day, and knew nothing about cutlery of any kind. All things considered, the idea just didn't appeal to his inventive fancy. Still, Heilborn persevered, and met several times with Nickerson during the summer — usually in the downtown Boston office of Henry Sachs, who persisted in cracking jokes about his brother-in-law's interest in such a harebrained scheme. Finally, almost in desperation — he had assured Gillette and Stewart that he could enlist Nickerson's help — Heilborn all but begged Nickerson to try his hand at the razor. This time, possibly only to put a stop to Heilborn's badgering, Nickerson gave in. He would think about it for a month, he said, and report on his findings.

Despite earlier misgivings, Nickerson soon began to see possibilities in Gillette's idea. "The more I thought about it," he recalled later, "the clearer the procedure appeared to me and the more certain I felt I could turn the trick." In quick succession, Nickerson envisioned machinery that would harden and sharpen the thin steel blades to a keen cutting edge. He also saw room for improvement on King Gillette's model, making the blade a bit wider and the handle of the razor somewhat heavier in order to give more stability to the flexible blade. And on September 9, 1901, a little more than a month after taking on what he had deemed at the time a highly doubtful project, he turned in his promised report to an anxiously waiting Jacob Heilborn.

"It is my confident opinion," wrote Nickerson, who seldom had opinions of any other kind, "that not only can a successful razor be made on the principles of the Gillette patent, but that if the blades are made by proper methods a result in advance of anything known can be reached. . . . I can see no reason why it cannot easily compete for popular favor with anything in its line ever put before the public."

Nickerson went on to observe that the key to the prospective razor's success was low-cost production of a high-quality blade, and said that he was certain of his own abilities to design and build machinery to manufacture such a blade. It would take him about four months to do so, said Nickerson, and the total cost for tooling up to commercial production would come to about $5,000. "In conclusion," he said, "let me add that so thoroughly am I satisfied that I can perfect machinery . . . that I am ready to accept for my compensation stock in a Company which I understand you propose forming."

Such enthusiasm from someone of Nickerson's proven mechanical abilities was all that Heilborn needed, and he now arranged for Gillette to meet the man who proposed to turn his invention into a marketable product. Years later, Gillette would have nothing but praise for Nickerson's contributions, and Nickerson would say of their first encounter that "I found Mr. Gillette a very affable gentleman with a kindly face and manner and immediately felt a strong personal liking for him." At the time, however, the two men viewed each other somewhat warily. Gillette, the dreamer, was quite willing for Nickerson to proceed with his work, but regarded the nuts and bolts of manufacturing as a minor — if still essential — detail. To the inventor, the idea was the most important thing. Nickerson, while not downgrading the idea, believed that his own role was far more critical. It is an age-old conflict between inventors and engineers, and even in his mellow old age, Nickerson was at pains to observe that a clear distinction must always be made between "the invention of the Gillette razor so admirably accomplished by Mr. Gillette and its practical development as carried forward by others [by Nickerson, that is], for the two things are quite separate and each required a type of mind and a training quite distinct."

Right at the start, the two minds collided over what to call the projected company of whose success Nickerson was so sure. Gillette, never one to indulge himself in false modesty, felt that Gillette Safety Razor Company had a nice ring to it. But Nickerson, when he considered the pivotal role he was to play in the company's fortunes, believed that naming it for the mere inventor would be a gross injustice; perhaps realizing that his own name would be an unfortunate one for a razor manufacturer, he stood up for the more neutral American Safety Razor Company. It is a measure of the original financial promoters' assessment of relative value that Nickerson prevailed. Gillette, however, had at least one major advantage over his colleagues — he owned the pending patent for the invention that underpinned the whole enterprise — and when the company was organized at the end of September, 1901, King C. Gillette was named president. Heilborn became secretary-treasurer and Stewart rounded out the three-man directorate.

Henry Sachs, the scoffer of old, had been converted to the safety-razor cause by Nickerson's contagious confidence, and with Heilborn and Stewart he set out to raise the $5,000 required for start-up costs. The company had been capitalized at $500,000, divided into 50,000 shares priced optimistically at $10 each. Of the total shares, Gillette got 17,500, Heilborn, Stewart and Nickerson split 12,500 among them, and 20,000 remained in the treasury. (Later, Nickerson would moan that he should have insisted on getting, if not as many shares as Gillette, then at least more than Heilborn and Stewart, whose contributions were not nearly so important as his own.) These were mere paper transactions, of course, and brought no funds into the company's coffers. To do that, and fully aware that no one was likely to shell out $10 for shares in an untried company, the promoters divided 10,000 shares of treasury stock into twenty 500-share blocks, which they proposed to sell at the bargain-basement price of $250 each. Even at that, the stock was hardly snapped up by eager investors, and those who did buy, frequently did so only as a favor to friends. Some invested for other reasons, such as the Pittsburgh bottle manufacturer who bought a $250 block from Edward Stewart in hopes that the soft-drink executive would in return buy bottles from him. The investment was made for the wrong reasons, but it turned out to be a good one for the Pittsburgher: four years later, when King C. Gillette maneuvered for control of the company, this same block of stock brought $62,500 in cash.

Such heady potential was hardly apparent at the start, however. By the first weeks of 1902 the promoters had unloaded just thirteen of the critical twenty parcels of stock, and only the timely intervention of Henry Sachs — who had been letting Heilborn and Stewart do most of the selling — brought the full $5,000 into the infant company's treasury. Out of gratitude for his efforts, King Gillette presented Sachs with 2,500 shares of company stock, taken out of Gillette's own allotment.

Happily for the budding razor entrepreneurs, Nickerson had not waited until the money was in to get on with his work. For a promised salary of forty dollars a week, he had agreed to devote half of each working day to perfecting the equipment for turning out blades and razors, and by December, 1901, he had all but completed the sharpening machine and rented a small shop area at 424 Atlantic Avenue, above a fish store and next to the wharf where Boston's garbage was loaded on crusted scows for dumping at sea. There, in what he recalled later as a "highly perfumed atmosphere," Nickerson labored through the winter and spring to fine-tune the processes for hardening and sharpening the thin steel blades that were the heart of Gillette's invention. Gillette, meanwhile, had assigned his patent application to the company, and Nickerson's own patent attorney, Everett D. Chadwick, had revised, broadened, and resubmitted it. The razor and blade that Nickerson was so busily working to produce were considerably different in appearance and detail from the model disclosed even in this new application, though the resulting patent would prove in time to be an airtight instrument against infringers.

Trying various types of abrasive wheels, experimenting with different cutting angles and grinding speeds, Nickerson moved confidently toward his goal, and by the end of May he reported to his employers. "The question is settled," he said. "It only needs money, courage and work to develop a proposition that can be made just as big as the people who manage it are capable of grasping. No man can set a limit to it."

These were heartening words for the razor's eager backers, and no one was more emboldened than Gillette himself. The previous November, at the same time that he had turned his patent over to the American Safety Razor Company, his fellow directors had agreed — possibly as balm for the inventor's bruised feelings at not having the company named after him — to print "King C. Gillette's Patents" on all forthcoming products and advertising. Now, buoyed by Nickerson's unbridled optimism, Gillette determined that this was not enough psychic recompense for his salient contribution to a company of such soaring promise. Calling a special meeting of stockholders, of which he himself was by far the largest, Gillette engineered a unanimous vote to change the corporate name to the Gillette Safety Razor Company. Possibly to soothe another wounded ego, William Nickerson was elected a member of the board of directors in the following month, as was Henry Sachs.

But success was not nearly so imminent as Gillette, Nickerson, and their colleagues believed. Courage and work were one thing; money was quite another. Nickerson's whirlwind development work had eaten up the first $5,000 and then some; according to Gillette's varied later accounts, the company that had just been stamped with his name was $8,000 to $12,000 in the hole. Nickerson, however, claimed that the figure was much lower, pointing as convincing proof to the simple deduction that no one in his right mind would have advanced such credits to so chancy an enterprise.

Whatever Gillette Safety Razor's true financial situation may have been, the company was clearly floundering for lack of capital to exploit its product, and periodic small loans by Henry Sachs were inadequate to take up the slack. Even Nickerson, the resident mechanical genius, tried his hand at finding financial backing, and managed to pin down a group of New York investors who were willing to put up a grand sum of $150,000 in exchange for a 51 percent controlling interest in the company's stock. When he got back to Boston with this proposal — which seemed reasonable enough to him at the time — Nickerson was somewhat taken aback when his fellow directors quickly turned it down, their suspicions about Nickerson's business sense amply confirmed.

Such airy refusal of proffered aid was a gallant gesture, compounded of steadfast hope for the future and the same spirit of bravado that moves a condemned man to brush aside his last meal and then decline a blindfold. Gillette, though frequently given to hyperbole, was probably not far from the mark when he spoke years later of this period and remarked, "We were backed up to the wall with our creditors lined up in front waiting for the signal to fire." But Gillette had seen his idea come too far to let it die at the hands of bill collectors, and was about to help engineer a stay of execution.

"We Offer a New Razor"

Young's Hotel was one of the more popular downtown dining spots for turn-of-the-century Boston businessmen, so John Joyce was hardly surprised when he happened to see King Gillette in the lobby one September day in 1902. Indeed, the two men had frequently lunched together at Young's, and though Gillette would say later that this particular meeting was a mere chance encounter, it is more likely that he had gone to the hotel that day in the desperate hope that he would find the portly millionaire who had so generously backed the ill-fated New Era Carbonator Company. Gillette had been considerably embarrassed at the outcome of that venture, which had been closed down just a few months before at a sizable loss to the investors. Joyce, having covered Gillette's portion of the investment, had taken a double drubbing, and when the books were closed Gillette owed his patron nearly $20,000. Small wonder that Gillette had hesitated before to ask Joyce for help in propping up the shaky razor company.

He had, however, given him one of the sample razors that Nickerson had turned out during his experimental work, and had kept him advised of the progress of his latest venture. Despite the sum of money between them — and Gillette would later repay Joyce the full amount owed, in cash — the two men were still on friendly terms, and Joyce cheerfully asked Gillette to join him for lunch. As they settled in at their table, Gillette couldn't have been more pleased to hear his host say, "King, what's the matter? You look worried."

He most certainly was worried, Gillette replied. In fact, he had just come from a meeting at Henry Sachs's office on Milk Street, where the backers of an apparently doomed Gillette Safety Razor Company had finally admitted to themselves that they were teetering on the margin of bankruptcy. What was worse, no one had come up with a way out. True enough, the directors had recently voted to float a $100,000 bond issue, but this was a move somewhat akin to a beleaguered general's summoning phantom reserves to his rescue. The little company could barely pay its rent, much less stand behind bonds redeemable in gold coin. Barring some miracle — or perhaps unconditional surrender to Nickerson's rapacious New Yorkers — it appeared that Gillette's years-long dreams were all but over.

As he unfolded his problems to Joyce, Gillette knew that the potential miracle worker was sitting just across the table from him. And so, of course, did Joyce, many times a millionaire from his sprawling Harvard Brewing Company and the giant Shawinigan Water & Power Company of Canada, and a man willing to take an occasional gamble on a new idea. Joyce had tried the sample razor, and was pleased with its performance. Properly exploited, he believed, Gillette's idea had great market potential, and it was certainly a better bargain than the now-defunct New Era Carbonator Company. He would, he decided, take a chance on it.

But if Joyce was a gambler, he preferred to play with sure cards, and proceeded to deal himself an almost unbeatable hand. He would back the razor company, he told Gillette, but there were certain conditions. Burned once in a venture with Gillette, he aimed to be more careful this time. If the company would issue $100,000 worth of 8 percent bonds, said Joyce, he would buy them — at sixty cents on the dollar. As a sweetener to this 40 percent discount, Joyce also wanted along with each bond an equivalent amount of company stock. And he would not, he added, take the full issue at once. Instead, he would buy the bonds at such times as the company showed that it needed additional operating funds. To cover himself still further, Joyce stipulated that if progress was not satisfactory he could call the whole deal off after he had paid in $30,000. With bargaining

such as this, Joyce had worked his way up from immigrant haber-
dashery clerk to become one of the richest men in Massachusetts.

Hard terms or not, the company's directors readily accepted the
proposition when Gillette laid it out at a meeting on October 1. By
October 10 the deal was closed, and Joyce, though not a director,
was given authority to countersign Gillette Company checks. Before
the year was out, he had put $9,500 into the Gillette treasury, nearly
twice what the company had had to work with during the entire
previous year.

His money worries over, Nickerson advanced rapidly to tool up
for commercial production, moving to larger quarters on the top floor
of 394 Atlantic Avenue. Now, however, he had worries of another
kind. In the earlier days, when funds were tight, he had felt little
pressure from his fellow directors. But with Joyce on the scene to
keep an eye on his investment — and with Gillette concerned lest
Joyce suspect that the razor might go the painful way of the carbon-
ating machine — Nickerson was goaded to start showing results. Joyce,
in particular, having shaved with one of the prototype razors, saw
no reason why they could not be mass-produced, and his impatience
rubbed off on the other backers. For Nickerson, it was a harrowing
time. "When things were dragging," he recalled later, "I not only had
to keep up my own courage, but I had to face the disappointment of
the parties in interest and sometimes their comments were very
cutting."

But Nickerson persevered, and by the middle of April — after the
bracing infusion of an additional $8,500 of Joyce's cash — he had
finished a second sharpening machine and was turning out sample
razors and blades that the promoters passed out for testing by curious
and courageous friends. Commercial production seemed near, and the
time had come to determine how much to charge for the product.
The time had come, too, for John Joyce to start asserting the authority that was his by virtue of his large financial commitment.

At a board meeting called to discuss pricing policies, the directors
decided that the blades ought to be retailed at one dollar per package
of twenty. It was difficult to decide what price tag should go on the
razor itself — or handle, as it was called at the time — and Nickerson,
Heilborn, and Joyce were named to a committee to study the question.

It would be Joyce's first act as a full-fledged director, for he, along with Gillette's old friend Ward Holloway, had just been elected as a board member.

After due consideration, the committee decided that three dollars was a reasonable enough sum to charge for the razor, but Joyce soon changed his mind and insisted that five dollars would be a better — not to mention a more profitable — price. "The rest of the directors were startled, not to say frightened, at this proposition," Nickerson recalled later. As well they might have been — at the time, five dollars was about a third of the average industrial worker's weekly wage, and a good straight razor could be had for as little as two dollars and a half. It seemed a bit bold, if not actually foolhardy, to set so high a price for a new article whose ultimate success would depend largely on mass marketing. But Joyce carried the day, announcing that it was fine with him if the other directors doubted that their product was worth five dollars, and that if they felt strongly about it he would prove them wrong by buying up all the razors they could make for two-fifty apiece, and sell them himself at a handsome profit.

With the price tag settled, and with Nickerson gaining ground in his drive for large-scale production, the Gillette safety razor moved closer to market. In July, 1903, the company signed an exclusive sales contract with the newly formed Chicago firm of Townsend & Hunt, which agreed to buy 50,000 razor sets — the handle plus twenty blades — by October, 1904, and to guarantee the purchase of 100,000 sets a year for the next four years. At the time, it seemed like a really major deal for both parties.

The general public — or at least that portion of the public that read the business journal *System Magazine* — got its first look at the razor in October, when a half-page advertisement appeared beneath a modest headline that straightforwardly announced: "We Offer a New Razor." Included in the ad were pictures of the razor, standing alone and nestled between blades in a plush case, but readers were advised: "You will have to see it to appreciate it." And the way to do that was to send five dollars to Townsend & Hunt, whose address just happened to be the same as *System Magazine*'s (one of the principals, George A. Townsend, Jr., was private secretary to the editor, who generously allowed his ambitious employee to handle Gillette's affairs on the side). A. W. Shaw, the obliging editor, did not think much of the venture, however, and discouraged Townsend, just as so many others had dashed cold water on King Gillette's early glowing hopes. Years later, Shaw recalled how Townsend, anxious to prove the new razor's virtues — and seeking, no doubt, to explain his recent inattention to Shaw's business and his lengthening lunch hours with his partner, Perry D. Hunt — took a sample razor to the older man's house one Sunday morning. Wrote Shaw: "I remember that he sat in the room adjoining the bath; that I lathered my face carefully and started in with the razor; that after I had tried to shave one side of my face in comfort, I walked to the door and tossed the razor to him and told him that I thought he had better stay with me." (Shaw also admitted that he had a particularly hard and wiry beard.)

With Shaw's reluctant blessing, Townsend decided to stay on as a secretary while waiting for the razor returns to come in; Gillette soon looked like a winner, and Townsend said goodbye to *System* and set up an office of his own to devote full time to razors and blades. To avoid confusion, Townsend & Hunt was soon doing business as the Gillette Sales Company, and three years later the partners sold out to the parent corporation for $300,000.

Public response to the first few ads for the Gillette razor seemed gratifying only because it started from a base of zero; by the end of 1903, the company had sold what might have seemed to some a minuscule fifty-one razors. But the important thing was that there were people out there willing to pay five dollars for a new kind of safety razor, and the backers who believed in the product were certain that these first few sales were harbingers of far greater things to come.

For King Gillette, however, savoring at last the taste of vindication, still more disappointment was in store. He may have been president of the company that bore his name, but he did not truly preside. Indeed, he was not even paid a salary, and still earned his living as a traveling man for Crown Cork & Seal, which now paid him $5,000 a year. Then in the fall of 1903, just as his razor began living up to the promise he had always foreseen, Crown Cork decided that its star New England salesman had done such a good job that he deserved more money and more responsibility. His salary was to be increased to $6,000; his job was to go to England and hold down a Crown Cork & Seal beachhead in London.

"I did not wish to go," Gillette recalled years later, "and urged the razor company to make a salaried position for me, so I might devote my time to the razor." But Joyce, whose funding had saved the company from ruin, would have nothing to do with this costly proposition. "I was president of the company," Gillette said bitterly, "but those in control refused to meet my wishes, giving as a reason the need of every dollar for development of the business."

On January 9, 1904, the directors of the Gillette Safety Razor Company met in John Joyce's Boston office and decided that from then on they would continue to sell their blades at a dollar per package, but that the number of blades would be quietly reduced from twenty to twelve — thus increasing their profit margin by a tidy 40 percent. At the same session, King C. Gillette resigned as president and nominated Ward Holloway to succeed him. Duly elected, Holloway joined the other directors in wishing their departing former president well, and Gillette sailed less than three weeks later from New York with his family and all his household goods aboard the steamer *Cedric*, bound for Liverpool. As a boy in Fond du Lac and Chicago, Gillette had dreamed frequently of travel to exotic lands; now he was off for what was to be at least a three-year stay in London, with all of Europe within easy range. But the sojourn that would have delighted the child only depressed the man, who left behind in the hands of others the enterprise that fulfilled nearly a lifetime of commercial striving. And somehow, in all the bustle and confusion of crating up his belongings for an ocean voyage, Gillette lost the drawings and the first model razors that he had made with such hope and care nearly a decade before.

3

Novel Blade, Novel Holder

"Hundreds of thousands are now able to shave themselves"

TWO MONTHS AFTER King C. Gillette and his family went steaming across the Atlantic to their new home in London, a satisfied buyer of one of the first Gillette safety razors penned a glowing testimonial to the new product. He had tried nearly every type of razor on the market, he wrote, but shaving with the Gillette had convinced him that it "is simply out of sight, although you can trust me to see to it that it is never out of sight when shaving time comes around. That it is a thing of beauty there can be no question, and that it will be my joy forever, is equally true. If some of my friends do not avail themselves of the opportunity of learning the true luxuries of shaving it will not be through any neglect upon my part in showing them the way." He was confident, he concluded, that the Gillette razor would "meet with the sale it so richly merits."

Other users volunteered equally lavish praise. The razor "gives you a clean, smooth shave that makes your face as soft as velvet," wrote one, adding that the whole thing was "a delightful sensation that I have never experienced with any other razor." Said another, who noted that his tough beard limited him to five or six shaves per blade: "I shall recommend this razor to my friends who are using safeties and consider that I am doing them, rather than you, a favor." Still another pleased shaver was a Kansas-born lawyer named Thomas W. Pelham, who was shown a Gillette razor in the summer of 1903 by Perry Hunt, about to join with George Townsend to form the Gillette selling agency. Pelham, who drew up the legal agreement between Townsend & Hunt and Gillette, had been a straight-edge user, but found that a Gillette razor cut his shaving time from twenty minutes to five; he was so zealous a convert, and so strong a believer in its commercial possibilities, that he would soon be devoting his full time to the razor company.

Perhaps the most effusive tribute that came to the new razor was from the nimble-fingered Harry Kellar, the first great American-born magician:

"God bless the man who invented the Gillette Safety Razor," he wrote. "I have for years suffered torture at the hands of all kinds of barbers, as I have a very hard beard and shave every day, until I discovered your marvelous razor. With the Gillette razor, shaving is a luxury and I am able to shave my face as clean and smooth as a baby's without irritating the skin. I want to thank you heartily for this priceless boon."

Some months later, as a further earnest of his boundless appreciation, Kellar wrote back to say that if he knew he could not replace it, he would not part with his Gillette razor for $10,000.

To a later age, whose men have always shaved themselves quickly and easily with a sometimes bewildering array of razors, blades, and variations thereof — not to mention whirring electric appliances — such enthusiasm for something so routine as a razor may seem quaintly amusing, almost silly. But we cannot measure the first achievements of the past against the more perfected accomplishments of the present. Put alongside a supersonic jet, the Wright brothers' little plane is a pitifully crude contraption, but that first flying machine lofting over the sands of Kitty Hawk still ranks as a wonder of the first order. In its own smaller way, the Gillette razor was no less miraculous. Indeed, among widely used inventions, it is almost in a class by itself, for rather than creating a need that did not exist before, it filled a long-standing need and offered a felicitous solution to a problem that had vexed mankind for thousands of years. William Nickerson was scarcely exaggerating when he said of the razor he had done so much to perfect that it was unparalleled "among the lesser of the great inventions," and hailed King Camp Gillette as a "benefactor of the race."

A new kind of razor was not exactly the class of benefaction that Gillette the utopian had in mind for the world, but Gillette the inventor was proud enough of his handiwork, and deemed it considerably more far-reaching than a mere handle for clamping in place a wafer-thin cutting edge. He was always careful, in fact, to distinguish between grand inventive conceptions and the mere mechanical devices that carried them out. In 1909, during one of the inevitable patent-infringement cases that arose in the wake of his razor's great success, Gillette jotted down a few hurried thoughts for the company patent attorneys. His ideas are worth noting in detail, for they illuminate the nature of the inventive mind.

To argue over mere technical details, Gillette wrote, "involves dangers of questions of degree — which should not be considered as a basic function of the inventor's conception." Furthermore, he said:

It is often true that invention involves underlying principles, purposes and questions of utility which are lost sight of in mere technical descriptions. To say that the Gillette blade only differs from other razors or blades in degree does not in any way describe the invention involved, or the principles or purposes that are inherent within it, and that are widely different from the principles and purposes of razors disclosed in the previous art.

It is manifestly true that no one — previous to the Gillette invention — had conceived the idea of producing a blade in which the purpose in view was to produce a blade that would be so cheap to manufacture that its cost to the consumer would permit of its being discarded when dull, thus avoiding the annoyance and difficulties of stropping and honing. Furthermore, it was true up to the time that the Gillette razor went on the market that there were hundreds of thousands of men who did not shave themselves, for the reason that they could not keep a razor in condition — they had not the knack or mechanical skill to strop and hone a razor, and there being no razor on the market that was of such low cost as to permit of the blade being discarded when dull and a new one substituted, they were obliged to be content to go to the barber, which involved large expense, annoyance and loss of time. It is to this fact that I the inventor attribute in large measure the instantaneous success of my razor, which success has few parallels in the history of invention. If the invention of this blade per se, could be considered in no other light than its having met the necessities of this large number of men who had never been able to afford the luxury of shaving themselves before, it must be conceded to be of the highest class of invention as would be the case if someone were to invent a machine to fly that would make it absolutely safe for anyone to use, where theretofore only experts [were able] to use [the] machines, and then only at great risk.

But the question of invention does not alone rest upon the fact that hundreds of thousands are now able to shave themselves who could not before, and do so without involving the question of skill in keeping their razor in condition, but it rests on its use by millions of men who have discarded other old style razors because the Gillette has reduced the art of shaving to such a cheap and simple process.

The inventor can surely be pardoned for this outpouring of pride. At the time he wrote this testament, little more than five years after the Gillette Safety Razor Company had gone to market with its first product, nearly two million razors had been sold; blades were selling at the rate of tens of millions each year, and the fast-growing Boston company was known all over the world. But the shaving public's ready acceptance of the Gillette razor had not been an unalloyed blessing, and the nascent enterprise had been nearly overwhelmed by its quick-fire success.

"Mr. Gillette suddenly returned from Europe"

In his minutes of the directors' meeting of June 17, 1904, Secretary Heilborn noted that John Joyce was "much disturbed about the small output of the factory." As well he might have been. For Joyce had not been putting his money — more than $45,000 so far — into King Gillette's razor idea out of any zeal for ministering to the needs of men who were unable to shave themselves or afford a barber. It was all a simple investment to him, of a piece with his other numerous interests in breweries, gas companies, and electric utilities. And now it showed signs of souring. As promised, Joyce would of course put in the remaining $13,389 for the discount bond issue that had bailed the company out of bankruptcy more than a year and a half before. But this final injection of cash would not cover the other outstanding debts — some $15,000 in all — nor would it be of any help in acquiring the additional machinery that William Nickerson now said he needed to get his production lines in good working trim. In short, just as the razor showed faint but lively signs of catching on, the company was virtually fundless once more.

Just three months before, a confident Nickerson had assured his fellow directors that production figures would be more than a match for demand, that he would be turning out stacks of razors and blades just as fast as Townsend & Hunt could sell them. More recent reports from the factory front were not nearly so sanguine. Because of faulty machines and processes, an alarming number of blades were emerging from the production line in a crumpled mess, and the company was hard pressed to produce even the minimal 1,250 razor sets required weekly just to break even. To make matters worse, this state of affairs caught most of the directors by surprise, for they had counted on a comfortable output of 2,000 sets a week, enough to show a respectable profit. Such, at least, Heilborn observed cuttingly, was the perform-ance that had been "practically guaranteed us by our Superintendent [Nickerson], and we now find that instead of being on that basis, that we have practically much experimental work to do before we reach a regular output of assured quality."

Nickerson, suppressing the smoldering anger that he always felt when meddlesome investors criticized his rate of progress, pleaded for time, a couple of weeks to troubleshoot and set things right. The others — Joyce, Holloway, and Heilborn — had no other choice, and agreed to give their mechanical expert another chance. There were certain conditions, though — he could spend no more money for machinery, and the $500 he was given for any expenses that might arise was to be considered an advance against salary. If he was to save the company, he would do it out of his own pocket. At the same time, the directors determined that they were bound to tell investors of the dire straits their company was in, and the next day a letter went out informing the small band of stockholders that "present indebtedness, together with outstanding contracts, is considerably in excess of the quick assets, in addition of which there is a liability of $100,000 in first mortgage bonds" (the sum owed to Joyce). Costly experimental work was still required, the letter concluded, and a substantial sum would need to be raised to get the company on a solid footing; in due time, the directors would unveil a program for financing the continued growth of the company.

King Gillette, of course, received word of the latest crisis while in London, languishing in what must have seemed like exile. Henry Sachs, leading light in the first capitalization drive, got his letter in Colorado Springs, where he had gone for his health and was in the process of setting up as a stockbroker and promoter. But separated as they were, they must have corresponded with each other about the pass the company had come to, for as two of the earliest active participants in the enterprise, they had grown to resent Joyce's overwhelming influence. They resented it even more in early August, when the stockholders were asked to turn half their shares over to the company, which would then sell the stock for not less than $1.50 per share and put the proceeds into the anemic treasury. To make this curious arrangement at least marginally palatable, stockholders were granted the "privilege" of repurchasing their own shares — presumably for $1.50 each. Those shares not bought by their previous owners would then be sold off "at the best possible price, but not less than seventy-five cents per share."

For Gillette in particular, the plan was an unmitigated disaster. Next to John Joyce, he was the largest stockholder, and he was also the least prosperous. If the proposal went into effect, he would be required to surrender fully half of the 9,000 shares remaining in his name (he had given a considerable amount of his stock to Joyce in order to meet the terms of the bond deal) and then pay out more than a year's salary if he wanted them back again. And if he didn't buy, there was little doubt in his mind that Joyce or some of his associates would, thus further consolidating their control over the company that Gillette understandably considered his own. Happily enough, a convenient escape hatch had been built into the directors' ingenious plan: the proposal would be carried out only if all the stockholders agreed to it, something that Gillette, for one, would never do. But this veto power was of small consolation to him as he pondered from afar the affairs of the company that he had been sweating over for nearly a decade. Something else was bothering him, too.

At the farewell board meeting held just before Gillette left for England, Joyce had laid out a proposition from a pair of Chicagoans who wanted rights to manufacture and market Gillette razors overseas. In exchange, they would put $100,000 into the business abroad, and pay the Boston company a royalty. King Gillette had been appalled by the suggestion. True enough, he had turned over his own personal rights to foreign markets in exchange for additional shares of company stock, but this had been a corporate formality, not a giveaway to strangers. In Gillette's eyes, his razor was to be a universal product, and he fully intended to enjoy maximum profits from worldwide sales. And royalties, no matter how generous they might be, are hardly in the same league with complete control. Bending to Gillette's impassioned urging, the directors had decided to take no action on the proposal, but now, at the same time that he was learning of the company's dismal financial condition, Gillette heard that the matter had come up again. And this time, there was a good chance that a foreign royalty arrangement would be made in his absence.

It was a time for decisive action, and Gillette took it. On August 20, 1904, not seven months since he had so reluctantly left the Gillette Safety Razor Company behind, King Camp Gillette took ship from Liverpool, bound for New York and Boston. This time, he left behind his wife and son, in a strange country.

Exactly when Gillette arrived back in Boston is unclear, though he said later that the trip took about ten days. If so, his timing could hardly have been better. For on August 29 his worst fears were all but realized when the board voted — on William Nickerson's motion — to give President Holloway full powers to execute an agreement granting overseas rights to the Gillette razor to Joyce's friends from Chicago. It is not clear, either, how Gillette responded to this move, though Nickerson hinted at an explosive situation when he wrote years later that "Mr. Gillette suddenly returned from Europe and not finding things to his liking, began taking an active part in the management of the Company and a contention developed between him and some of the directors." According to Gillette, whose role as inventor and company namesake was surely a weighty one, he "merely protested against the proposed disposition of our foreign rights and won my point." Indeed he did, and he won more, too. When the directors held their next formal meeting on October 6, they not only heard Holloway report that the matter of a royalty agreement had been dropped, but they also voted in a new slate of officers: Joyce as president, Gillette as vice-president, and Holloway as secretary-treasurer. Equally significant — for Gillette, at least — each officer was granted an annual salary of $18,000.

At long last, the inventor's chronic financial worries were over. Already, he had made a quick trip to Baltimore to quit his job at Crown Cork & Seal, and some of the officials of that company had been so impressed with prospects for the razor venture that they bought 4,000 of Gillette's shares at a premium price of $20 each. "It seemed," Gillette said later, "as though I were walking on air, I was so rich and independent, for I was to have $80,000, which was more money than I had ever had before." And the first thing he did with this unaccustomed treasure was repay John Joyce the $19,700 he still owed from the defunct New Era Carbonator Company. Now he would no longer be personally beholden to the man whose policies for the razor company seemed so frequently at odds with his own. Then he began quietly buying up Gillette company stock — which was available for considerably less than what his Baltimore friends had paid — until his holdings reached 14,000 shares. He wasn't fully in control, but he was in a much stronger position than he had been earlier in the year, when he had been obliged to leave the country because his own company wouldn't give him a paying job. On October 10, Gillette sailed for England once more, to settle his affairs in London and bring his wife and son back home. Before he returned to Boston, the abundant success of his inventive enterprise would be all but guaranteed by the sovereign powers of the United States of America.

"We began to get inquiries from prospective users
in every part of the United States"

In the same article of the Constitution that authorizes the Congress to declare war and issue coinage, the government is also empowered "to promote the Progress of Science and useful Arts, by securing for limited Times to . . . Inventors the exclusive Right to their . . . Discoveries." Thus it was that on November 15, 1904 — the very day that the Gillettes boarded the steamship *Baltic* at Liverpool for the return trip to Boston — the United States Patent Office at last granted letters patent numbered 775,134 and 775,135, covering King C. Gillette's "new and useful improvements in razors." For the next seventeen years, the Gillette Safety Razor Company was to have exclusive rights to the manufacture and sale of a novel article comprising, among other claims made in the tightly drawn patent application, "a detachable razor-blade of such thinness and flexibility as to require external support to give rigidity to its cutting edge."

Considering the progress that the company had made since the dark days of summer, and assuming that infringers could be kept successfully at bay, the patent was a virtual license to print money. Nickerson, who seemed always to perform best when under extreme pressure, had worked out the production-line kinks, and had developed a new blade-grinding process that John Joyce would later credit with rescuing the company. No stockholders had risen to the dubious bait of turning in half their holdings for resale, nor was such bizarre financing necessary: with the factory situation straightened out, sales began to soar, and by the end of 1904 Gillette had sold nearly 91,000 razor sets and more than 10,000 packages of extra blades for the year. In December alone, the company sold close to 20,000 sets of razors and blades. Meanwhile, with their machinery running day and night, the directors bought a six-story building in South Boston, and by the spring of 1905 the company's ornate letterhead featured — along with a razor and a festoon of blades — an engraving of the new plant, belching black smoke from its chimney and grandly captioned: "The largest Factory in the World devoted to the exclusive manufacture of razors." It was a long way from Nickerson's experimental shop above the fish store, and more distant still from King Gillette's brainstorm of just a decade before.

Two keys to the company's rapid sales growth were distribution and advertising, areas in which it was destined nearly always to excel. In early 1904, at the time Townsend & Hunt began doing business as the Gillette Sales Company, the company began phasing out the mail order business and selling its goods to wholesale houses as well as directly to the hardware, cutlery, jewelry, and sporting goods dealers that were seen at the time as the primary outlets for razors and blades. From the very start, it was company policy to set aside about twenty-five cents per razor for advertising, which soon moved from specialized publications such as *System* into *Judge, Review of Reviews,* and other general circulation magazines. In April, 1905, with sales running far ahead of the previous year, the ad budget was boosted by increasing the per-razor allotment to fifty cents.

By latter-day standards, and even by the standards of their own day, early Gillette ads were not particularly hard-sell. But they were successful nonetheless, stressing as they did the then-novel feature of "No Stropping, No Honing," and promising from ten to forty shaves per blade. The whole notion was an appealing one to men accustomed to flaying themselves with temperamental straight razors or shelling out a quarter or so for a barbershop shave: "It takes but a moment to insert a new blade," read one 1904 ad. "You cannot cut yourself or fail to give yourself a smooth delightful shave. Think of the cleanliness, the comfort, the security from infection of shaving yourself and of the satisfaction of being free from the barbershop habit. Think of the waits you save — and the dollars." As an added bonus, the ad went on to offer six fresh blades in exchange for twelve dull ones. (At the time, only customers were advised not to hone or strop their used Gillette blades. The company itself did both, and sold the resharpened blades as new. The practice was halted in 1906.)

A few years after these maiden advertising campaigns, the attorney Thomas W. Pelham, by then vice-president of the Gillette Sales Company and a director of the parent corporation, explained the strategy behind them. "Our manner of advertising," he said, "was to get the user to demand of the dealer that he supply him with the article. Our advertisements also stated that if the user could not procure the razor from his dealer to write to us, and we would supply the demand direct." Both consumers and dealers got the message: "Immediately after the advertisements appeared," said Pelham, "we began to get inquiries from prospective users in every part of the United States, and within a short time thereafter we began to get inquiries from the dealers, stating that they had received calls for the Gillette safety razor and asking for terms and prices." And as demand increased, terms and prices became a problem.

Young King Camp Gillette posed soberly for a photographer sometime during the Civil War. *Courtesy of George Gillette*

At thirty-nine, Gillette's dreams had not yet turned to razors and disposable blades. *Courtesy of George Gillette*

In Gillette's version of utopia, ten thousand buildings such as this would house a hundred million people. *Drawing from* The Human Drift

By 1897, Kingie Gillette was three years old, and his doting father was obsessed with razor blades. *Courtesy of George Gillette*

K. C. GILLETTE.
RAZOR.
APPLICATION FILED DEC. 3, 1901.

NO MODEL

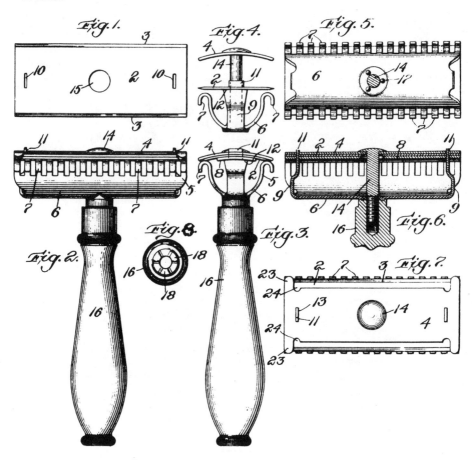

The first patent drawings showed a razor and blade somewhat different
from the final production model.

William Nickerson's assistant, Frank Brown, could be rightly proud of this 1901 blade-grinding machine.

The first advertisement for the Gillette safety razor promised twenty to thirty shaves per blade.

By 1905, the company's letterhead featured an engraving of the recently occupied South Boston factory building.

When John Joyce had decreed that the retail selling price of the standard Gillette razor set was to be five dollars, several other company directors had feared that this was a bit steep for the average wallet. Many dealers, watching the growing popularity of the new razors and blades, felt the same way, and began edging their prices down, some of them offering Gillette sets for as little as $3.69. This may have been a bargain for consumers and for retailers looking for loss leaders, but it augured nothing but headaches for the Gillette Safety Razor Company, which hoped to achieve national distribution by guaranteeing that all dealers would make a comfortable profit on each razor and each package of blades sold. With large retailers trimming prices to levels that other dealers could not economically match, there would be considerable reduction in the number of outlets handling Gillette's products, and a proportionate slowing down of the flow of goods to consumers. Such, at least, was one of the common rationalizations offered at the time by Gillette and other manufacturers of patented goods when they sought to compel retailers to maintain a set selling price. And on a more practical level, there was the ever present possibility that widespread price cutting would also drive wholesale prices downward, and eat into a manufacturer's own profits.

Happily for Gillette, if not for thrifty shoppers, a legal remedy was at hand. For the courts had consistently held that patent rights went beyond the simple manufacture and sale of an article, and included also the absolute right to dictate the retail price. Any dealer selling below that price would be infringing the patent just as surely as if he made and sold an exact copy of the product.

Despite his persistently exotic social and economic beliefs, King C. Gillette was capable of shrewd and decisive business judgment, and he was quick to see that price maintenance could be a critical ingredient of his company's ultimate financial success. A monopoly enterprise, after all, stands to gain little by selling its goods at cut-rate prices. In mid-April, 1905, Gillette discussed the problem with Thomas Pelham, and a few days later he had a long session with an official of the Bissell Carpet Sweeper Company of Grand Rapids, which had been particularly successful in forcing retailers to hew the price line. Following this meeting, Gillette wrote to Pelham and instructed him to prepare the wording for a warning notice to be placed on all razor and blade cartons. And lest there be any doubt about his resolve, he observed that "the more stiff and firm you are in maintaining a minimum selling price to the public, the stronger you will be and firmer your support from the legitimate dealer."

Within a month or so, all blade and razor cartons tumbling out of the Gillette factory in South Boston carried a plainspoken warning that anyone selling the goods for less than the price set by the manufacturer was infringing Gillette's patents and was subject to prosecution. At the same time, the company launched a relentless campaign against dealers defying the discount ban. Gillette salesmen in the field, along with retailers who abided by the fixed price, kept vigilant eyes on newspaper ads and store windows, alerting Pelham immediately to any signs of price cutting. Usually, a stern letter from Pelham — who could, as necessity or the spirit moved him, sign himself as a sales manager or as an attorney — would push straying retailers back into line, and in the handful of cases where friendly persuasion failed, the company didn't hesitate to drag the offenders into court, where they were invariably slapped with an injunction barring further price slashing.

Most cases of price cutting were relatively simple, involving retailers who had merely to be advised that Gillette really meant what it said about prices. Others were a bit more complicated, and took considerable time and diligence to unravel.

It was Frederick A. Grant, a Gillette salesman covering the Midwest out of Chicago, who first came upon the trail of Sam Farbstein. In calling on some of his regular customers in May, 1911, Grant found to his dismay that he had been preceded by a smooth-talking competitor who was peddling Gillette blades at a rock-bottom fifty cents per package of twelve, considerably below the company's factory price to even the largest customers. Informed of the mysterious price cutter, Pelham concluded that someone must be unloading a supply of stolen blades; when they were sold out, he reasoned, the problem would solve itself. By mid-July, however, the Chicago sales manager, J. Frank Rebuck, began getting calls from dealers who reported that a salesman had been offering blades at fifty cents and sixty cents per package, and razors at from $2.50 to $3.00. This was something more serious than a few random blade sales, and if it continued, Rebuck knew that the company would be in for a wave of retail price cutting and angry demands from other dealers that Gillette match the discount wholesale prices.

Learning the name and alleged address of the price-cutting salesman, Rebuck "played a little detective work," as he wrote to Pelham, and after posing as a potential buyer of cut-rate Gillette goods, he found that the salesman represented one Sam Farbstein of Saint Louis. Farbstein, he was told, had considerable dealings with one of Gillette's own major wholesale distributors, the Simmons Hardware Company. Rebuck immediately wired Pelham in Boston, telling him of Farbstein's activities and warning that his rumored sale of a thousand razor sets at just $2.50 was causing quite a stir among loyal Gillette dealers.

Pelham quickly fired off a telegram to salesman Grant, on the road at Mattoon, Illinois. "Proceed immediately to Saint Louis," he said, "investigate and report fully."

In Saint Louis, Grant went directly to the source, and was able to report to Pelham that Farbstein "conducts a cheap variety jewelry store under the name of 'The Crystal.'" But everything seemed to be in order at the store: Grant browsed about and found that what few Gillette razors and blades Farbstein carried were being offered at the full retail price. "If this party has other stock outside of what he carries in showcase," said Grant, "it will be difficult to get a line on him." More definite information was needed.

Grant's next stop was the Simmons Hardware Company, where the trail grew warmer. Farbstein was indeed a Simmons customer, Grant found, and had "been a source of annoyance for a very long period." It seemed that he was a sort of junk dealer, whose specialty was buying damaged goods which he put into shape and sold as new merchandise. Though Simmons had never sold Farbstein any new Gillette products, one company official recalled that there had been possibly a hundred damaged razors included along with a batch of salvage goods bought by Farbstein from the company some weeks before. But this thin thread of information did not begin to explain where Farbstein was getting blades and razors in such quantities that he was severely cutting into Gillette's own sales efforts. By mid-August, Grant was reporting that Farbstein was on the road throughout Kansas and Nebraska, as well as in Saint Louis and Chicago, selling dealers any quantity of blades and razors they desired. "Farbstein is causing a great deal of disturbance throughout this territory," Grant informed Pelham, "and if we do not stop him the dealers will take advantage of the opportunity and buy all their goods from him."

Back in Boston, Pelham was more than a little frustrated. His usual warning letter to Farbstein had gone unanswered and unheeded, an affront to Pelham's abilities as Gillette's chief legal officer; and as dealers began canceling orders with Gillette salesmen because they were getting better bargains from Farbstein, Pelham's reputation as an effective sales manager was threatened too. To make things worse, Farbstein was spreading the word that he was buying his blades directly from Gillette, explaining the low price by claiming that the company was dumping overstocked goods at bargain prices. This was hardly the case — the factory was, in fact, hard pressed to meet the expanding demand. But it sounded plausible enough, and Pelham hesitated to take a tough line against dealers who bought from Farbstein lest they suspect that Gillette was merely trying to keep its own prices firm and rob customers of legitimate bargains. So instead of threatening legal action, he sent all midwestern dealers a form letter, which warned: "It is quite probable that the Gillette Razors and Blades offered to the trade by Farbstein have been damaged by fire or water or possibly that they are second-hand goods. RAZORS OR BLADES OBTAINED FROM SUCH SOURCE OF SUPPLY ARE NOT GUARANTEED BY US, IN ANY WAY."

The fact was that Pelham had no idea where Farbstein was getting his merchandise. Though he had no proof, he suspected that it was stolen, probably from one or more of the larger wholesale distributors. But none of these dealers took kindly to his hint that laxness in their security had caused them to become suppliers of a hot-blade operation, and they were growing a bit impatient at Gillette's inability to get to the bottom of things. "What have you done in reference to the Farbstein matter?" wrote one dealer after the case had dragged through the summer and fall and into December. "It seems rather strange," he added icily, "that you are unable to trace where these goods come from, as all of your goods have serial numbers."

Indeed they did, but one of Farbstein's "peculiar methods," as salesman-sleuth Grant put it in one of his many reports to Pelham, was to remove telltale numbers from the packages of Gillette merchandise he handled. Through numbers stamped on the metal, some of the razors had been traced to a couple of large Saint Louis wholesalers, among them Simmons, but the unmarked blades were another story, and toward the end of 1911 Pelham had to confess to an irate hardware distributor that "we have been wholly unable to trace the blades." Finally, fired by reports that Farbstein had unloaded something like eight thousand packages of blades since the beginning of the year, Pelham himself went to Saint Louis in April, 1912, and met with the chairman of Simmons Hardware. All clues pointed to Simmons as Farbstein's primary source of razor blades, he said, adding that he had no doubt that the blades were somehow stolen from the company's giant warehouse. At last moved to action, Simmons hired a Pinkerton detective to shadow Farbstein "in his daily haunts and at home," and agreed that all blades shipped to it by Gillette should be secretly marked.

But it was neither gumshoes nor cryptic markings that finally brought Farbstein's price-cutting career up short. On June 4, the Simmons vice-president, G. W. Simmons, advised Pelham that "as we were making no particular headway, I took the thing in my own hands." Holding up and searching a couple of truckloads of silver plate that had been sold to Farbstein, Simmons found a package of a hundred dozen Gillette blades tucked away in an odd corner. Called to Simmons's office, the salesman who dealt regularly with Farbstein whipped out a check for the legitimate price, and explained lamely that he had intended to turn it over to the company later. Simmons, suspecting that the salesman was in league with Farbstein and had the check only to cover himself in case of detection, fired the man on the spot. Farbstein, offered a choice of keeping the blades or taking back his check, sheepishly chose the blades — probably, Simmons chuckled, because he had already sold them at a price lower than the legitimate one he now unexpectedly had to pay. In the future, Simmons assured Pelham, Farbstein would get no blades unless he paid the full price. Other wholesalers were informed of Farbstein's methods, and Pelham reported to his midwestern salesmen that "we have effectively stopped the source of supply" of cut-rate goods to Sam Farbstein. It had taken more than a year, but Pelham was at last able to get back to the simpler price-cutting matters that could be handled with mildly threatening letters or a gentlemanly lawsuit or two. Meanwhile, he had engineered an even more important and sweeping victory — this one in the United States Circuit Court of Appeals — and in the process considerably strengthened his position in the company. But as happened so frequently in the history of the Gillette razor, triumph came only in the wake of a near rout.

"I came within an ace of landing in jail"

Almost as soon as Gillette razors and blades went on sale, various rival products began to appear alongside them on dealers' shelves. By 1906 safety razor buyers had at least a dozen brands to choose from, and Pelham advised the Gillette directors in July of that year that all of the competitors "are multiple blade razors and all are imitators of the Gillette, and all are gathering what help and benefit they can from the Gillette advertising." Many of them, too, were considerably undercutting Gillette's zealously maintained five-dollar selling price, and some of the more popular brands — among them the Ever Ready, Gem Junior, and Enders — sold for only a dollar. They had, Pelham reported, "made considerable inroad on the Gillette business."

Strangely enough, the company's patent attorneys seemed unconcerned about these competitors, even though nearly all of them were infringing on Gillette's patent claims. One attorney, the New Yorker Hubert A. Banning, counseled a wait-and-see attitude, all but arguing that it was somehow unseemly to sue a rival concern until it had become large and well established. Many of the competitive companies, he pointed out, operated out of small shops with only a few employees, and could hardly be considered serious challengers to the commanding lead that Gillette had already taken in its field.

Pelham, charged at the time only with marshaling Gillette's sales drive and keeping price cutters in line, was quick to observe that Gillette, just three years before, had had only a tiny factory and a handful of workers, and advised the directors to launch a merciless drive against anyone seeking a foothold in the market that Gillette had so recently carved out for itself. "Our theory is," he said, speaking for the quasi-autonomous Gillette Sales Company, "that we should never permit them to reach the dignity of competition, but that we should hit them hard and hit them in the beginning, otherwise some of them will enlist capital and we will have to fight for our market." Gillette must, said Pelham, turn on its incipient competitors with a "vigorous campaign of destruction by suits, purchase, or other method of keeping them out of the field." Tough words, to be sure, but Pelham wrote from the firing line, and saw unmistakable signs that Gillette sales were beginning to fall under the pressure from upstart rivals. He was, he said, pleased to note that the company's patent attorneys had at last made a move against one competitor, the so-called Zinn razor, though before six months had passed he would realize that instead of wiping out a competitor, the suit was about to destroy the Gillette Safety Razor Company itself.

Like the Gillette, the Zinn was a five-dollar razor. Made in New York by the brothers Martin and Arthur Zinn — doing business as the Gem Cutlery Company, and the manufacturers, too, of the Gem Junior razor — the Zinn came with twenty-four single-edge, flexible blades, and was bidding to make fair progress against Gillette. In attacking Zinn, however, Gillette's attorneys did not move against the manufacturer, but hit instead at the Lawrence, Massachusetts, hardware firm of Sanborn & Robinson.

According to testimony given later in the summer, it all started in March, 1906, when Maurice J. Curran, who was John Joyce's partner in a variety of enterprises — including a wholesale spirits house — stopped by at John T. Maguire's liquor store in Lawrence. A native of Palmer, Massachusetts, Curran had met Joyce at an early age, and the two men had soon gone into business together. Closer than most partners, they were married to sisters, and their families lived for a time in an almost communal mansion in Andover. They shared in most of their investments, too, and Curran had an interest along with Joyce in the razor company; he was more than a little interested, therefore, when John Maguire remarked almost jokingly that he had seen some Zinn razors on a shelf at the Sanborn & Robinson hardware store. Curran asked Maguire to buy one of the razors and bring it to the office of Curran & Joyce, and on March 30 this razor became the basis for a patent-infringement complaint filed by the Gillette Safety Razor Company against the proprietors, Edward M. Sanborn and James B. Robinson. To Everett Chadwick and Hubert Banning,

Gillette's top attorneys at the time, it seemed like a reasonable enough maneuver — if they won their case against these two obscure hardware dealers, retailers everywhere would be put on notice that they sold the Zinn or any other infringing razor at their peril, and Gillette would be armed with a formidable legal club in any future court proceedings. Unfortunately, Chadwick and Banning had neither done their patent homework nor reckoned with the prowess of Clifford E. Dunn, the able New York patent attorney and sometime inventor retained by Gem Cutlery to defend Sanborn & Robinson and the Zinn razor.

Quite simply, Dunn was able to build a case that seemed all but to demolish the sweeping claims of the Gillette patent. Through incisive examination and cross-examination of witnesses, aided mightily by his own mechanical gifts, he constructed a legally convincing body of evidence that the *Gillette* razor could be in possible infringement of numerous prior patents, and that its startling success in the marketplace was due more to high-powered advertising than to actual novelty.

Pelham, asked by the suddenly worried directors to look into the case as it neared its conclusion, was appalled as he pored over the record. Advised by a knowledgeable patent attorney that Gillette had "no shadow of a chance" of winning its suit as presented, he rushed an urgent message to company executives: drop the suit as soon as possible or face the almost certain loss of all patent protection. At the same time, the ambitious Pelham asserted his firm belief that the Gillette razor patent was eminently defensible if handled by wise and competent attorneys, and suggested that in the future the company's critical legal affairs would be best entrusted to "the direction of someone financially interested in the Gillette enterprise and not be left to an attorney who would have nothing to gain except his fees or the glory of winning his case," someone who would "give the matter the best that there was in him." Someone, in other words, like Thomas Pelham.

President Joyce wasted no time in taking Pelham up on his not-so-subtle suggestion, and by the end of January, 1907, Pelham was empowered to take any necessary steps to see that the infringement suit was dropped as quietly as possible. ("You can of course readily appreciate that Mr. Banning and Mr. Chadwick would feel a little humiliated and hurt if this action is to be dismissed," Pelham wrote to a fellow attorney, "but the interests of their clients must come first.")

Providentially, the Zinn razor had meanwhile been withdrawn from the market for economic reasons, so Pelham was able to write coolly to the Zinn attorney, Clifford Dunn, that he had decided to drop the suit because it was no longer of any real importance. His one condition was that the Zinn brothers must agree "not to advertise the fact that we have dismissed this action, nor to use it in any way for commercial purposes or otherwise." And of course, Gillette would pay all of Dunn's fees for handling the case. Dunn, perhaps influenced by the fact that Pelham had also offered him a lucrative retainer to represent Gillette after the matter was settled, advised his clients to accept the proposition, and on March 11, he and Pelham signed a notice of dismissal on behalf of their respective clients. And to keep the possibly damaging record from the eyes of future competitors, the two attorneys arranged to have it removed from the files of the court.

They made another arrangement as well, and on March 15, 1907, Dunn wrote to Pelham in the name of his firm: "We have your letter of March 14th with respect to retaining our services on behalf of the Gillette Safety Razor Company and the Gillette Sales Company, and in reply beg to say that we accept your proposition." And before the summer was out, the Gillette directors had put Pelham in full and official charge of all their legal affairs.

With the advice and counsel of a former adversary, Pelham moved to establish once and for all the validity of the Gillette patents. He and Dunn went to great lengths to keep tabs on potential competitors, even to commissioning a private investigator to snoop on their activities. "Was out trying to do what some people might call housebreaking and last night I came within an ace of landing in jail," he wrote from Ohio in May, adding that "by a good imitation of too much aboard which caused a mistake in location, I escaped." Over the next couple of years, the company filed an occasional suit against infringers, but chary of bringing the basic patent claims to final adjudication, Pelham held back on pushing the actions to their ultimate conclusions, preferring to wait for the right time and place to strike for clear-cut victory. The chance came in late 1909, when the Clark Blade & Razor Company of Newark, New Jersey, went to market with a product strikingly similar to Gillette's. This time around, Gillette was more than prepared for an elaborate attack on its patent claims. Anticipating all the arguments that they knew would be brought to bear against them, Dunn and a battery of other company attorneys had painstakingly rehearsed the history of razor making and laid out in close detail the unique features that set King C. Gillette's invention apart from all others.

When the dust of the hard-fought Clark infringement suit had finally settled in May, 1911, Gillette walked away with ironbound ratification of its patents. Summing up his decision, the judge declared of Gillette's razor that it is "of the greatest utility and has had an enormous sale. This of itself, if the case were doubtful, would constitute an important factor in its determination, but the patent is well able to stand without such aid. It disclosed a novel blade and a novel holder, and their combination in a novel manner." And if Everett Chadwick had been humiliated when his doubtful case against the Zinn razor was dismissed at Pelham's urging, he at least had the satisfaction of seeing that it was his own revised version of Gillette's first patent application that had at last stood up so well in court. Indeed, Chadwick's carefully phrased claim for "a detachable razor blade of such thinness and flexibility as to require external support to give rigidity to its cutting edge" was the leading edge in the war against infringing products, and was so strictly worded — by the standards of its day, at least — that it was an almost impenetrable barrier to serious competition.

Gillette wasted no time in informing the trade of its courtroom triumph, and when Clark's appeal was turned down the following year dealers throughout the country were reminded pointedly that "there are various razors and razor blades — both single and double-edged — which clearly infringe the Gillette patent, and we trust, now that the validity and scope of the Gillette patent has been determined by the U.S. Circuit Court of Appeals, that any dealers that may have handled such infringing razors or blades will immediately discontinue handling the same." Most of them did, and for nearly a decade, until the basic Gillette patents expired, the company would use this landmark decision as a truncheon against intruders in the fast-growing safety razor field, a field that had expanded far beyond the borders of the United States.

4

An Epoch in This
Company's History

"He stropped away himself for dear life"

NO ONE HAD BEEN more aware of the worldwide appeal of the Gillette razor than King C. Gillette when he scurried back to Boston from London in the late summer of 1904 to block the imminent sale of overseas rights to his product. The razor had already been patented in a number of foreign countries, ranging from Britain and France to Chile and Argentina. The custom of shaving, after all, knew few national or cultural boundaries, and Gillette had every reason to believe that if his razor caught on at home it would spread throughout the world. Indeed, Gillette was probably his company's first foreign missionary: when he embarked so reluctantly to take up his duties for Crown Cork & Seal, he had carried with him a good supply of razors and blades for sale in England, enabling the fledgling Gillette Safety Razor Company to claim grandly on its letterhead that it had European agents, the Gillette Company, Limited, with headquarters in London. Gillette had also taken along his brother-in-law, Charles A. Gaines, to work with him in both the bottle-top and razor lines, and

when Gillette returned to America to devote his full time to the razor
company, Gaines stayed on to mind the London business. But it was
soon apparent that the European market demanded more formal attention, and in early 1905 Jacob Heilborn was dispatched across the
Atlantic to set up a London office and explore the general European
situation. Operating at first out of the same office space that Gaines
and Gillette had used for their Crown Cork & Seal affairs — and using
their old cable address of "Stoppalite London" — Heilborn was soon
doing considerable business, both in Britain and on the Continent. And
by the end of the year, Gillette had made another significant move
when it opened its first overseas factory. This step, though, was not
taken by choice, nor did the plant last for long.

In a number of countries, patents lapse if they are not "worked" —
that is, the product must actually be manufactured in the country
granting the patent — within a certain period of time, usually three
years. Happily for Gillette, England as yet had no such provision, but
France was a different story. There, the deadline fell on the next-to-
last day of 1905. Heilborn had been dickering with a French manufacturer to make Gillette razors and blades under contract, but this
plan had been stymied by a combination of disagreement over terms
and an October fire that had wiped out available space and machinery
in the French plant. Something had to be done quickly, and in November, Arno A. Bittues, a former service superintendent at the
Boston Gas Light Company, was sent to Paris to set up a production
line.

Heilborn, somewhat suspicious by nature, was a bit taken aback
when the ebullient, twenty-nine-year-old Bittues, flashing business
cards imprinted "London and Paris," showed up for a visit at the
London office, and he tried several times to ply his unexpected guest
with liquor to find out what he was really up to. "Thinks I am checking his methods or something of that idea," Bittues wrote cheerfully.
But in fact, Bittues was indeed concerned only with the French operation, and after moving on to Paris he looked at several buildings before
settling on space at 24 rue Cauchy, the home of a bicycle-seat manufacturer who was doing business as the American Saddle Company.
After a whirlwind installation of machinery — some shipped over from
the United States, some rented from American Saddle — Bittues man-

aged by the end of the year to put Gillette's first foreign factory on stream, just in time to save the French patent from revocation.

Or so he thought. French courts found otherwise a few years later when they ruled that the rue Cauchy facility had been established only as a stopgap to protect the patent, and was not a serious attempt to make razors and blades in France. Indeed, before a year had passed, Gillette was out of the American Saddle plant and resettled with its machinery in the factory of the French cutler who had agreed to make the company's products in the first place. Whatever the merits of the case, Gillette's French patent was eventually nullified after hard-fought litigation — not for want of novelty, but for lack of working. Bittues, meanwhile, had gone on to Montreal in 1906 to launch a Canadian plant, and stayed on as managing director of the Gillette Safety Razor Company of Canada, Limited.

In Germany, because of the complexity of that country's patent laws and a variety of different patents granted to Gillette — not to mention the welter of infringement suits in which the company was soon embroiled — it was not exactly clear when the cutoff date for patent working might be. But another provision of German law made patents liable to cancellation if a large demand was supplied by goods made abroad. Demand for Gillette goods was growing in Germany, and in early 1907 Jacob Heilborn was in Berlin, writing back to Boston that "we should be manufacturing as soon as possible," and advising that Berlin would be a better factory site than Hamburg. Things did not progress quite so quickly as Heilborn had in mind, but by the end of 1908, Gillette razors and blades were being shipped out of a small factory in Berlin. At about the same time, the finishing touches were being put on a British plant, at Leicester, and by 1909 Gillette could boast three European factories. Each was under the wing of the London sales office, which was in charge of all Gillette business in Europe.

With such an organization behind him, the peripatetic Heilborn ranged throughout Europe, lining up distributors and trying to drum up more business for the Gillette safety razor, which was well on its way to worldwide distribution. And to the extent possible under existing laws, the company maintained its selling price in foreign countries as well as at home, although this sometimes tended to dampen sales growth. Such, at least, was the explanation offered to Sales Director Pelham sometime later by one of his representatives who had tried with little success to make a dent in the Spanish market. In Spain, he said, men would rather spend a bit less for a mediocre razor than pay more for the superior Gillette article. "You probably remember the kind of gunpowder the Spaniards had in the Spanish-American War," he added. "It was something cheap that would almost explode. It is a good deal the same with razors."

There was considerable competition in Europe, mainly from low-cost German-made razors, but Heilborn pressed on, carrying the Gillette banner far and wide. And in his travels, he frequently crossed paths (if not swords) with one Alfred Keene, his counterpart at the AutoStrop Safety Razor Company, a corporation destined to play a large part in Gillette's future.

The AutoStrop razor, developed by the ingenious American inventor Henry Jacques Gaisman, was a kind of compromise between Gillette's disposable blade idea and the more traditional safety razors with blades made to be resharpened. The AutoStrop's main sales pitch was that its blades did not have to be thrown away as frequently as Gillette's, that they were designed for restropping — an operation performed easily by threading a special strop through the razor's hinged blade holder, and then moving the handle rapidly back and forth. Even Heilborn, loyal as he was to his own product, admitted to Keene that the AutoStrop idea was a fetching one. Indeed, Keene reported to Gaisman early in 1909 that Heilborn, calling on a potential customer, had disparaged the AutoStrop as a "toy"; then, according to Keene, Heilborn looked at one of the razors in the dealer's display, conceded that "people like to strop it, as it amuses them, and he stropped away himself for dear life."

Heilborn and Keene were convivial competitors, frequently traveling and socializing together and engaging in good-humored banter as they crisscrossed Europe peddling their respective razors. Once, at a friendly dinner in London, Keene remarked that it seemed somewhat strange that Heilborn wore a beard. "I said to him," Keene noted with characteristic clumsiness in one of his frequent letters to Gaisman in New York, " 'It is a funny thing selling a Gillette and you do not take a shave.' And his answer was that was what all his customers say to him, and he always replied that he does this to advertise the Gillette, because it shows how ugly a man can look by having a beard." Keene, following through with the joke, gave Heilborn an AutoStrop razor, and told him that he hoped he would see the error of his ways.

It was a good, leisurely life for American businessmen in Europe in those languid days before World War I, and Heilborn made the most of it, hobnobbing with the likes of the impresario Oscar Hammerstein and running up expenses that would in time bring him to grief with Boston headquarters. First and foremost, though, he was a company man, and if he and Keene talked business much of the time, he was always careful not to spill any secrets. Anything he said to Keene, after all, was likely to get back to AutoStrop's Henry Gaisman, a fact which Gillette officials sometimes used to their advantage. On a European visit in the spring of 1910, for example, Thomas Pelham ("Mr. P. is quite a sport," Keene wrote in his report, "and played poker, baccarat, etc., to such an extent that I had to lend him $100") confided to Keene, among other things, that Gillette had sold 750,000 razors during the previous year, nearly double the actual sales figure. It never hurts, Pelham knew, to have your competitors think you're doing far better than you really are.

Pelham also mentioned that if he had his way, he might "make some arrangements" with AutoStrop, possibly even buying out the company and combining forces. But such a move was unlikely, he said, because Gillette's directors "are purse proud, and it is hard to get [them] together." He did not mention just how hard it was, but Keene got an inkling a few months later in a letter from Gaisman: "Have just seen in the daily papers," he wrote, "that the Gillette Company have what appears to be a very serious internal quarrel which has taken the form of a litigation in the courts between the two principal owners."

"*I am schooling myself to avoid personalities*"

The two principal owners, of course, were King Gillette and John Joyce, whose feud had been simmering off and on since Gillette returned and settled into his full-time executive post at the razor company. Friends before they had become business associates, the two men tried gamely to get along, but their aims soon began to clash. Details of their conflict are sparse, but the depth of feeling — on Gillette's part, at least — is evident in a letter written to Henry Sachs in Colorado Springs in 1908. Speaking darkly of "those who combined against us — that is Mr. Joyce and his friends and the Baltimore people," Gillette went on to say:

I have done all that any one man can do to build up this company, and since the first inauguration of the company I have gone through many varieties of hell — but in the face of discouragements and the treachery of those about me I have stood by my guns, believed in the proposition, and secured my present position [he was by then president once more] against opposition that would have downed many a man. . . . There are some people to whom a dollar is larger than the biggest heart that ever beat, and to whom the sight of a dollar will make their conscience shrink until nothing is left but a human beast of prey. They think everything is right that is done within the law; to them business is business, and when the dollar glitters, friendship and moral right can go to the devil. Such are some whom I have had around me, such are the type of some around me now. They are not honest and they are dangerous.

For his part, Joyce would later accuse Gillette of "fraudulent and improper conduct," and charge that he had acted against the best interests of the company and its stockholders in pursuit of his own selfish ends.

The contention between the two camps had started in earnest when Gillette blocked Joyce's pet proposition to sell overseas rights to the razor. In the long run, of course, Gillette turned out to be eminently right, and foreign sales and profits have consistently been a priceless boon to the company. At the time, however, Joyce had ample logic on his side — the company had scarcely enough resources to do its job at home, and it seemed almost a godsend that outsiders were willing to put money into the development of overseas markets and give Gillette a share of the proceeds. It appeared to Joyce that Gillette had not only been overbearing, but also wrongheaded in pushing his own strongly held views on the other directors. Joyce also had his doubts about Gillette's insistent and costly scheme to make a considerable portion of the company's products in Newark, New Jersey, and his obvious desire to move the whole operation there.

The Newark project had been set in motion at the same time that Gillette was making plans to move out of its cramped quarters on

Atlantic Avenue and into a spacious, six-story building in South Boston. At first, it all seemed reasonable enough: a Newark mechanical engineer named Leach King had been working with King Gillette's brother Mott in making a bottle-capping machine that the prolific Gillette had recently patented, and Gillette soon had them working for the razor company as well. "Brother Mott," as he was always addressed in letters from "Brother King," was put in charge of procuring boxes for the razor sets, and Leach King was set to designing and building machinery, for both the Boston factory and the French, Canadian, and German branches. It soon became apparent, however, that King Gillette wanted the Boston-Newark connection to expand far beyond a mere service function. As early as June, 1905, in fact, he was corresponding with Leach King about an imaginative plan to make razor blades out of wire — which would, by some process not then or since known, be mashed out to the correct width and thinness. Within a year, Gillette said openly that his long-range goal was nothing less than a total move of the Gillette Safety Razor Company to Newark.

Joyce balked at any such notion, feeling that it was both needless and too expensive, and as president and largest single stockholder, he was able to keep a rein on Gillette's plans. But he did not reckon on, nor could he prevent, what his lawyers would later describe as Gillette's "fraudulent purpose to devise a scheme and create an instrumentality by which he, while a minority stockholder . . . could permanently control the management and operation" of the company. Gillette himself, of course, saw things in a different light, and wrote to his friend and ally Henry Sachs that his innocent purpose had been merely to protect his own interests and those of his family and friends.

Whatever his purpose, Gillette had able counsel, and when the ingenious Inventions Securities Company was organized in the fall of 1906, its chief architect was the future Supreme Court Justice Louis Brandeis, at that time a prominent Boston corporate attorney who had been involved with the Gillette Company's legal affairs almost from the beginning. The idea behind the new company was simple enough: it existed for the sole purpose of holding stock in the razor company. And supersalesman King Gillette was soon able to round up enough shares, including his own and his family's, to give the Inventions Securities Company control of 32,668 shares of Gillette Safety Razor, or more than half of the 65,000 outstanding shares and considerably more than the 24,117 shares held by Joyce and his partner Maurice Curran. For Gillette himself, it was a costly venture. To consolidate his own control of the holding company, he borrowed $62,000 from the First National Bank of Boston to buy the stock that the Pittsburgh bottle manufacturer Charles L. Flaccus had picked up for a mere $250 just five years before. But it was well worth it. As president of Inventions Securities — which was soon reorganized as the Gillette Securities Company — Gillette had considerably more corporate clout than he had enjoyed as a minority stockholder-director with only a moral claim to a major voice in shaping company policy.

Gillette first flexed his new muscles in early April, 1907. Just a year before, in a power play that had convinced him of the wisdom of acquiring voting control of the company, he had been eased out of his vice-presidency and into the secretary-treasurership to make room for Harvey Coale, one of the Baltimoreans who had bought stock from Gillette and then proceeded to join forces with Joyce. Meanwhile, Coale had sold his stock and withdrawn from the company. Gillette easily had himself elected vice-president — Ward Holloway took over as secretary-treasurer — and later in the summer he managed to change the corporate bylaws to expand the board of directors from five members to seven. This, of course, enabled him to fill the board with hand-picked associates, and set the stage for his total takeover.

Meanwhile, events were conspiring against the razor company's fortunes. A combination of copycat competitive products and bottle-necks at the Gillette factory had set sales on a roller-coaster ride: blade output, after seesawing up to more than 80,000 packages in August of 1907, plunged to less than half that figure in September. From coast to coast, dealers were firing off desperate letters and telegrams begging for more and bigger shipments. It was a problem that would plague the company for several more years, and it only increased the tensions between the Gillette and Joyce factions.

In October, Gillette made his move. With typically dramatic flair, he resigned as a director and officer, knowing full well that it would hardly do for the inventor, namesake, and controlling stockholder to be playing the part of disgruntled outsider. Besides, he had carefully orchestrated the whole move in advance. On cue, the directors voted with fine irony that John Joyce, his archrival, should persuade Gillette to withdraw his resignation. Having no other choice, Joyce did so, and by mid-January King C. Gillette was elected president of the Gillette Safety Razor Company, a post he would hold almost until his death a quarter of a century later.

For a while, it seemed that all was well. Joyce took Gillette's new position — and his own downgrading to the vice-presidency — with outward good grace; Gillette, his boardroom battle won, began taking an avid hand in the company's long-range and day-to-day operations. He was particularly concerned with technical matters that continued to dog the Boston manufacturing operation, and for solutions he looked more and more toward Newark. By early 1908 he had installed Leach King in rented factory space there, and was corresponding with him about a proposal to improve blade production by turning out the blades in a long, continuous strip rather than by the individual method that was causing so many problems in Boston. "It can readily be seen," he wrote to King, "that if this process could be utilized it would mean an enormous saving for our company and put us in a position where we can make some money on our blades, which up to the present time we have never been able to do."

Gillette also put Leach King to work designing and producing a new, more compact "pocket edition" razor, and he himself paid particular attention to the appearance of the product. Once, he sent King some rough sketches of possible handle patterns, one of which, he said, was taken from a bracelet he had bought in Italy for his sister Fanny: "This bracelet was made after the pattern of a Grecian column in one of the old temples, and bent into the form of a bracelet. It is one of the most beautiful and artistic pieces of work I have ever seen." Dabbling in every phase of the operation, Gillette relished being president, and by mid-1908 he could write to his brother-in-law Charles Gaines, who had returned to London on business, "I feel more contented and more interested in the company than ever before since the company was started."

Contributing to Gillette's newfound happiness was the departure from the company of Ward Holloway, who had frequently been at odds with Gillette on company policy. In failing health, Holloway had sold his Gillette stock to John Joyce, who took over Holloway's duties as treasurer. Gaines, in responding to his brother-in-law's letter, said he was pleased to learn that Holloway was no longer with the company. "I have not," he said, "for a long time, been able to believe that he was strictly honorable in his business dealings." But he was even more pleased to find Gillette and Joyce "drawing closer together and understanding each other better."

The two were indeed united in their common desire to put the company on a profitable footing. But Joyce continued to argue against Gillette's wildly escalating plans for Newark, and felt that money spent there, as well as the considerable funds that Gillette was squirreling away as surplus for use in yet-undetermined projects, should be paid out to the directors as dividends. What the president and his friends on the board were doing, Joyce believed, was attempting to hold down dividends in order to lower the market value of the company stock, thus forcing Joyce and his allies to sell out their holdings.

Whatever Gillette's motives, it is probable that he was indeed keeping an unreasonably tight lid on dividends. The 1908 payout, for example, came to $130,000 — the same amount distributed to shareholders during each of the previous two years — at a time when the company was left at year's end with combined cash reserves and surplus of some $900,000.

If Joyce felt that Gillette was depriving him of his rightful share of the pie, Gillette believed that Joyce was displaying an appalling lack of gratitude for all that Gillette had done for him in the way of free stock and ground-floor entry into the razor and blade bonanza. "I am schooling myself to avoid personalities and to think the best possible of those I am associated with," Gillette wrote to Henry Sachs in early 1909, but he added pointedly: "I have never received a share of stock or a dollar from anyone I am or have been associated with. On the contrary, my supposed closest and best friends and associates have proved themselves most ungrateful in their attitude toward me." Toward these ingrates, Gillette's attitude was clear. "I shall take mighty good care," he assured Sachs, "that those who have made me suffer shall never again be placed in a position where they can make me feel the knife."

For a time, the dagger thrusts had come uncomfortably close. When Holloway withdrew from the company in 1908, he and his wife also sold their considerable shares of the Gillette Securities Company to Joyce and Curran, giving those two Gillette antagonists a position in the very holding company that had been set up as a counter to their influence. Their holdings came nowhere near to matching those of Gillette and his cronies, but their presence was nonetheless nettlesome, and Gillette feared it as an opening wedge that might lead to eventual control. Happily, Louis Brandeis had provided Gillette with a prepared position to fall back on in just such an eventuality. The year before, he had set up still another holding company — the more personalized King C. Gillette Company — and Gillette now proceeded to transfer his and his cohorts' shares in the Gillette Securities Company to the King C. Gillette Company. Joyce and Curran, of course, were not given the opportunity to make the exchange, and soon found themselves in the cold once more. As Gillette put it so primly in a letter to Sachs, the King C. Gillette Company "will not take the shares of those whom it does not wish to be associated with."

With a house-that-Jack-built control of the holding company that controlled the holding company that owned a controlling interest in the razor company that was the point of the whole Byzantine exercise, Gillette exulted to Sachs that he was at last able to "push things ahead without continual obstruction." And what he seemed to be pushing hardest was the proposed New Jersey venture.

By early 1909 the company had bought — over Joyce's objections — a twenty-acre parcel of land alongside the Pennsylvania Railroad tracks about midway between Newark and Elizabeth. Gillette was especially pleased with the property, which had been picked out by his brother Mott and cost the company $65,000. He was even more pleased with the steel-making and manufacturing complex that was intended to rise there in plain view of the scores of passenger trains passing by each day. Indeed, he and Dr. Leonard Waldo, perhaps the nation's foremost authority on steel technology at the time, intended to erect nothing less than the most advanced plant in the world for the production of high-grade steel. Built of brick, glass, and steel, operated entirely by electricity, the plant would be a technological marvel, turning out steel not only for Gillette razor blades, but for outside customers as well. "We would be specialists in high-grade steels for special purposes," Gillette explained to Henry Sachs. "Every razor going out would carry at least one page in each instruction booklet calling attention to the fact that the Gillette S. R. Co. were specialists in high-grade steels." And there was now no question in Gillette's mind that Newark would soon be the home of his whole company.

"Eventually," he wrote, "all our business will be done there — the making of razors and all that pertains to same." He added that he planned to move to New Jersey himself just as soon as the factories there were completed.

Gillette had projected originally that the steel mill might begin operating sometime in early 1910. But as summer dragged into fall, it became obvious that steel expert Leonard Waldo — whose $12,000 annual salary was as much as Gillette and Joyce were paid at the time — was not making the kind of progress expected of him. He had done considerable metallurgical work, but it wasn't until late August that he got around to having the plant site graded. At last even Gillette's allies on the board joined Joyce in doubting the wisdom of the Newark scheme, and in November, Director Charles Gaines — who had returned from London to become general manager of the Gillette plant in Boston — was sent to New Jersey to investigate the stalled steel plant. As Gillette's brother-in-law, Gaines tried hard to see the good side of the project, but after careful consideration he advised that the whole thing should be suspended. Gillette, perhaps realizing by now that he had made a costly mistake, went along with the recommendation, and by February the property was put up for sale.

Joyce may have felt vindicated when the Newark venture was scrapped, but he continued to fume over the machinations that barred him from exercising what he believed to be his proper controlling interest in the company. And in May, 1910, he and Maurice J. Curran filed suit against the Gillette Safety Razor Company, the Gillette Securities Company, the King C. Gillette Company, and King C. Gillette himself — along with those shareholders and directors allied with him — demanding that voting power be stripped from the holding companies and returned to the individual owners of razor company stock. Now the lines were clearly drawn, with the capitalists Joyce and Curran on one side and the inventor Gillette on the other. The whole future of the company hung in precarious balance.

Despite the rancor of the legal proceedings, which threatened to become almost Dickensian in length and complexity, the razor and blade business went on. William Nickerson — so distressed during the early days of the Joyce-Gillette imbroglio that he had sold most of his company stock — proceeded with plans for an automatic honing machine that would greatly improve the blademaking operation. Gillette himself, even in the heat of boardroom battle, developed a new razor which he said could be profitable to the company at a retail price of just one dollar. And in a prophetic move that heralded a long and close relationship between the Gillette Company and the sports world, Gillette advertising began to feature testimonials from baseball heroes of the day — who were presented with gold-plated, engraved razor sets as a reward for their cooperation. The great Honus Wagner praised the Gillette razor, and so did John McGraw, the manager of the New York Giants. According to an ad appearing in October, 1910, McGraw would not be without his Gillette, "especially when I am on the road with the team. It makes shaving all to the merry."

Then in May, another legal shoe clunked to the floor at Gillette's executive offices when the United States Patent Office, following years of objections from Henry J. Gaisman, the AutoStrop razor inventor, granted to King Gillette a patent for a razor with a blade-clamping mechanism strikingly similar to the one used in the AutoStrop. Inasmuch as Gillette's invention had been judged to predate Gaisman's, the competitive AutoStrop razor was now an infringement of the newly awarded Gillette patent. A lawsuit was clearly in order, and even if the action failed to drive AutoStrop out of the market, it would still have a certain harassment value, and might make many dealers think twice about handling the AutoStrop razor. In any event, after sparring with Gaisman for so long in the Patent Office, Gillette was now bound to uphold its rights in court. There was, however, a slight problem.

In the very first days of the old American Safety Razor Company, Gillette had agreed that he would assign to the corporation all rights to any improvements he might make in safety razors. Now, "in view of the action brought by Mr. Joyce and Mr. Curran," Gillette steadfastly refused to assign the critical patent to the company, even though the directors had already laid out thousands of dollars in legal fees to obtain it. Joyce was furious, but given a slate of directors who, in his words, "vote in accordance with [Gillette's] wishes," there was little he could do when the board decided to pay all expenses for prosecuting the suit, while leaving the patent in King Gillette's hands.

For Joyce, conditions had become intolerable. He owned the largest individual interest in a company whose product was bidding fair to become a worldwide standard, a company with almost limitless potential. Yet he was constantly bedeviled by the company's seemingly eccentric founder, whose goals seemed increasingly capricious, unclear, and contradictory. Joyce was thankful that the Newark scheme had been nipped before it got out of hand, but he lived in constant dread that the imaginative Gillette might someday carry through an even more disastrous venture. And what, Joyce wondered, did Gillette mean when he insisted that he as an individual had the right to manufacture and sell the razor at issue in the Gaisman suit? Could it be that he was threatening to start a rival company, independent of Joyce's investment? Joyce did not know, but he fully believed that Gillette was capable of just about anything.

Lesser men might have given up the battle, sold their shares, and withdrawn from the company — which may well have been what Gillette was hoping for. Joyce was, after all, several times a millionaire from his other varied enterprises, and was not solely dependent for his fortunes on the razor company. But Joyce could be as scrappy as Gillette, and chose instead to resort to the ultimate argument of wealthy men: he offered to buy out the opposition — which may also have been what Gillette was hoping for.

There was no regular, ordered trading in Gillette common stock at the time, so there was no clearly established value per share; when trades were made, price was negotiated between individual buyer and seller. Joyce proposed to buy the stock at an attractive $87.50 per share, and to pay an equivalent sum for stock in the Gillette Securities Company and the King C. Gillette Company, both of which would then be dissolved and their shares converted into stock in the razor company. Those owning shares in the holding companies were also given the option of exchanging their stock for shares in the razor company — but either way, John Joyce stood to be the final winner.

If accepted, the offer would mean the end of King C. Gillette's hard-won control of the company. It would also end the bickering that had dragged on for half a decade, and it would make Gillette a rich man in fact as well as on paper.

For Gillette, the decision was a fairly easy one. Weary of corporate infighting, his long-sought goal of great personal wealth now clearly in view, he took Joyce up on his offer, and urged his associates to do likewise. By year's end, the Gillette Safety Razor Company was in

Joyce's hands, and General Counsel Pelham was assuring stockholders that "the management under Mr. Joyce will be conservative and able," and at the same time trying hard not to imply that it had been otherwise under Mr. Gillette.

Gillette, meanwhile, had sold more than two-thirds of his shares to Joyce, taking in some $900,000 on the transaction. He had also agreed to turn over to the company all pending and future patents, and not to work for any competing razor company; in exchange, the directors agreed to pay Gillette $12,000 a year for five years, with the stipulation that he could be away from the office as much as he cared to. Independently wealthy now, Gillette could do as he pleased, untroubled by the day-to-day cares of commercial enterprise. He could turn to other interests, which even in times of corporate turmoil had continued to range beyond the business of razors and blades.

"Promoters are the true socialists of this generation"

Radical reformers of the utopian stripe must have been nonplussed in 1905, when a familiar face began staring out at them from razor-blade packages and magazine advertisements trumpeting the overwhelming virtues of the new Gillette safety razor. The cheeks were a bit fuller now, and the mustache had been trimmed back a bit, but there could be no mistake: this was the same King C. Gillette — could there be anyone else named King C. Gillette? — who just a decade before had rocketed to esoteric prominence with the publication of *The Human Drift*. Here, his hair parted neatly down the middle, wearing a wing collar and a sparkling stickpin, was the man who had once proclaimed a movement to lead humanity out of economic darkness and into a shining world of idyllic peace, justice, and equality — and now he was shamelessly hawking razor blades. Granted, he was doing it with a certain amount of style, and his readers of old may have detected a familiar ring in some of the ads, many of which bore unmistakable traces of Gillettian rhetoric. "Like a triumphant army onward, marches the Gillette Safety Razor to Success," said one, adding grandly: "The Gillette Safety Razor is one of the greatest mechanical inventions of the 20th century. It *was* a necessity and *now* a success." Still, all this was a far cry from summoning downtrodden masses to economic paradise, and it was apparent that the onetime president of the utopia-bound Twentieth Century Company had sold out his old ideals and switched allegiance to the crass world of commerce, had jettisoned his views on the evils of competition, the rapacity of capitalists, and the wastefulness (if not outright sinfulness) of advertising.

He had, in fact, done nothing of the kind. For even as he was mixing it up in bare-knuckle corporate power plays, even as he urged ruthless action against competitors, King Camp Gillette did not abandon his utopian vision. And in 1906, just when he was scheming to outwit his associates at the razor company, he burst into print once more, this time in *National Magazine*, a respected journal of public affairs whose many advertisers sometimes included the Gillette Safety Razor Company. Though he did mention his "now well-known razor," Gillette's latest literary work had nothing to do with shaving. Titled "World Corporation (Unlimited)," the article was billed as a synopsis of a larger work in progress, and along with recounting the story of the Scranton hotel room, it remains the most cogent expression of Gillette's social goals, which he fully believed could be reached "within the lifetime of more than nine-tenths of those now living." In addition, Gillette displayed again his serene self-confidence: it never even entered his mind, he said, that his reasoning might be faulty.

The 1906 article was indeed a prelude to a more lengthy work, but before this appeared, there would be more — much more — to be said about Gillette's plans for a better world. In 1907, another preliminary book on the Gillette social philosophy rolled off the presses, its frontispiece graced with the same distinctive photograph that served along with the subject's bold signature as a trademark for the Gillette Safety Razor Company. The book had not actually been written by Gillette himself — he was, after all, busy enough with his more worldly affairs — but by an ardent disciple and collaborator, the now-forgotten novelist Melvin Linwood Severy, who had become one of the few really close friends that Gillette would have in his life. Eight years Gillette's junior, Severy was also an inventor, though his curious musical instruments, the choralcelo and vocalcelo, were hardly crowned with the same success that came to Gillette's razor. But Severy, who lived in a Boston suburb, had not been drawn to Gillette as a fellow inventor, but as a social philosopher, and the brief biographical mention in the book makes no note of the razor, referring to Gillette only as the "inventor" of the system which Severy was equally certain would save the world.

Titled *Gillette's Social Redemption*, the thick, 783-page volume more than measured up to the first sentence of its preface: "This book is not intended to be interesting," wrote Severy with disarming candor, "nor has it been written with the idea that it will be consecutively read from cover to cover." Indeed, it was hardly written to be read from page to page, or from sentence to sentence, and must surely rank as one of the most tedious philosophical tomes ever composed in the English language. In *The Human Drift*, Gillette had taken for granted the reader's knowledge that industrial society had come to a poor pass and was in need of major overhaul; in *Gillette's Social Redemption*, Severy — with the advice and consent of the master — sought to catalogue illustrative examples of all the myriad ills that cried out for radical solution. Quoting liberally from vivid reports of man's worldwide inhumanity to man, outlining the evils of political and corporate corruption, he filled his pages with tales of atrocious cruelty, pausing after one outburst to observe simply, "It is needless to multiply instances of the more than fiendish crimes of the unspeakable Turk."

One critic, who can be pardoned for failing to plow through the whole concoction, was moved to say of the Severy-Gillette book: "Sensational 'stories' from daily newspapers, even of the 'yellow' type, are seriously treated as historical materials, without rational criticism. All the muckrakers are here invited to unload their unsavory burdens, and the result is a sort of literary dumping-ground." In the New York *Times*, a long-suffering reviewer noted charitably: "It may be that some of the world's scandals are omitted from this large and handsome book, of whose paper and print it is possible to speak well. . . . Never, perhaps, have social conditions been so thoroughly denounced, and assuredly never before have so many human blemishes been assembled and systematized and indexed for ready reference." As for the authors, the reviewer concluded that they "are unable to communicate their ideas," and noted that their portraits showed them to be "nice-looking gentlemen, whose features scarcely reflect the age, labor, and care which accompany deep thought."

Undaunted — or perhaps strangely inspired — by the lack of critical enthusiasm, Severy and Gillette proceeded as planned and published yet another preliminary book, *Gillette's Industrial Solution*, the following year. With a mere 598 pages, this work was not quite so ponderous as its predecessor, and as its title implied, it proposed answers to the evils posited in the previous companion volume. As if to give cachet to its theories, the book also featured a photograph of Gillette — said to be his favorite photograph of himself, it shows him in a snappy Panama hat, leaning comfortably against the back of a straight chair — over the unmistakable diamond-and-arrow trademark of the Gillette Safety Razor Company. Gillette himself had selected this insignia — accompanied by the slogan "Known the World Over" — not long before, possibly because he felt it symbolized more than just his industrial ambitions. Shown a number of possible designs, he had rejected those that embodied blades or razors, but his eyes lit up when he spotted the one featuring his name alone, its letters pierced by an arrow and enclosed in a diamond-shaped background. As the company draftsman who created this trademark recalled some years later, Gillette "asked me the meaning of the arrow through the letters. I told him my idea was that the arrow was forging ahead, carrying Gillette with it. He told me I need not go any further as I had struck upon the design that pleased him."

The design pleased other company executives as well, though it is doubtful that any of them anticipated or approved of its incidental use in promoting their president's balmier economic theories. As the adjacent caption in *Gillette's Industrial Solution* said: "The argument most frequently used against Socialism is that its sponsors are dreamers, impractical, or those whose failure in life has made them dissatisfied with present conditions. As a successful inventor and the head of one of the largest corporations in the world [a gross exaggeration, to be sure], King C. Gillette is an eloquent refutation of this theory."

Be that as it may, the book was essentially a windy and even more chaotic rehash of *The Human Drift*, complete to the plan of a vast industrial metropolis at Niagara Falls. As an alternative to this, it detailed the astounding claim, made almost in passing in *Gillette's Social Redemption*, that the entire human race — at the time estimated at about 1.5 billion — could live and support itself in Texas, with enough land left over to equal the combined areas of England, Wales, the New England states, Maryland, Delaware, the District of Columbia, and New Jersey. Severy granted that existence would be crowded, but added cheerfully, "*Modern* man is a social being, and his happiness increased by the presence of his fellows: indeed, the high rate of insanity which obtains among ranchmen, whose duties keep them for long periods without any other society than that of sheep, dogs, cows and other domestic animals, demonstrates conclusively that the craving for companionship has, in modern man, a deep psychic lodgement, and cannot safely be gainsaid."

Not least of the boons in store for mankind under the Gillette system of organization, wrote Severy, would be the total abolition of advertising, which would leave behind only "memories which would voice themselves something like this: 'None genuine without the name of Smith on every can.' 'If it isn't Jones's it's a fraud.' 'Beware of imitations. Unscrupulous men are counterfeiting Brown's products. Look out for the Trade-Mark on every package. No goods pure without it, etc., etc.' " But strangely enough, at the very time these words were appearing in print, the man who had inspired them was playing a somewhat contradictory role: King C. Gillette, looking for all the world like a slightly dissolute sideshow barker, was appearing in ads that shouted: "If my razor wasn't good enough for me to use I wouldn't ask you to try it!" Gillette seemed to be living in two different worlds, though it may well be that those worlds were not quite so far apart as they seemed.

In a lengthy 1912 memo to his fellow directors, Gillette advised them in no uncertain terms that "*the whole success of this business depends on advertising.*" And the whole point of Gillette's advertising, he said, was to pummel weaker competitors into submission, leaving Gillette in near-total control of the market. "All it requires for us to drive them from the field," he said in the steel-tipped language of a military commander, "is to train a Gatling gun on them — they could never stand the fire." Later, becoming even more bloodthirsty, he cautioned, "We must be the aggressor — we must be continually advancing and drive them back at the point of the bayonet, and our ammunition must be money for advertising."

Could this be the King C. Gillette of social redemptions and industrial solutions speaking? Was it the same man who had once declared roundly, "I dispute the proposition that competition is the life of trade?" It could be, and it was, but the inventor-businessman-utopian had in the meantime been able to rationalize — to his own satisfaction, at least — his apparently schizophrenic views.

He did it, characteristically enough, in still another book, the promised follow-up to his article in *National Magazine*. It was titled simply *World Corporation*. He had found time to write this one entirely on his own, and if he did not disavow his previous collaborations with Severy, he advised readers that this latest volume superseded all previous works on the subject. He was also careful not to mention his razor-related activities, though there was surely no mistaking that familiar face and signature on the opening page.

As he had in *The Human Drift*, Gillette continued to maintain that centralization of industrial enterprise was an inevitable trend in the modern world. In the natural course of events, he said, centralization would beget centralization, until at last every giant corporation would be merged into a single immense entity, a mystical, almost living organism which Gillette was pleased now to call the World Corporation. During the evolutionary process leading to this end, said Gillette,

men of quick perception and great financial and executive ability [men, in other words, like himself] become the seers and prophets of their generation. They see far into the future, and discount that future by coming to the front as promoters, and by securing options on competitive plants of industry and bringing them together into great noncompetitive corporate bodies they are able to make enormous profits. . . . These profits are legitimate under our present system, and these far-seeing men not only deserve what they make, but they deserve the thanks of every individual in the world, for their work of organization is that of the pioneer who blazes the way for greater things to follow.

It was a beautifully simple proposition: by driving his competitors to the wall and forcing them out of business, by striving for a safety-razor monopoly and growing rich in the process, Gillette was merely acting as a benefactor of mankind and hastening the advent of the millennium! It was almost as though the unfortunates whose businesses he might destroy or absorb in the process should be grateful for the opportunity to participate in the inexorable and beneficent drift toward total centralization. "Promoters are the true socialists of this generation," Gillette wrote, "the actual builders of a cooperative system which is eliminating competition, and in a practical business way reaching results which socialists have vainly tried to attain through legislation and agitation for centuries." It is tempting to guess what J. P. Morgan might have made of such talk. Or Eugene V. Debs, for that matter.

Considering Gillette's continued attentiveness to the minutiae of the razor business, it is perhaps well to wonder just how serious he really was about these more cosmic pursuits. On the other hand, it could just as easily be asked how a man who consistently preached such heady social and economic gospel could really have been all that engrossed in something so comparatively pedestrian as an instrument for removing whiskers. But the fact is that he was equally interested in both, and regretted the failure of the one as much as he rejoiced in the success of the other. And in his own way, he pursued his social vision with the same practical zeal that impelled him in his chasing after the razor rainbow.

His main purpose in publishing *World Corporation*, in fact, was to announce that he had actually incorporated – in what was then the territory of Arizona – a company of the same name. And he fully believed, as he said in his book, that "World Corporation will displace all governments. Nations will be helpless in its grasp. Absorbing, controlling, and eventually directing industrial life, it will tear down the barriers of caste and nationality and combine in one brotherhood all the people of the earth for one common purpose." There were three directors of this ambitious enterprise – Charles A. Gaines, Gillette's brother-in-law; Edward S. Crockett, a Boston attorney whose office at 6 Beacon Street doubled as the corporation's world headquarters; and Gillette himself, whose title was president.

This was not, however, a post he intended to hold permanently. Overcome with uncharacteristic modesty – and, in fairness to the genuine depths of his beliefs, he was seeking a highly able man for the job – Gillette offered the presidency to none other than Theodore Roosevelt, recently of the Executive Mansion in Washington, D.C. To make it worth the old Rough Rider's while, Gillette said that he would become one of twenty volunteers to pay Roosevelt $50,000 apiece in advance – a full million dollars in all – to assume the post for a four-year term. "I make this offer," he said, "feeling that the position would carry with it greater honor than to be President, King, or Emperor of any nation in the world."

It was an exquisitely woolly proposition, as was the whole naive notion of an all-embracing world corporation. Neither Roosevelt nor the nineteen requisite philanthropists rose to Gillette's challenge; the World Corporation, like its predecessor, the Twentieth Century Company, withered and died aborning, its fall mourned only by a minuscule knot of zealots.

The Gillette Safety Razor Company, of course, was quite another story, and the self-styled "Inventor of the System of World Corporation" drew a great deal of satisfaction from the global spread of his more down-to-earth invention. But considering his grander ambitions, there is an almost poignant ring to the 1913 advertising brochure that sonorously declared: "The message of Solon to the Greeks of old was 'Man Know Thyself.' The message of Gillette to all the world is 'Man Shave Thyself,' and he has not only pointed the way but provided the means to make this possible."

He had indeed, though it is as understandable as it is ironic that only his withdrawal from active management gave the company the internal stability required to capitalize on the shaving revolution made possible by his invention and his persistence.

"Have this framed; it marks an epoch in this Company's history"

Almost as if to ratify the transfer of power and control from King Gillette to John Joyce, the company was recapitalized and reorganized as a Massachusetts corporation in mid-1912, though this had scant impact on operations. Gillette, the titular president, soon moved to California, which he used as a base for years of restless roaming throughout a world that embraced his razor but shunned his social nostrums. Joyce, the man in charge now, was vice-president, and while he set broad policy and took an active interest in company affairs, day-to-day operations were the responsibility of professional managers rather than inventors or promoters.

The old fighters, the men who had been with Gillette from the beginning of his dream, were mostly gone. Ward Holloway, perhaps the first to hear of the disposable blade idea, was dead at an early age, leaving Gillette with bitter memories of real or imagined betrayal; Edward Stewart, the first to have faith enough in Gillette's razor to try to raise money for it, had turned on his old friends and sued them for allegedly cheating him out of his fair share of the bounty. From his healthful retreat in Colorado Springs, the early investor Henry Sachs continued to bombard Boston headquarters with comments and suggestions, but was frequently regarded as a meddlesome minority stockholder to be humored because he was a friend of the founder. Even Jacob Heilborn — "fine fellow or damned good actor," as William Nickerson had once called him to his face — had not long survived the new regime. Joyce had frequently marveled at Heilborn's large expense accounts, and at the end of 1912 things finally came to a head over a costly and unauthorized trip back to Boston. After Heilborn returned to London, where he usually put up at the posh Savoy Hotel, the executive committee wrote and asked for his immediate resignation. Thomas Pelham, who saw him not long afterward, reported that Heilborn was "not only shocked but dazed" at the news. For a while, Heilborn thought of getting back at the company somehow, and even considered going to work for Henry Gaisman at AutoStrop; in the end, he withdrew quietly, retired in London, and changed his name to Hilborn. Only Nickerson, who had proved more than once that he was no businessman, stayed on as a remnant of those earliest days of struggle, confining himself primarily to the mechanical matters that he knew best.

Chief among the men now running the show was Frank Joseph Fahey, who had been finishing up his high school education in Baltimore at the time that King Gillette was visiting with William Painter in the same city and talking over inventive ideas. By 1896, following three years with a Cleveland railroad company, Fahey (who pronounced his name "Fay") had signed on with a Chicago-based grain and cotton broker, and later became the firm's managing partner in New York. He had been so impressed with Gillette's new safety razor that in 1906 he joined the Gillette Sales Company as a director and the advertising manager; by 1909, his mania for hard work and tight organization — he was not hindered, either, by his marriage to John Joyce's daughter — had made him a director and the assistant treasurer of the parent company in Boston, and when Gillette sold out to Joyce, Fahey was elected treasurer. In fact if not in name, he was the chief executive officer of the Gillette Safety Razor Company, and for nearly two decades to come, Fahey and salesman-lawyer Thomas Pelham would run the company virtually in tandem, and with seemingly brilliant efficiency.

As head of the all-important sales force, Pelham was the more visibly active of the two, and with good reason. Since the first big surges in 1904 and 1905, razors and blades had been selling at a fitful pace, with blades somewhat stronger than razors — which is how it should have been, for King Gillette had always seen blade sales as the key to prosperity. As early as 1906 a company memo noted, "The greatest feature of the business is the almost endless chain of blade consumption, each razor sold paying tribute to the company as long as the user lives," though the company did not start making money on its blades until at least two years later, when prices were raised back to a dollar per package of twelve after a disastrous experiment at selling them at ten for fifty cents.

The price boost was made with some trepidation. "In order to overcome any objections that may be raised by the consumer," Gillette had written to his brother-in-law Charles Gaines, "or at least to overcome such objections as may be made as far as possible, we hope to have a better blade, and have it machine polished, which will improve its appearance very greatly." Not long afterward, a relieved Gillette had been able to advise Henry Sachs that "our dollar blade proposition went into effect without a hitch. No complaints from trades people at all and few from users — makes a difference of fully $500,000 profit in year for us on our present blade output." The key to the whole enterprise, then, was to boost razor sales, and the blades would almost take care of themselves.

To that end, Pelham drove himself as hard as he drove his sales staff, making frequent, grueling tours of the hinterlands to drum up business and inspect the company's competitive front lines. "Am wearing out the soles of my shoes rather than the seat of my pants," he wrote back to the executive committee from Kansas City, two weeks shy of winding up an eighty-three-day circuit of the country in 1913. And on the same trip, he sent back such encouraging news as

"Detroit is certainly a Gillette town and if we had conditions everywhere appearing as they are in Detroit, our factory would be pushed to its utmost to meet the demand." From Milwaukee, he reported that "Gillette business is very good," and said of a wholesale drug firm there, "They remembered my visit in 1905 when I got them to put in 12 Gillettes, and they thought they were good sports to take so many." San Francisco, like Detroit, was a Gillette town, and so was Los Angeles. In Seattle, he had some misgivings about the local salesman's wardrobe, but soon set him straight. "He was wearing a winter ulster, which I told him he ought to shed," wrote Pelham in early May. "He also had a Norfolk suit which will just pass, but his hat — well, it was loud, and he now has another."

"Am just a little tired," Pelham confessed in Cincinnati, near the end of a trip that took him to several dozen cities, but he still had energy enough left to take on an underhanded competitor, a so-called demonstrator who had set himself up in rented floor space in an established retail store.

"I found a German infringing razor on 5th Street near Race Street," he said. "Usual kind and usual display and methods. I handed out my card. Man looked white. I said: 'You know it is an infringement.'

"He said: 'Yes. How long will you give me to get out?'

"I said: 'Today.'

"He said: 'I'll go.'

"Incident closed."

Back in Boston after his nearly three months on the road, Pelham could survey the ever growing Gillette empire with a strong sense of satisfaction. Razor sales may have plateaued somewhat — not until 1915 would the record volume of 1911 be matched — but blades were beginning to go at a steadily increasing pace, rising by something like a million packages each year. Still more growth was made possible in 1914, when William Nickerson, always the ingenious tinkerer and refiner of machines, perfected the equipment for automatic blade honing, a process that had previously involved several hand operations. During the same year, the company came out with a variant on its mainstay standard razor. Dubbed the Bulldog, this model came with a thick, heavily knurled handle which Pelham told his salesmen was intended for the "solid-framed, athletic chap. . . . It goes with his stout walking stick, his Bulldog pipe, his man's size pocket knife and his thick fountain pen."

Nor was the women's market overlooked. In mid-1915 Gillette introduced its Milady Decollete — "brought out after frequent requests from Palm Beach, Virginia Hot Springs and other pleasure resorts," the field force was solemnly assured. It was the first razor designed and marketed specifically for women, and was billed in the extensive national advertising campaign as the "safest and most sanitary method of acquiring a smooth underarm." This was, apparently, a somewhat ticklish subject in those barely post-Victorian times, and Gillette salesmen were sternly ordered: *Do not use the term 'shaving'* as applied to this operation." Men could shave with impunity; women merely smoothed.

Spurred in part by the hoopla attending the introduction of these new models, razor sales moved up in increasingly larger annual increments. The 1916 total of 782,028 was more than double the number of just two years before, and 1917 saw the million-razor barrier breached for the first time. Meanwhile, blades sales had soared accordingly, to nearly ten million dozen. Beyond all peradventure, Gillette had proved itself in the marketplace, offering a product that was not only superior to the old straight razor that it sought to supersede, but better, too, than the scores of imitators seeking to capitalize on its success. The name of Gillette had become almost a generic word for safety razor, though the company zealously guarded its trademark, lest it sink into the public domain.

Freed of the internal bickering and rivalries that had marred its first decade, the Gillette Safety Razor Company was moving ahead as a smoothly managed, modern corporation. But turbulent shapes from the past continued to surface from time to time, largely in the form of Henry Sachs and his relentless sniping at company executives. Early in 1916, as Treasurer Frank Fahey would later write to King Gillette, Sachs had even gone so far as to write "confidential letters to some of our people in the factory here telling them things about my personal affairs and predicting that I would not be with the Company after this year."

Considering that Fahey was then in the process of divorcing John

Joyce's daughter, it was not exactly an unreasonable prediction, though Fahey's agile survival of that domestic storm did not blunt the attacks from Sachs. Later in the year, Fahey complained to Gillette that Sachs had visited the Boston offices not long before, and after a quick tour of the plant had announced that "our factory is fine but our management rotten."

Fahey traced Sachs's somewhat vindictive discontent to an incident of several years before, when Sachs had been denied access to company information beyond that furnished to other stockholders. But Fahey was certain of the president's full confidence and concluded, "I appreciate it is not necessary for me to defend myself with you, Mr. Gillette. . . . My record in this company is an open book that he who runs may read, and I am working harder today for its continued success than at any time since I came here about nine years ago."

He very probably was, though there would come a time when Fahey's opened book — and Pelham's, too — would reveal some rather curious records. Meanwhile, the two would soon be doing their work for a new set of owners.

John Joyce, in steadily declining health, turned sixty-eight in the fall of 1916, not long after his lifelong bosom friend and partner, Maurice J. Curran, had written to King Gillette that Joyce often spoke wistfully of Beverly Hills, California, where he had maintained a vacation home for a number of years. "I do not think it will be very long before he will pack his traps and leave for there," Curran said, and indeed it wasn't. And on January 26, 1917, Joyce died there, an Irish immigrant who had made good beyond all boyish dreams. At the Gillette Safety Razor Company — hardly the largest of Joyce's varied industrial interests — the directors noted his death "with deep sorrow," hailing his "wide experience and clear judgment acquired in a life-time of devotion to large interests and his quick intuition and temperament [that] made him an associate whose departure we mourn."

Along with their mourning, of course, they were also apprehensive about the future of the company, now that the largest stockholder was dead. But their anxieties were soon put to rest by the advent of John

Edward Aldred. A longtime friend and associate of Joyce's, Aldred was head of the New York investment banking firm of Aldred & Company, and had joined Joyce nearly two decades before to form the giant Shawinigan Water & Power Company, of which he was now president. Joyce had told him about Gillette's razor in its very earliest days, but Aldred had been unimpressed; when he learned that Joyce had put money behind the invention, he "made a little mental note that Mr. Joyce was beginning to fail a little." Later, when Joyce took him on a tour of the Boston factory — "There was a lot of buzzing going on," Aldred recalled — and let him take a quick peek at the company's profit statement, Aldred made a mental note of another kind. And with Joyce's death, "the wheel of fortune turned around, and there arose an opportunity whereby I became intimately related to the Gillette Company."

The Aldred-Gillette relationship was consummated in September, 1917, when the Aldred concern, after buying out shares held by the Joyce estate and firming up control with purchase of additional shares from Maurice Curran, reorganized the company as a Delaware corporation and gave stockholders in the old Massachusetts company three shares in the new corporation for each share of the old. Frank Fahey, who had been retained along with the rest of the old management, always called September 20 — the date this deal was finally sealed — a "red-letter day" in Gillette's affairs, and years afterward wrote a melodramatic account of an incident which he said took place in his South Boston office after the final papers had been signed at the downtown Old Colony Trust Company: "Our President, Mr. King C. Gillette, seeing the calendar in my office, tore off the date sheet, handed it to me with the remark, 'Frank, have this framed; it marks an epoch in this Company's history.' " Gillette, with his flair for the theatrical, probably did say something like that, and Fahey, company man that he was, took the remark to heart — the dutifully framed calendar page hung on his office wall for more than a decade.

Momentous as it may have been in a narrow corporate sense, Aldred's 1917 takeover at Gillette was a lilliputian maneuver when measured against the new epoch of human history that began earlier in the same year when the United States was drawn at last into the great war that had been thundering across Europe since the first guns of August, 1914. And from his Olympian perch as inventor of the system of world corporation, King C. Gillette must surely have pondered that nations would not have taken up arms if only they had first embraced his utopian scheme, though it is perhaps ironically fitting that the bloody cataclysm of World War I proved in the long run to be a boon for the Gillette Safety Razor Company.

5

Familiar to All Men

"The trip home was without incident"

ON AUGUST 4, 1914, at midnight European time, Britain's ultimatum to
Germany ran out, and the two great powers found themselves at war;
on both sides of the English Channel, field marshals and generals
dictated orders setting in well-oiled motion the mightiest military
machines yet known to man. Ten days later, across the Atlantic
Ocean in Boston, Thomas W. Pelham issued orders of his own to his
strategically deployed sales staff. "WAR DECLARED!" his General
Letter No. 13 trumpeted in screaming red type. "The Gillette has
declared war against all previous Sales Records." August, Pelham assured his men, "will be a 'hummer.' September, October, November
and December, 1914 will make previous Gillette Sales look like 30¢.
Make your fight to that end."

On August 7, just days after field-gray hordes of Kaiser Wilhelm's
infantry had poured across the neutral Belgian frontier, Pelham had
written to Charles A. Gaines, now returned to the Gillette factory
in Leicester, England: "Is there any opportunity of getting the British

Government, the French Government or any of the other nations of Europe [Germany, perhaps?] to adopt the Gillette as part of the equipment of soldiers, sailors or officers?" It was only a suggestion, Pelham said, adding that if it had merit he was sure Gaines would follow through.

In retrospect, several brutal conflicts later, it may seem to have been somewhat tasteless for Pelham to model his sales letter after a bona fide declaration of war, and perhaps ghoulishly opportunistic of him to see the coming bloodbath as a main chance to sell razors to the belligerent armies. But under the circumstances Pelham was driven to extraordinary measures, and he was acting virtually alone. Frank Fahey, who happened to be in England that fateful summer, had become seriously ill, and did not know until weeks later that there was even a war on — a war that Pelham judged would be "of some considerable length" and "very disastrous to the commercial life of the several countries involved." And Pelham was not, after all, a statesman, but a sales manager whose job was to look after business.

After years of faltering — the company's sales policy in Europe, Pelham had written to King Gillette after a visit in 1913, had been "the lazy man's way" of selling to a few large distributors and depending on them to do the rest — the company was on the way to getting its European house in order; now, everything seemed about to be undone. With the warring powers decreeing a suspension of credit and a moratorium on debt, international commerce had become a bootless enterprise, made even more difficult by attacks on merchant shipping and the stemming of movement across hostile borders. The Paris warehouse and sales office, opened with such ill-timed optimism in the summer of 1914, were both shuttered by fall. The French contract manufacturer — whose performance, in any case, had long been a source of dissatisfaction to Gillette — found that his plant in Nogent-en-Bassigny was in the middle of the war zone, cut off from markets as well as supplies.

One consolation was that the German company, whose output had also been of somewhat dubious quality, had already been quietly dissolved by the end of 1913, its equipment shipped off to the British plant — which became the source of much of Gillette's razor and blade supply to the rest of Europe. But the Leicester factory was soon reeling from manpower and material shortages, not to mention the wrenching halt in Continental trade; after limping along for a time, the plant was liquidated in 1915, leaving Boston and Montreal as the sole makers of Gillette razors and blades. (Clever Germans stepped into the gap later on, however, and Europe was flooded with counterfeit Gillette blades, their wrappers featuring a decidedly Teutonic-looking King Camp Gillette. "The one concession that the German fakirs have made to decency," sniffed the well-known American writer Isaac F. Marcosson, "is that they have omitted the words 'Made in U.S.A.' from the wrapper and box.") As the war wore on and the lines stabilized, Gillette was able to capitalize on America's "too proud to fight" posture, and began serving some of its European markets directly from the Boston plant, though this was complicated somewhat by the fact that dealers in some Allied and neutral nations had been supplied by Gillette agents in Germany who insisted that despite the ill fortunes of war their exclusive contracts were still valid.

Possibly the knottiest problem arose in the Russian market, covered since 1910 by a Hamburg distributor who at the outbreak of war was selling Gillette's goods at a somewhat sluggish annual clip of 15,000 razors and 100,000 packages of blades. By the agent's own admission to Gillette, hostilities had brought his activities in Russia to a standstill, but he still maintained that his contract was in force and that he was entitled to commissions on whatever business Gillette drummed up in Russia through its own or other channels. The company turned the matter over to German attorneys who eventually dissuaded the agent from pressing his flimsy case. Thomas Pelham, meanwhile, took personal command of the Russian situation, though he was unable to do anything to help the hapless Bruno Below, a German salesman for the Hamburg distributor. Trapped in Moscow when war came, Below was shipped off to Siberia to await the armistice.

With $50,000 worth of Gillette razors and blades in his baggage, the intrepid Pelham set out in the spring of 1915 for imperial Russia, via Norway and Sweden. After loading his cargo on peasant carts, he crossed the Russian border and arrived in Petrograd in mid-May. There he set up a Russian sales agency and sold all his wares for cash. Later, after he had returned home and repeat orders began pouring in, shipments to Russia began taking ever more roundabout routes, with some goods going by train to Vancouver, by ship to Vladivostok, and then by parcel post to the agent in Petrograd. By late 1916, Russian demand for Gillette razors was so brisk that the agent fired off a rush order for 80,000 razors and 600,000 dozen blades. Hard pressed to fill the needs of all its growing markets, Gillette parceled out this order in weekly registered mail shipments of 5,000 razors and 25,000 blade packages, and after six weeks was prepared to send the balance of the goods via Pelham's old Norway-Sweden route. Thirteen tons of razors and blades had already been tightly packed in tin-lined cases when word came that the Russian government, plagued by revolutionary troubles, had canceled its permission to bring the goods in by the proposed passage.

Pelham, not easily thwarted when it came to pushing Gillette's interests — or his own, for that matter — scouted out another way, and mapped an itinerary which, had his caravan contained exotic spices and teas or silks and jewels, might be termed an epic commercial journey. In mid-March, after shipment to the docks of Vancouver by American Express, the full carload of Gillette goods was put aboard the *Empress of Asia*, and with Pelham on hand to supervise his goods, the ship set sail for Yokohama, Japan. "The service was most excellent," Pelham recalled later. "The food was good, well prepared and also well served." He was also pleased to find that most of the passengers aboard the vessel were "users and advocates of the Gillette razor."

Pelham was unimpressed with Yokohama and the other Japanese cities he visited while awaiting the transshipment of his cargo to Dairen, in Japanese Manchuria. For one thing, few men in Japan made enough money to buy Gillette razors, and because of racial characteristics, "only a few of them need to shave" anyway. Industrially, Pelham judged that Japan was merely "an imitator and a manufacturer of cheap goods," a judgment he also passed on Germany. China, too, left much to be desired in his eyes, and while he was impressed with the European-dominated commercial section of Shanghai, he found that "the native city is like all other Chinese cities, very dirty, very badly built and very thickly populated." As in Japan, the market for Gillette goods in China seemed minimal.

At Dairen at last, Pelham caught up with the 164 stout cases of Gillette razors and blades bound for Petrograd, and after photographing them for his records, he watched as they were lugged by mule cart and on the backs of Manchurian coolies from dockside to a nearby warehouse. There, by prearrangement, the cases were broken open and their cargo of specially prepared ten-and-a-half-pound burlap-wrapped parcels removed for mailing to the Russian agent. Pelham himself, after seeing his mass of bundles to the post office, moved on through Mukden and Changchun to Harbin, where he boarded a train of the storied Trans-Siberian Railroad for the journey to Petrograd. During his long transit through Siberia, he was "much surprised to see the many large and well-built cities and to see the amount of development in the agricultural lands." The crimson flag of revolution was visible everywhere, he noted, but "no evidence could be seen of the Revolution that had taken place." After nine days on the train, he reached Petrograd in mid-April and spent two weeks meeting with his Russian agent, A. G. Micheles. He also saw plenty of signs of revolution, among them the May Day festivities, which he said drew a crowd of one million people to watch an awesome parade of marching children and workmen, women and girls, "black men from Turkestan, Mohammedans, Tartars from the Caucasus, Kurds from the Trans-Caucasus, Mongolians, Manchurians, Laplanders and people from every part of Russia," all wearing the red badge of revolution, and all potential Gillette customers. "Russia," he concluded, "is one of our greatest markets for the future."

His Russian business finished, Pelham left Petrograd on May 4 and went north through Finland, where he crossed the frozen Tornio River — the ice broke the following day — into Sweden for an inspection of the mill that even in wartime was supplying Gillette with the high-grade steel needed to make razor blades. He had planned originally to cross the North Sea to England, and then travel south through France and Italy, but given the unlikely choice of making the passage as a common seaman aboard a neutral Norwegian tramp steamer or as a passenger on a British cargo ship that would be an easy target for German U-boats, he called off this side trip and opted instead to head directly for home on a Norwegian vessel bound for New York by way of Halifax, Nova Scotia. He arrived back in Boston in mid-June, some three months after setting out from the Gillette factory with his carload of razors and blades. "The trip home," he noted, "was without incident."

Pelham had been lucky. Germany's increasing harassment of supposedly neutral shipping had at last brought the United States into the war on the side of the Allies. The American Expeditionary Force was girding to cross the Atlantic to take its place in the fields and trenches of France, and its troops would be armed not only with Springfield repeating rifles, but with Gillette safety razors as well.

"*Every man in Khaki ought to have one*"

On a bright clear day in 1918, a German sniper peered from the concealment of his trench near Verdun and took expert aim at a distant and unsuspecting American army private named Hynes. Gently catching his breath, squeezing his trigger ever so carefully, the German got off a good, clean shot that smashed through the upper left pocket of Hynes's olive-drab field coat, directly over his heart. Miraculously, the young soldier — who was, coincidentally enough, a worker in civilian life at the Crown Cork & Seal Company in Baltimore — was only slightly bruised. Instead of plowing into his chest, the sniper's bullet had pierced the lid of Hynes's Gillette service set, penetrated its steel mirror and razor blades, and then ricocheted off the handle of the three-piece razor.

Hynes was among the handful of World War I troopers whose lives were saved when their razors deflected deadly shrapnel or small-arms fire, but he was only one of the several million American servicemen outfitted with Gillette safety razors during their military service. For many of them, it was a first introduction to the relatively rare custom of frequent self-shaving, a custom whose widespread acceptance was necessary before the Gillette razor and blades could begin to approach their full sales potential.

The company had targeted the military market long before the war, and in its advertising had quite early sought to feature military men — along with hunters, fishermen, and other outdoor types — as symbols of the masculine business of shaving. "Jack afloat or ashore is neatly shaved; it's part of the U.S. Navy regulations," read a 1910 ad in *Town and Country*. The Gillette razor, the ad continued, is "a godsend to a sailor. It is as popular with the officers as with the men." But the raising of mass armies, with millions of men in uniform and under strict military discipline, offered boundless opportunities, a virtual captive market for a product such as Gillette's — as the canny Thomas Pelham had realized right at the start.

Almost from the day the first shots were fired, military leaders on both sides of the lines had seen the advantages of clean-shaven troops. Not only was regular shaving a good hygienic measure during endless months in the trenches, but it also assured a close fit for the gas masks that were used with growing frequency as the conflict wore on. Beyond that, a fresh shave was a morale builder, and it is perhaps significant that French infantrymen were sometimes said to pride themselves on how *infrequently* they shaved, and that the slang word for French soldier was *poilu*, meaning hairy. Among British soldiers, at least, Gillette razors were particularly prized, and the effects of slain Germans were routinely rifled on the chance of turning up the scarce blades.

By the time America tossed its helmet into the deadly European ring, United States Army regulations required every soldier to provide himself with a shaving outfit of some kind, and though other manufacturers — most notably AutoStrop and Eversharp — had entries in this market, it was the more compact Gillette with its disposable blades and no complicated stropping attachment that was by far the most practical and popular. And to further tailor its wares to the serviceman, the company even put its standby pocket edition in a newly designed case that featured on its cover the insignia of both the navy and the army, managing to include in one embossment the superimposed branch symbols of the infantry, cavalry, artillery, and engineers. According to Gillette's early advertising, these service sets had been in the works since 1916, when a young company executive had seen the need for them while on active duty as an officer with General John J. Pershing on the Mexican border. "When Uncle Sam jumped into the Big War the Gillette was ready to do its bit," a *Collier's* ad boasted in the fall of 1917, and home-front readers were advised, "If your dealer does not have this Set, send us $5 and your Sammie's address and we will make *free delivery* direct to his hands from our Paris Office or to any American Cantonment from our Boston Office." And as the ad said, "Every man in Khaki ought to have one."

Soon, every man in khaki — and every man in navy blue and marine drab, too — would have a Gillette safety razor, with the compliments of the United States government and best wishes for long and continued use from the Gillette Safety Razor Company.

With raw recruits pouring into training camps in stunning numbers, high military officials had concluded by the end of 1917 that uniform efficiency would best be served if every man was issued his shaving equipment rather than providing it on his own. At five dollars, a Gillette service set was still a heavy expenditure for many civilians, and it was all but impossible on a lowly private's pay. No doubt the high command's decision was arrived at with considerable help from Gillette, and by March, 1918, the company had booked with the War Department orders for 519,750 razors — more than had been sold in any single year up until 1916 — and 710,000 dozen blades. Even King C. Gillette, a worldwide symbol of the clean shave, got into the selling act, and on February 28, Frank Fahey wrote him in Los Angeles, thanking him for "seeing the Depot Quartermaster and lining them up for the Gillette Razor." In the same letter, Fahey couldn't resist bragging: "We might say here that we have a stranglehold on this business from the Government by being first in the field before the other razor companies began to get active." By the end of the war, this stranglehold had put some 3.5 million razors and 32 million blades into military hands — at considerably below the normal factory price, but nonetheless profitably — and made the men of the American Expeditionary Force the most cleanly shaved soldiery in history.

There were a few minor snags along the way, to be sure. Some doughboys, untutored in the mysteries of safety razoring, complained on their first try at it that the blades were so dull that they just would not cut whiskers at all. Things were set right when seasoned veterans advised that it was always best, before clamping the blade in the razor, to remove the inner wax-paper wrapper as well as the decorative green outer envelope bearing the King C. Gillette portrait and signature. From then on, it was easy, not to mention obligatory. "Any soldier," a wounded veteran told the Cleveland *Plain Dealer* in early 1918, "particularly an officer, who wants to improve his standing will keep his face shaved. The men who really want clean faces somehow manage to shave even under gunfire. The American soldiers in particular pride themselves on clean-shaven faces. I have seen thousands of troopers with blood-stained and trench-dirty faces, but beneath the blood and dirt you found clean-shaven faces." He had also, he added, seen soldiers "torn to pieces while shaving themselves," and he did not mean by the blades.

To ensure that the survivors had more pleasant memories of shaving gear, Gillette capitalized once more on the national pastime, and in 1917 the company's recently reinstalled Paris representative helped organize a soldiers' and sailors' baseball league, supplying much of the equipment and offering a razor set to every player who belted a home run. It was, said the Paris edition of the New York *Herald* as the 1918 season got under way, in "the right spirit and it does baseball good. Now, boys, bat out for that blade!"

Within little more than eighteen months, the needs of modern warfare had initiated millions of men into the rites of easy self-shaving, a custom they carried back into civilian life with considerable encouragement from Gillette. In 1919, the company launched a series of campaigns in which teams of young women traveled to nearly every large city, staging demonstrations and offering tips on how to get the best performance from Gillette razors. That same year, the company opened lavish service stores in San Francisco, New York, and Chicago, where retail customers could purchase Gillette goods and get answers to questions or complaints. At about the same time, Gillette motorized its sales force with the purchase of a thirteen-car fleet of jaunty Franklin convertibles, the diamond-and-arrow trademark blazoned on their sides.

On all sides public applause greeted the spread of Gillette's self-shaving gospel. The influential *Collier's* editorialized with a presumably straight face that "shaving as it is practiced in America today marks a step forward in civilization." The advance was made possible only by the safety razor, which "transformed shaving from a fairly long, decidedly unpleasant and slightly dangerous operation to one that was finished before the bathwater had ceased running."

It was a tempting proposition for legions of men, not least among them Sinclair Lewis's quintessential post–World War I American, the incomparable George F. Babbitt, never one to shun the mechanical blessings of modern civilization. On the memorable April morning in 1920 when he is introduced to the world, Babbitt is wakened by "the best of nationally advertised and quantitatively produced alarm-clocks," and then pads sleepily into his well-appointed bathroom to rake his ample cheeks with a safety razor. And though Lewis doesn't say so, it almost had to be the nationally advertised and quantitatively produced Gillette, which on April 1, 1920, had blanketed nineteen midwestern cities — among them, it may surely be imagined, Babbitt's own Zenith — with full-page newspaper ads expertly tailored to the spirit of the age. "If there's one thing characteristic of American life, it's the American sleeping car," said one, noting that in Pullman washrooms "there are some things that all big-brained, red-blooded men agree on. And the *Gillette* Safety Razor is *one* of them. Twenty million men of all breeds, all classes, in every country on earth are using Gillettes *every day* of their lives and *liking* them." Alert dealers, the ad concluded, "always hand out a Gillette when they see a regular man coming."

Perhaps so, but the time was fast approaching when dealers could also reach for a variety of lawful imitations: the United States patent that had given Gillette seventeen years of protection for its flexible blade idea was set to expire on November 15, 1921. The company, some said — and others hoped — would not long survive the flood of identical razors and blades that would pour into the market on the very day the patent ran out; the best that Gillette could expect to do was to slash its long-standing five-dollar price to the bone and trim its lush profits to mere subsistence levels. As it happened, the company did neither: Gillette executives had come up with a far better battle plan.

"*We practically dominate the Gillette-type blade business of the world*"

As they filed into the darkened room festooned with spring flowers and paper streamers, the members of the Gillette Safety Razor Company sales force, who had assembled in Boston for their 1921 convention, had a distinct feeling that they were in for more than the standard words of welcome and inspirational pep talk. They knew it for certain when they glimpsed at the front of the room a velvet-draped platform topped by nine miniature "stages," each with its own individual curtain. After greeting the conventioneers from behind a podium made in the form of an upended razor, the vice-president and treasurer, Frank J. Fahey, handed over his gavel — which was not, for some reason, in the form of a razor — to his longtime colleague Thomas W. Pelham, who unobtrusively signaled a company electrician to press the appropriate button. As if by magic, the velvet curtain on the first small stage was rolled up, revealing two unopened razor-set boxes against a backdrop of gold brocade. At the next sign from Pelham, another button was pushed, this one wired to cause one of the onstage boxes to lift its lid, exposing to the sales force's wondering gaze the first look at the New Improved Gillette safety razor. And so it went, from stage to stage, until all the models in the new line were unveiled. If an informant of the advertising trade magazine *Printers' Ink* can be believed, the men "abandoned all sales convention dignity, and cheered each new disclosure to the echo."

And well they might have. The new razors they saw for the first time that day were destined not only to hold Gillette's commanding position in the shaving market, but to make it even stronger. The manner of their development and public introduction, according to *Printers' Ink*, showed a "high degree of business generalship" on Gillette's part, and when the campaign was over, the old familiar razor that had done such yeoman service for so long was consigned to "the limbo of discontinued styles," dragging behind it the host of imitators that had sought to capitalize on Gillette's expiring patents.

The shaving public got its first glimpse of the new razor on May 16, little more than a month after the introductory theatrics at the sales convention, when Gillette kicked off a two-million-dollar advertising push to launch the product in style. The new improved model, the ads stressed, had made all other razors obsolete just as surely as more modern steamships had pushed aside Robert Fulton's first paddle-wheeler, just as certainly as Edison's light bulb had squeezed out previous attempts at making incandescent lamps. "Measured by the precision of the New Gillette," said one, "any other razor you've ever known is crude" — and no exception was made for the old standby Gillette. While carefully and correctly conceding that the future could hold in store things yet undreamed of, the veteran razor builder William Nickerson assured salesmen that the new model had "reached about the limit of development" in shaving instruments, though he cheerfully admitted that there was always room for improvement in blades.

The new improved Gillette razor was indeed a major technical achievement, built with more precision than the old ones and providing a more rigid and efficient shaving edge. But it was more than a mere mechanical marvel: it represented a major marketing victory, the first of many for a company that would in time gain a worldwide reputation for its product innovation and marketing strategy.

Plans for a new razor of some kind had been on the drawing boards since as early as 1916, but they got under way in earnest in the closing days of 1918, when Frank Fahey summoned his corporate lieutenants to discuss what actions the company might take to prepare for the coming expiration of its patent. There were, he said, three options: The first was to develop an improved design that could be sold at the customary five-dollar price. The second was to reduce manufacturing costs so that the traditional razor could be sold profitably at a reduced price. The third was to come up with a new, cheap razor to compete head on with the army of imitators that would surely arise after November 15, 1921. The committee appointed to study the question almost immediately chose the first course, and determined at the same time to make no change in the familiar three-hole blade design. Consumers, they feared, might be leery of any alteration in such a widely used, standard article.

Meeting frequently and as secretly as possible — a popular gathering spot was the company's photographic laboratory — the committee members tested and considered a number of basic razor designs, and a patent on the final concept was granted on January 13, 1920. By the fall of the same year, committee members were actually shaving themselves with several different refinements of the proposed new razor, in order to determine such things as the proper width and spacing of the rakelike teeth on the razor guard. On September 16, at the seventy-fourth meeting of the group, the verdict was unanimously in favor of the experimental razor designated Model B. The selection process had surely been far more scientific and formal than King Gillette's almost random putterings of a generation before, though not nearly so sophisticated as what was yet to come.

Meanwhile, Thomas Pelham had been working on marketing and distribution plans, leaving nothing to chance. And while the main element in his strategy was the higher-priced new improved model, he was at pains to protect his flanks against cut-rate competitors, too. At the same time that the new razor went on sale, Gillette would introduce old-model razors, done up in cheaper packages, with only three blades instead of twelve, and dubbed the Brownie, all for one dollar. For the market in between, regular old-model sets were offered at two-fifty and three dollars. For the first time, Gillette razors would truly be within the financial reach of any man who wanted one. And in the bargain, would-be competitors who were said to be stocking bonded warehouses with tens and hundreds of thousands of cheap foreign-made Gillette imitations would be beaten at their own game before they even had a chance to play. "Six months before it is possible for anyone else to manufacture under the old patent," marveled *Printers' Ink*, "the company is coming out with a genuine Gillette for a dollar. So far as is humanly possible, the expiration of the patent is to be turned from a liability into an asset."

It was indeed. Retailers, offered credits on new improved razor purchases for each "old" razor on their shelves, eagerly stocked up with the new models, and when the spring-to-Christmas advertising barrage opened up, customers at the 250,000 establishments offering Gillette products had a wide range to choose from. And choose they did, in record numbers. At the Gillette New York City service store, it took a traffic policeman to control the crowds that gathered to see the display of new Gillette goods. In the first two months on the market, 500,000 new improved razors were sold; and the public bought up three million Brownie sets — each one a continuing consumer of blades — in just six months. Production capacity at the Boston plant, which had peaked during the high-volume war year of 1918 at 26,000 razors and 700,000 blades a day, was jacked up to a daily rate of some 40,000 razors and a million blades.

When the all-important figures were totted up at the end of the year, the campaign had proved successful beyond all the imaginings of its planners. Razor sales hit more than 4.2 million, just shy of the 1918 total with its inflated, one-shot War Department bonanza; blade sales stood at a record 19.5 million dozen. Earnings and dividends, too, edged to all-time highs and continued rising, filling the company's treasury and enriching its growing list of stockholders.

And so it went, through much of that heady, expansive decade of jazz and Prohibition, of flivvers and flappers, and Gillette was happily in the thick of it all, capitalizing on its heavy advertising and on such independent hyperboles as the claim made in 1927 by Albert M. Johnson, chairman of the board of the National Life Insurance Company, that the increasing life expectancy of the American male was due in part to the safety razor. "By cutting off his whiskers," said Johnson of the average man, "he unconsciously adopted a more youthful attitude; he felt younger, he kept younger, he dressed younger." The company did its part for the female population, too, coming out in 1924 with a scaled-down standard razor dubbed the Bobby Gillette. "Every bobbed haired Miss should have one," the advertising said, noting that a newly bared neck "must be kept smooth and white." As a bonus, the Bobby was "ideal for keeping the underarm smooth and clean."

To be sure, Gillette was not without its competition, but it was far and away the mightiest entry in the razor and blade field. Henry Gaisman's AutoStrop puffed along with only a relatively minor share of the market for its so-called Valet razor. The American Safety Razor Corporation — maker of the Gem, Ever Ready, and Star brands, and no relation to the original Gillette company of the almost identical name — was fairly big on the low-priced end of the market, but this was of little moment to Gillette, whose output was larger than that of all its competitors combined. In fact, the company frequently managed to outmaneuver even the cheapest of cut-rate razors by arranging combination deals with banks, hotels, consumer-goods manufacturers, and other concerns looking for a desirable premium to give away with their products or services. The first such arrangement, worked out in 1922 with the William Wrigley, Jr., Company to introduce P.K., its new brand of gum, accounted for a million razors; later combination deals would reach as high as ten times that number, with the razors selling for as low as fifteen cents. And no matter how the Gillette razor got into a user's hands, or at what price, it was a potential consumer of Gillette blades, which were intended from the very beginning to be the backbone of the company's profits. Indeed, William Wrigley himself, meeting Gillette stockholder Henry Sachs at a dinner not long after the P.K. introduction, said jokingly that Gillette should have given the razors to Wrigley for nothing, "on account of the new blade business that would accrue." In writing to Pelham of the incident, Sachs said he informed Wrigley that "his P.K. gum could only have been introduced by the Gillette razor." Both men had laughed at this, but Sachs hastened to say that "the P.K. was in my opinion the best gum they produced." Not to be outcomplimented, Wrigley replied that his new Gillette was the best razor he had ever used.

Wrigley was surely clamping genuine Gillette blades in his razor, and early in January, 1924, he would have found that a change had been made in the way his favorite blades were packaged. Faced with rising costs — and with public demand that wax-paper inner wrappers, dropped a few years before as an economy measure, be reinstituted — the company decided to raise its prices by the simple expedient of again reducing the number of blades in each package. Accordingly, blades were put up in packs of ten and five instead of the long-familiar twelve and six, and the price remained one dollar and fifty cents respectively, or a dime a blade. This was considerably more than the nickel-per-blade retail price that Sachs, with tacit encouragement from Gillette himself, had urged upon Pelham not long before, and Sachs, for one, was worried that customers might balk at paying the same price for fewer blades. But he was mollified by the saleswise Pelham, who informed him confidently that "the new packets will go wonderfully well. The public demands blades wrapped in wax paper and within a short time the public will forget that they used to buy twelve blades in a packet and will be quite content with ten blades in a packet." He was cheered even further by Pelham's assurance that the new packaging policy would eventually bring in an additional $2.5 million a year. Small wonder, considering that the actual cost of making the blades was only about a penny apiece.

Pelham's prediction may have been near the mark at the time, but the fact was that a large number of shavers, both at home and abroad, were beginning to look for cheaper blades. And there were plenty of blade manufacturers waiting eagerly in the wings to supply this demand, usually by making up private-label brands for large distributors or retail chains. This practice was particularly true in Europe, where the average wage earner had considerably less income than his American counterpart, and it was in Europe that

Gillette made its first decisive move to contend with cheap competition. Rather than fight the enemy, Gillette chose instead to join him — or rather, buy him out. In April, 1926, Vice-President Fahey made a whirlwind trip to Berlin, where he managed to purchase a controlling interest in the Roth-Büchner Company, a longtime Gillette competitor. This was, Fahey assured King Gillette in one of his periodic reports, the only operation that was "making headway in the cheap blade market over there, and we were most fortunate in securing control of it." Just how fortunate was shown eighteen months after the purchase, when Fahey boasted of the new acquisition that "their business is 35% ahead of that for last year and they have done exactly what we planned for them — that is to go after all other cheap blade distribution in Europe and bring their sales to a standstill." There was no reason, Fahey added grandly, why Gillette and its German satellite "cannot eventually dominate the blade business of the world." Already, Roth-Büchner was churning out blades bearing 250 different private labels.

Ironically, one of the stumbling blocks to this global dominion was the New Jersey–based Otto Roth, Incorporated, a Roth-Büchner subsidiary which was not included in Gillette's control of the parent company in Berlin. Otto Roth was such a troublesome rival that Gillette tried for some time to plant an agent in the Roth factory to find out details of the competitive operation. When this cloak-and-dagger approach failed, Gillette decided to beat Roth in its own bailiwick by making low-cost blades of its own, and accordingly, in 1927 the Rubie Blade Corporation opened its doors in New York City. (Rubie was a brand name that Gillette had used overseas, and with similar intent, for nearly twenty years.) Rubie's mission was to capture such private-label mass marketers as Woolworth's, Kresge's, Montgomery Ward, Macy's, and Sears, Roebuck by selling them blades, as Fahey said, "at a price below what the little fellows have to get from them."

It was a brilliant, if ruthless, maneuver, and one that promised great profits. As for the blade itself, Gillette did not set up a new plant in which to crank out Rubie blades: it supplied them from its own Boston factory, in the form of blades rejected for failure to meet the rigid Gillette standards of quality. At only a negligible cost, this put the company in a position to engross the lower as well as the upper ends of the blade market, placing Gillette almost beyond the reach of even the most determined opposition.

In fairness, it should be noted that only the *best* of Gillette's rejects were put into Rubie's various wrappers, and that these blades were in any case as good as or better than most of the other manufacturers' products. When it came to shaving edges, even Gillette's bad blades were pretty good — at least by the standards of that time. And Pelham, anticipating that some dealers might well maintain that their common origin made Rubie blades the equal of the Gillette brand (or, perhaps more damning, vice versa), advised salesmen to inform such cavilers that "the Rubie Blade is the best imitation blade on the market, but of course, is not comparable to the Gillette Blade."

The Rubie gambit did not go unmarked in Newark, where Otto Roth, after stubbornly holding on to its independence until defeat seemed inevitable, threw in the towel and sold out to Gillette — whose attorneys prudently got prior clearance from the United States Department of Justice — at the end of 1927.

Earlier in the same year, Gillette had made plans to attack the market from yet another angle: by producing four types of Gillette-brand blades, each with somewhat different shaving characteristics. To distinguish one from the other, notches would be cut in the familiar curved ends, and the standard currency-green package would be augmented by brown, blue, and red wrappings. Changing market conditions — and difficulties in achieving markedly different edges — scotched this project before the blades could be distributed, and the company decided to concentrate its new efforts on Roth-Büchner, Rubie, and Otto Roth. In the spring of 1928, Fahey could scarcely contain himself when he wrote to King Gillette, "We are pushing them all ahead with 'WIM and WIGOUR,'" adding that his earlier hope was at last coming true. "By these three moves," he said more soberly, "we practically dominate the Gillette-type blade business of the world."

They did indeed, and in the United States, where safety razors had become so common that they were frequent grist for cartoonists' mills, some 80 percent of the nation's shavers used Gillette razors and blades. Such, at least, was the conclusion of an extensive survey made in late 1927 by Batten, Barton, Durstine & Osborn, recently retained as Gillette's advertising agency. (Apparently, BBD&O's predecessor had not heeded the half-whimsical advice given by an unfortunately anonymous Gillette advertising staffer: "Don't approach the Gillette problems in the spirit so usual with New Yorkers — that nothing ever really happens outside of New York, and that those living beyond 155th Street are entitled to a whole lot of sympathy.")

Whatever their source, whether from Gillette or some look-alike competitor, the familiar rectangular blades with gently rounded ends and three neat holes piercing the lengthwise axis had become ubiquitous in America. And so, it seemed, had certain domestic problems associated with their wide and frequent use.

"Take one pound of young, tender blades, wash and rinse"

After lathering his face with what Sinclair Lewis so artfully described as an "unctuous brush," George Babbitt began to shave. Suddenly he was brought up short. The razor pulled at his cheek. The blade was dull. "Damn — oh — oh — damn it," he moaned, and then:

He hunted through the medicine-cabinet for a packet of new razor-blades (reflecting, as invariably, "Be cheaper to buy one of these dinguses and strop your own blades,") and when he discovered the packet, behind the round box of bicarbonate of soda, he thought ill of his wife for putting it there and very well of himself for not saying "Damn." But he did say it, immediately afterward, when with wet and soap-slippery fingers he tried to remove the horrible little envelope and crisp clinging oiled paper from the new blade.

Then there was the problem, oft-pondered, never solved, of what to do with the old blade, which might imperil the fingers of his young. As usual, he tossed it on top of the medicine-cabinet, with a mental note that some day he must remove the fifty or sixty other blades that were also temporarily, piled up there. . . .

Gillette most assuredly disapproved of the variety of little dinguses designed for home restropping of its blades, and of the hardware and cutlery stores that sometimes offered low-cost resharpening services. There was little that could be done about such penny-pinching defiance of the "NOT TO BE RESHARPENED" injunction printed on each blade, though King Gillette himself, according to an article written (with a considerable assist from the writer Franklin Fargo) for the January 15, 1927, issue of *Liberty*, suggested that "each blade-user shall replace the blades in the original package, take them to be resharpened, and then never call for them." Another disposal method from Gillette-Fargo: "Keep a jar of strong salt solution at hand and drop the blades into it until they corrode and may be thrown out without danger to anyone." Or to any animal, for that matter: hog raisers who slopped their stock with municipal garbage complained that pigs sometimes perished from swallowing blades tossed in with the potato peels and coffee grounds by heedless householders.

Ludicrous as these concerns may seem to a later age, they were not entirely pointless. By the mid-1920's, Pullman car washrooms were equipped with slots in which traveling men could drop their used blades, and many hotels had installed special containers to accommodate the guests who needed to dump a dulled blade. Not until some years later did makers of home bathroom fixtures provide medicine cabinets slotted to conduct discarded blades into the nether regions between walls. And until this convenience became commonplace, safety-conscious men and women took a lively interest in what to do with defunct razor blades that were still sufficiently sharp to pose considerable domestic danger.

Surely the most effective method was simply to replace the blades in their original cardboard container, which when filled would be dropped into the nearest wastebasket with hopes for a safe journey to incinerator or city dump. But those who shunned simple solutions frequently came up with more imaginative options, which they gladly passed on to newspapers that occasionally staged suggestion contests. Wrote one zany entrant to a Cleveland paper in 1926: "Take one pound of young, tender blades, wash and rinse. Dry them, peel, and slice very thin. Prepare one pint of water that has been sifted and mixed, by boiling for two hours and carefully straining. Add blades and parboil for forty minutes. Drain and mash. Season with salt, vinegar, mustard, and pepper. Form into patties and fry in coal oil."

In 1927, the New York *Telegram* went on a similar quest for answers to the burning question. One reader rather sportingly suggested that used blades be mailed to King C. Gillette. The sportswriter

Joe Williams, asked what he did with his old blades, replied: "I take two in warm water before retiring every night." Eddie Cantor, no gag writer at hand, could only mumble, "I just throw them away, that's all," which was a lot less inspired than Flo Ziegfeld's "I give them to my valet. He shaves with them." According to the *Telegram*, Ziegfeld's valet was unavailable for comment. Certainly the most notable respondent was H. L. Mencken, recipient of a Western Union telegram reading, "Seriously, what do you do with your old razor blades." Almost by return wire, the sage of Baltimore replied: "Put them in the collection plate."

Surely, the lowly razor blade had been enshrined in the national consciousness.

Just as opinions differed when it came to getting rid of old blades, there was wide disagreement about how long a blade should be — or could be — used before being mailed to King C. Gillette, consigned to a concentrated saline solution, or slipped into the collection plate. In the blade's very earliest days, Gillette had made much in its advertising of the durability of its shaving edges, proudly printing the 1905 testimonial of a Sioux City, Iowa, bank auditor who had shaved sixty-two times with a single blade and was still going strong at the time of writing. Later, as the safety-razor idea became generally accepted, the longevity factor was played down, both as a practical matter — even the keenest edge grows disappointingly dull with use — and to boost blade sales. After all, at twenty to forty shaves per blade, as promised in many early advertisements, the average buyer of a razor set could go for as long as two years before buying replacement blades, and then be out of the market for another year or two. This was hardly a purchase pattern designed to exact proper tribute from razor owners.

In practice, of course, few shavers sought to husband their blades to the last dim vestige of keenness, and BBD&O's 1927 survey showed that the average American — who shaved, by the way, 4.4 times a week — was able to squeeze out 8.5 shaves per blade. The number of shaves reported most frequently by the survey subjects, however, was three, considerably more gratifying from a sales standpoint.

There were, to be sure, marathon shavers, men who prided themselves on their ability to use a razor blade for as long as humanly and metallurgically possible. And having done so, they often took great glee in informing the manufacturer of how infrequently they changed and bought blades. The record holder may well have been W. N. Walters, a hardy construction contractor from Roanoke, Virginia, who wrote in 1926 that he had used a single Gillette blade for eight years, shaving with it fully five times a week. Far less ambitious (or masochistic, as the case may be) was a Newark insurance man, W. H. Doolitell, who on December 31, 1926, replaced with appropriate ceremony a blade he had used daily for the entire year.

Nor were American shavers the only ones caught up in the craze for extracting maximum mileage from their razor blades. One Oskar Jähnisch, a Viennese, was at a party one night in 1921, when a devotee of barbershop shaves maintained that a safety-razor user could expect to get no more than five shaves per blade. Jähnisch, a Gillette partisan since 1908, impetuously made a wager — how much, he did not disclose — that he could get five *years'* worth of daily shaving from a single blade. In May, 1926, the triumphant Austrian advised Gillette that he had won his wager, adding, "By this record I convinced many of your adversaries of the goodness of your blades and razors."

The experience in England, apparently, was not quite so spectacular. In 1926, when the staid *New Statesman* made a passing comment on the short life of razor blades, a reader wrote in to say that he got close to fifty good shaves from a single Gillette blade. The editor replied drily that the correspondent must have an uncommonly soft beard. Another Briton who contributed to the deluge of letters that poured into the *New Statesman's* office maintained that a good blade should last for a year, but only if properly resharpened — which was definite heresy in the Gillette scheme of things. The consensus seemed to be that five shaves per blade was a good average, with one reader claiming that the Gillette article manufactured in Boston was greatly superior to its British-made counterpart.

And from Italy came the final word, from none other than Benito Mussolini, an advocate of the clean-shaven face as well as a wearer of a smooth head. This would-be Caesar — and dedicated Gillette user — told Thomas B. Morgan of United Press in 1926: "I have to use a new blade every time I shave, for there are no blades made that can stand more than one shave on my beard." That the herald of a new and glorious Roman empire could be so partial to a single-shot American product was ample testimony to the worldwide primacy of the Gillette razor and blade.

At about the same time, Alfred A. Gaipa, manager of the company's Italian branch, wrote Frank Fahey from Libya: "Our product is as well known here as in the heart of Europe. From here our Arabian merchants take Gillette into the interior." They apparently had been doing so for several years. When Major W. T. Blake, the globe-circling pioneer aviator, touched down in the desert in 1922, he was cordially greeted by nomadic tribesmen, one of whom "wore a Gillette razor suspended from his right ear."

"I am bringing back an order for fifty thousand razors from the Kaffirs of Africa"

After the armistice of 1918 had opened shipping lanes to merchant commerce and freed production lines to meet pent-up civilian demand, Gillette had quickly regrouped its forces to ensure that Englishmen and Italians, Austrians and Arabs, and men of every other nation in the world would have access to the blessing of shaving themselves with genuine Gillette razors and blades. And Thomas Pelham had no intention of returning to the prewar way of relying mainly on independent distributors — many of whom dealt at the same time in competitive products — to hoist the Gillette flag throughout the world. "It is very evident," he had written to Charles Gaines in London a little more than a month after the German army had first coursed into Belgium, "that after the war is over our entire selling plans will have to be changed." Now, instead of depending on outsiders to move its goods, the company would establish branches and subsidiaries whose sole concern would be the marketing of Gillette razors and blades.

Two such sales organizations, in London and Paris, were already in place and girded for renewed action. And in Paris, at least, the company had seen to it that its representatives would be given headquarters of a kind the high-living Jacob Heilborn would surely have appreciated. In 1917, when a half-million Parisians had fled their city in fear of German besiegement, Gillette had providentially signed a fifteen-year lease on choice office space at 3 rue Scribe, for the distress rental rate of $320 a year. Not long after the war, the building was bought by the Royal Bank of Canada, which offered the company $250,000 to bow out of the lease. Back in Boston, Frank Fahey declined, and in the face of persistent pressure was writing to his Paris manager as late as 1926 that "if the Royal Bank of Canada want us to move from our present comfortable, low-priced quarters at 3 rue Scribe, they should find us correspondingly comfortable, low-priced quarters elsewhere." As for the ever increasing amount that the bank would pay its stubborn tenant to move out, said Fahey, such a windfall would merely cause unwanted tax problems.

In less bargain-basement offices, Gillette moved quickly to set itself up in other countries of Europe, and by mid-1919 had established wholly owned subsidiary companies — from the very beginning of its overseas expansion, the company had determined wherever possible to have one hundred percent ownership in its foreign companies — in Italy, Belgium, Switzerland, Spain, and Denmark. In addition, the newly formed export department in Boston had assigned its own men to handle Gillette affairs in South and Central America, Africa, Asia, and Australia. To see that all was in order worldwide, Gillette's thirty-year-old foreign sales manager, Edward V. Hickey, set out in the spring of 1920 on a globe-girdling inspection trip that took him through Europe and then to Egypt, India, around the coast of Indochina to Japan, and back to Boston by way of Vancouver and Montreal. He found Gillette razors and blades everywhere, he reported, and added that those manning the company's overseas outposts were to a man "filled with Gillette spirit."

Also in 1920, Gillette took steps to begin manufacturing once more in England, though not with one hundred percent enthusiasm. A new British patent, awarded in 1917 and covering the new improved razor, was up for expiration in 1921, and the records of a late October meeting note that "after considerable discussion as to what might be considered a good excuse for not working it was decided that the only way to play safe and insure the maintenance of our British patent would be to take immediate steps towards the commercial manufacture of the new razor holder in England." And this time, the decision was to locate the plant close to the commercial hub of London rather than in a provincial town like Leicester. By December, millwrights were setting up machinery in a former military motor-truck factory at

Slough, some thirty miles out from London, and the first razors for the British market were delivered from the plant on February 1, just two days shy of the patent working deadline.

The unsettled monetary and economic conditions that continued in the wake of the late world war kept something of a rein on Gillette's overseas sales in Europe and elsewhere in the world, but progress was encouraging enough for the company to pursue an expansionist policy and form additional subsidiaries in such countries as Brazil, Germany, and Austria. By 1925, Gillette had set up forty-four branch offices and agencies, ranging from Bagdad and Beirut to Manila, Shanghai, and Valparaiso. By any standard of commercial enterprise it was an impressive achievement, one that moved a contributor to the twenty-fifth anniversary issue of the company house organ to geographic rhapsody: "Had Aladdin rubbed his magic lamp," he wrote, "and wished to be transported to a Hindu town along the Ganges, to Addis Ababa in Abyssinia, or Port Elizabeth, Hankow, Osaka, Irkutsk, Kiev, Trondheim, Nome, or Mendoza, he would have found a dealer or shopkeeper ready to supply him with Gillette razors or Gillette blades."

And in Shanghai, Aladdin would have found a young man so eager to own a Gillette razor that he offered to strike a bargain most peculiar by Western standards. Unable to come up with the necessary five dollars — which was probably close to his monthly wage — seventeen-year-old Yun Sen wrote to a Gillette agency and proposed that he be permitted to make his purchase in three monthly installments, including a fifty-cent carrying charge. As proof of his honest intentions, he swore that "if I fail to carry out my words, my corpse will be exposed in an abandoned creek. Heaven be my witness." There is no record of whether or how this transaction was concluded, but it is tempting to hope that some kindly soul in the Gillette organization was moved to present Yun Sen with a razor free and clear.

Italians, too, were lively prospects, if only because their leader — he of the single-shave blades — made no secret of his disapproval of beards and mustaches. "I am anti-whiskers," Il Duce informed Thomas Morgan in 1926. "Fascism is anti-whiskers. Whiskers are a sign of decadence. Glance at the busts of the great Roman Emperors and you will find them all clean-shaven — Caesar, Augustus. When the decline of Roman glory began, whiskers came into style. It is true of all periods. The Renaissance was a beardless period. Whiskers were the rule in the old decadent regime, which Fascism replaces with youth of clean-shaven faces." Nor was Mussolini the only noted figure addicted to shaving the Gillette way. The Bombay *Times*, noting in 1929 that a delegation of workers calling upon Mahatma Gandhi had found the diminutive charismatic happily shaving himself, asked editorially: "Are we to take it that Mr. Gandhi's sweet, unruffled temper is a tribute to the superlative excellence of the Gillette Safety Razor?"

Not all foreigners were pleased with Gillette's steady progress, and when the British War Office decided in 1926 to replace old army-issue straight razors with an order for 200,000 Gillette razors, great bellows of patriotic outrage were heard from the press and the floor of the House of Commons. The furor subsided only after it had been patiently explained that all the razors would be made in the company's British plant by British labor, and that this, indeed, was why Gillette had won out over two other American companies that had submitted lower bids for the contract. Gillette's bid was, however, lower than its British competitors', and the company sweetened the deal by offering a trade-in allowance for the 100,000 straight razors held by the British army. One diehard member of the House of Commons was hooted down by his fellows when he maintained that the cause of smooth shaves would better be served by keeping the old razors in service.

Commercial resentments die hard, too, and a couple of years after the brouhaha over Gillette's army contract, it was claimed that British manufacturing plant or not, Gillette was bringing in enough of its American blades each year so that if they were spread out they would "cover England eight times over." Considering that the man making the charge was an official of Darwin's, Limited, a Sheffield razor and blade manufacturer, it was suspected by many that this graphic verbal tableau was a bit exaggerated. But it was left to one William J. Pope of Cambridge, perhaps a waggish don, to disclose just how exaggerated it was. Writing to *The Times* about what he termed this "disquieting revelation," he revealed that his own calculations, based on the population and land area of England and the size and weight of a razor blade, indicated that if the Darwin's charge was true, Gillette blades were being dumped on the kingdom at a rate of nearly 800 million tons per year. At that clip, he observed, every man, woman, and child in the realm was spending more than £150,000 a year to keep himself or herself supplied with some twenty million blades, weighing in at about twenty tons, consumed yearly per capita. "Whilst disclaiming any desire to interfere with the innocent amusements of the people," he concluded, "I feel that this safety razor business is being overdone. A mere million blades per annum should suffice to keep the normal individual clean-shaven."

Gillette was not, of course, shipping any such number of blades to any country, but production was steadily rising. In 1925 — for competitive reasons, 1925 was the last year in which the company regularly revealed its unit sales — close to fifteen million razors and more than half a billion blades went to market, a considerable number of them outside the United States. By the following year, export sales accounted for perhaps 35 percent of the company's total dollar volume, and Pelham was confidently predicting that the figure would hit 50 percent in five years' time. As economic conditions stabilized, Pelham could step off the steamer *Majestic* in New York after a 1927 trip overseas and say that "the safety razor business is good all over Europe, and I am bringing back an order for fifty thousand razors from the Kaffirs of Africa." The war, he said, had "made Europe a continent of clean-shaven faces," and Gillette had every intention of capitalizing on this grooming phenomenon. Even in Communist Russia, Pelham added, beards were giving way to the smooth shave.

Russian beardlessness was not, however, slated to be a boon to the capitalist Gillette Safety Razor Company, despite Pelham's rosy pre-Bolshevik vision. The coming of the Soviets had changed the picture considerably. To raise funds as well as to keep the balance of payments in line, the Soviet Union levied high tariffs on imports, and the price tags of Gillette razors and blades were in any case beyond the reach of the average peasant or proletarian. Even so, Gillette products were well known in Russia. In fact, a German-owned company near Moscow was turning out razors and blades under the name of Swedish-Gillette. The spurious blades wholesaled at the equivalent of eighty cents for a package of ten, versus the going price of about fifty cents for a single, genuine Gillette blade (a few of the latter trickled in, mainly from Germany and Scandinavia).

Despite the many obstacles in its path, Gillette was diligent in its pursuit of the elusive Russian market, and came tantalizingly close to building a factory there. An old Russia hand explored the country on Gillette's behalf in 1928, and determined that the best plant site would be Leningrad. In the beginning, at least, he estimated the market at a modest 250,000 razors and one million packages of blades a year, but advised that lower prices could expand that base considerably. Among the problems was the fact that the Soviets strongly preferred that manufacturing be carried out with Russian raw materials and stipulated that the government must be given half the plant's earnings in return for the franchise to operate in Russia.

Still, the company pressed on, and in December, 1929, after three weeks of hard and concentrated bargaining — the shortest time on record for such negotiations, the New York *Times* reported — Gillette became the first American industrial company to be granted a concession to build and operate its own facility in the Soviet Union. Unfortunately, this deal with a Communist power was subject to the vagaries of capitalist economics, and in the aftermath of the stock-market crash the directors voted a quiet end to the Russian project.

Even without access to Russia, there was still the rest of the world to concentrate on, and Gillette did so with increasing vigor throughout the 1920's. In Australia alone, the company sold more than a million razors in 1928, and as that year drew to a close, Gillette was carrying on its books foreign orders for six million razors, about four million of them destined for Europe. And more than developing markets overseas, Gillette was also developing a corporate philosophy, an approach to foreign markets that would prove wise in the long run even if it was not always followed. Many American companies, said Pelham in 1926, "make of exporting a mere 'dumping ground' for surplus production." Not so at Gillette, which pursued a policy of aggressive expansion throughout the world and believed, as Pelham told the New England Export Club in 1926, that "export trade and export customers are worthy of the same attention as domestic business."

To see that proper attention was paid to foreign customers, Gillette generally preferred to put its own man, an American wise in the ways of the American way of doing things, in charge of each overseas branch. (For years, the Belgian manager was the aptly named William F. Shaver.) Office and sales staffs were composed of natives, and to keep the branches on their toes, upper-echelon executives from the American parent company paid periodic visits, checking on procedures or making goodwill calls on important customers. Pelham made many such inspection trips, and so did Fahey. And so, on occasion, did the founder himself, King Camp Gillette, whose arrival at a Gillette dealer's — or anywhere else, for that matter — could be almost as startling as the appearance at a candy counter of the flesh-and-blood Smith Brothers.

"I keep up my interest in many things"

Following a leisurely week in Constantinople in the spring of 1927, Mr. and Mrs. King C. Gillette went by train to Budapest, stopping off along the way at Sofia and Belgrade. In Sofia, Gillette met with his company's local representative, who was proud to report to the president that more than sixty stores in that Bulgarian city were carrying Gillette products. (He might have been prouder still to know that Gillette, a few days later, would write to Frank Fahey that his man in Sofia was a "very bright and pleasing personality.") In Budapest, too, on a Sunday morning while his wife attended a church with "a great reputation for its music," Gillette was joined by the native agent for an inspection of several retail shops where Gillette goods were sold, even on Sunday. "You would have thought," wrote Gillette, "I was the King of Bulgaria rather than King Gillette, at the reception I received. It was a most interesting and enjoyable morning."

Gillette may indeed have been greeted with the deference usually reserved for crowned heads of state, for in his own time, he had become an almost fabulous figure, perhaps more universally recognized than any man in all history. His portrait and signature had been printed and circulated tens of billions of times, and with each passing year hundreds of millions more razor blades wrapped in his likeness and boldly penned name fanned out even to the most distant quarters of the globe. His fame was greater than that of any living prince or potentate, any emperor or elected president. He had not, as he had once assayed to do, led the world out of social and economic darkness, but had instead taught all mankind to shave, and his very name was almost synonymous with the implement used in that grooming ritual.

As early as 1909, he had been stared at and greeted by strangers on London streets where just five years before he had walked as an obscure American salesman with bottle caps in his sample case and a scarcely realized dream in his head. Before another decade was out, legend had so far outstripped the man that there were many who believed that he did not exist, that King C. Gillette, face and name, were merely artful trademarks. Even as close to home as Montreal, where Gillette had attended a dinner given in his honor in 1918, a contributor to the company house organ noted wonderingly that "there were many guests of the evening who, before Mr. Gillette was introduced, had thought him a myth; that there was in reality no such person."

There most certainly was such a person, and wherever he went in the world he was recognized, even though time had worked changes on the face framed by the camera at a New York photographer's studio in 1906, when the final, familiar trademark portrait was snapped. And Gillette hardly sought to hide his identity. Always kept amply supplied with blades, he often passed out samples to people he met, much as John D. Rockefeller dispensed shiny dimes — though Rockefeller's coins, of course, were not stamped with his own likeness. On a grand tour around the world in 1922, Gillette was surrounded and cheered by the villagers of Touggourt, in the Sahara south of Biskra. While stranded there by a sandstorm — only a system of walls and dikes kept the desert from burying the small settlement — he went to a shop to buy canned food with which to supplement the Arab rations (and possibly handed out a few blades on his way). "I noticed on a show case in this store several Gillette razors and some cartons of blades," Gillette was pleased to record. On another jaunt, Gillette was hailed by townsfolk in Hammerfest, Norway, the northernmost permanent settlement of civilized man. And in Spain, in 1929, a young gypsy street musician stopped playing his harmonica long enough to show an American tourist his collection of pictures of world monarchs, gleaned from a variety of sources. Among them was the king of the United States — who was, of course, King C. Gillette, on a razor-blade wrapper.

If Gillette was a king, he was without a real kingdom, for his top-lofty title as president of the Gillette Safety Razor Company was only in name. He took, naturally enough, a lively and continuing interest in company affairs, and from the time he made the permanent move to California sometime in 1913, he was kept abreast of corporate problems and progress through almost weekly copies of financial reports and letters from Frank Fahey, with whom Gillette had developed a rare and warm personal relationship. "Our Annual Meeting was held yesterday," wrote Fahey to Gillette on January 9, 1917, "and the new Board of Directors organized today, electing Mr. Gillette President, Mr. Joyce and Mr. Curran Vice-Presidents, and myself, Treasurer." In the main, though, Gillette's role was a ceremonial one, limited to cameos at sales conventions, where he generally confined himself to praising the salesmen for their dedication and reminiscing that he, too, had once lived the lonely life of a commercial traveler. Occasionally, though, he strayed from this set piece. In 1921 he proceeded to read a lengthy paper, in which he marveled at what his invention had wrought and presented an ingenious formula by which he proved that the monetary value of the time saved each year by men shaving with his razor was equal to the entire capital of the United States Steel Corporation.

Gillette was quick to admit that the razor company had grown and prospered far beyond his original expectations, and there were times, too, when he felt that the corporation had outgrown him, had passed the founder by. Writing to Thomas Pelham in early 1922, Henry Sachs commented on a letter he had received from Gillette, recently returned from a visit to Boston headquarters. Gillette seemed pleased about the factory operation and general business conditions, said Sachs, but he added, "As I read between the lines of his letter I wonder if he is not unduly sensitive about something — just what, I don't know."

It may well have been that Gillette, like many men who have launched and helped to build large enterprises and then have withdrawn from active management, felt left out, unappreciated by those running the show in his stead. He said as much to Fahey several years later, when he proposed that on an upcoming world trip he be commissioned to make official calls on Gillette agents and customers. He had made much the same proposal some years before, he said, explaining that "I think at that time my suggestion was mistaken by some of those to whom the matter was referred — anyway the proposal was not favorably received — and as a result I took the position that the Company was not favorably impressed." And he added somewhat testily that when making such calls on his own initiative, "I enjoyed it very much — and strange to say, was received in many places with great pleasure."

In any event, Gillette became a roving goodwill ambassador for his company, and on his almost yearly — and sometimes nearly yearlong — trips abroad would gladly show his famous face wherever it might do the company some good. "I found our European managers much pleased at your having visited them when in Europe," wrote Fahey after one such sojourn. The man in Prague was particularly impressed, Fahey advised, "and said your visit with him gave him additional inspiration to go out and sell more goods."

Gillette's frequent and extensive travels were the fulfillment of a boyhood dream — one of a number of boyhood dreams, it seems — but as the boy became an old man he was plagued with nagging doubts about his purpose. "I sometimes think we are overdoing this traveling business and missing things more worthwhile," he confided to Fahey from Vienna not long after his fanciful masquerade as the king of Bulgaria in Budapest. "But I also think it keeps me from growing stale — otherwise old. For I keep up my interest in many things — whereas at home back in Cal. there is always too much family — and one has little time to really live their own life. To me it is a terrible thing for anyone to live the lives of other people and neglect their own desires and interests and things they want to do. And usually these other people have nothing to do themselves and only expect to be amused. It kills me to put myself into such a life day after day — so I prefer to travel."

When not traveling the world by steamship, railroad, or motorcar, Gillette had a number of other diversions to occupy his time in California — not the least of them, of course, the numerous relatives and in-laws who had followed him westward. At one time or another, his mother and mother-in-law, two sisters, brother Mott, brother-in-law Charles Gaines, and assorted others came to share the salubrious climate of southern California. And of course, there was always young Kingie, Babe, who despite the avid encouragement of his father — or perhaps because of it — never seemed to hit his stride as a bearer of the family tradition of inventive tinkering.

Gillette's first regular base in California had been the Beverly Hills Hotel, and for years he occupied a spacious house on the hotel grounds. But as early as 1914 he purchased a spread of land at nearby Lindsay and established the Gillette Ranch. In most parts of the West, a ranch is devoted to horses, cattle, or sheep; in California, a ranch is as likely to be given over to agriculture of some sort. At the Gillette Ranch, where young King Gillette was financial and business manager, the staple product was navel oranges, which went to market with the Gillette diamond-and-arrow trademark inked on their skins. Young Gillette, to be on the safe side, had written to the razor company for permission to use this widely known symbol, but was assured by Pelham that it was registered by the razor company only for use on cutlery, soap, and brushes. The Gillettes, he advised, could use it on any other kind of goods they desired, just as an unrelated Concord, New Hampshire, Gillette Company was using the self-same sign on its line of hot-water bottles.

Later, in the 1920's, Gillette moved from oranges into dates, a foodstuff which had struck his fancy during trips to the Near East. On a sixty-acre plot of ground near Indio, he and a partner planted the newly introduced Egyptian variety called Saidy, along with the garden variety Deglet Noor so common in the region. Their plantings were interspersed with grapefruit trees, though some accounts have it that their grapefruit trees were interspersed with dates.

Agriculture was not the only field to engage Gillette's fertile imagination in the years following his departure from the active affairs of the razor company. In the early 1920's, he took an interest in a Boston concern called the Pollock Pen Company, whose product was a fountain pen filled by means of a disposable ink cartridge rather than the conventional refillable rubber bladder. It seemed almost of a piece with his throwaway-blade idea, and the impressed Gillette bought stock in the company and accepted a directorship. Apparently, wiser heads had warned him against getting involved in this venture, and when Henry Sachs heard that he had gone ahead and put money behind the novel pen, he wrote to Pelham that "Gillette seems to be growing a bit forgetful in his older days." Later, as the caveats proved true and Gillette grew disenchanted with both the product and the company's management, he sold his holdings for what he could and resigned from the board. He was highly indignant when he learned a few years afterward that the company — reorganized under another name — was approaching prospective investors and claiming that the eminent King C. Gillette was still among the directorate. "I have none but the best wishes for the success of the pen company," he advised, "but I cannot allow my name to be used in connection with its exploitation."

Gillette did use his name in connection with other enterprises in which he was more closely involved. One was the short-lived Gillette-Schmidt Gear Shift Company, built around automotive inventions made by one Benjamin F. Schmidt. Backed by Gillette, Schmidt probably worked in the well-equipped experimental machine shop that the aging inventor had set up in hopes that it might inspire his son to prove himself worthy of the family's inventive mantle. In any case, Schmidt was granted a number of patents for improvements on equipment used in oil-well drilling — in gratitude and payment for Gillette's aid, he assigned part interest in his inventions either to Gillette personally or to the gear-shift concern.

Oil was also involved in another Gillette-backed enterprise, the Shale Rubber Products Company, whose goal — which may or may not be apparent from its name — was to extract synthetic rubber from oil shale. Considering that the most modern technology has yet to come up with a feasible method for recovering oil from shale economically, the company's aim was surely an imaginative one. Gillette poured about $9,000 of his own into two years of experimental work before formally organizing the concern as a Delaware corporation in 1928 and generously drawing William Nickerson, Frank Fahey, Thomas Pelham, and two other high Gillette Company executives into the venture with him. But it was soon apparent even to Gillette that rubber was not likely to become a chemical counterpart of the razor blade. The trouble was, he said in a letter to his fellow investor Fahey, that the expert chemist the company had hired — like Benjamin Schmidt, he puttered in Gillette's well-appointed shop — lacked suitable imagination, lacked the drive and flexibility that Gillette and Nickerson had both displayed in such full measure in the razor's time of gestation. Experts, said Gillette, too often "lose all elasticity in reasoning and cannot get out of a particular orbit." That was the problem with the expert Gillette had banked on in the shale venture. "He may be the finest of chemists and have a great understanding of rubber," Gillette groused, "yet stand right next to a great discovery and never see it because he is prejudiced in favor of common practice." In any event, shale oil proved to be a dry well, and the company quickly followed the well-worn path to that great corporate boneyard that held the remains of so many wildly speculative enterprises spawned during the frenzied 1920's.

Meanwhile, young King G. Gillette had sought on his own to follow in his father's enterprising footsteps, though with much poorer judgment and even worse luck. Early on, he had been involved in a minor way with the shale venture, but soon went after bigger game, guided by a certain Walter Arnold, the "inventor" of a radio device designed to locate hidden treasure. Using his ingenious equipment, Arnold assured the younger Gillette while pocketing unspecified sums of his money, it would be possible to unearth a fabulous store of buried pirate gold. Gillette was a believer, though the only thing he was left to show for his misplaced devotion was a $50,000 lawsuit brought against him later by the smooth-talking Arnold's ex-wife, who claimed that she had been hurt in an automobile accident while riding with her former husband in search of the pirate treasure. At the time, she said, Gillette was her ex-husband's employer, and was thus responsible for her injuries. Mercifully, a judge ruled otherwise, and King G. Gillette was spared at least one further indignity.

Young Gillette may have had cause to wonder about the outcome of zany investments, but an indulgent father saw to it that he did not lack for a roof over his head. In the spring of 1928, at about the same time that Kingie was preparing a defense against the damage suit brought by the treasure hunter's aggrieved ex-wife, the elder Gillette bought a twenty-room mansion for his son and daughter-in-law. The purchase price was $125,000, and the Los Angeles *Examiner* described the place as "one of the finest homes in Beverly Hills."

Expensive though it was by the standards of the day — or of any day, for that matter — the Beverly Hills house was merely a bagatelle among King Gillette's real estate purchases. Like many who rise to riches from propertyless obscurity, Gillette had turned to land for certification of his surprising wealth. By the late twenties he could with justice be called a real estate baron as well as the Razor King. The Gillette Ranch — eleven hundred acres in Tulare County — was his first notable foray into land acquisition, but it paled in comparison to his purchase in 1924 of a prize parcel of land at Pershing Square in downtown Los Angeles, where he planned to build a monumental office building. The transaction cost Gillette close to $1.5 million, but his personal representative, L. E. Lounsbery, was quick to say that it was well worth the price. Gillette, he said, was firmly convinced that "Los Angeles business frontage is one of the soundest fields for investment to be found anywhere. He is absolutely sold on Los Angeles and believes this city has a boundless future." Gillette had already made some less spectacular land buys in Los Angeles, and confirmed his faith in the city still further two years later when he bought, for $840,000 that included the trade of thirty-two hundred undeveloped acres in Santa Barbara County and some small lots in Hollywood, yet more choice footage at Eleventh and Broadway. It was, said the *Examiner*, just one more earnest of Gillette's "absolute faith in Los Angeles real estate."

The late 1920's were a time of high promise and prosperity, and Gillette enjoyed it to the fullest. In 1927 he had two chauffeurs and three Pierce-Arrow limousines, and when he saw that his traveling days were numbered he moved to set himself up in opulent California quarters. At Calabasas, on the northern march of Los Angeles, he built a rambling, Spanish-style house complete with courtyard and gatehouse; because his eyes were growing sensitive to bright light, Gillette had his bathroom tiled and outfitted all in black. At Balboa, overlooking Newport Harbor, he raised a fourteen-room, three-story "beach house" complete with an oversized bathtub for his 250-pound frame, and a specially shelved room in which to display his wife's large collection of miniature figures, many of them ivory. He never completed his move to Balboa, though — the house was built quite close to the water, and Gillette did not like the sudden spells of fog and the pounding waves so common to that part of the coast. There is even a story, surely apocryphal, that the proud owner arrived at the house at the head of a train of moving vans during a violent summer storm, took one look at the towering seas, and motioned his caravan to backtrack to Beverly Hills.

Gillette also found Palm Springs to his liking. So much so, in fact, that he saw possibilities for a similar resort community in nearby Palma Village (now Palm Desert), where he bought 480 acres and proceeded to clear the heavily overgrown land for grapefruit cultivation while awaiting the inevitable rush of well-heeled vacationers in search of home sites. It was tough going to clean out the creosote bushes, mesquite, and smoke trees that infested the property, and Gillette, out on a ramble in the wild land one morning, was gone for so long that a worried search party went to track him down. And their concern was surely well grounded — during the clearing operation, workers had killed a total of five hundred rattlesnakes, one of them five feet long, thick as a man's arm, and shaking twenty-three ominous rattles.

Gillette drilled some of the first irrigation wells in the Palma Village area, and in nearby Indio he and a partner bought still more land, some of which is even now known as Gillette Park, a monument of sorts to his foresight. For King Gillette believed in California as perhaps only a wanderer can, and as yet saw no need to recant his confident words in 1926 to a Boston financial reporter: "Business is good in California, and with the state's climatic advantages in mind I can see nothing ahead but permanent prosperity."

Even so, he had continued to look ahead for something that far transcended a mere business boom.

"What has made us the slaves of money getting?"

Possibly because of the always heady political climate of southern California, Gillette's faith in perpetual prosperity — and his devotion to roomy mansions, sleek Pierce-Arrows, and regal travel — had done little or nothing to rout the essential belief in corporate utopia that he had slipped into his mental baggage by at least the early 1890's. Indeed, on his frequent courses through the world, Gillette was sometimes moved to contemplate the backward social systems of the ancients, untouched by ideas of democratic cooperation. Consider classical Athens "at the height of its so-called glory," he once wrote to the ever attentive Frank Fahey. "There lived in the fifth century before Christ 200,000 so-called nobles and 400,000 slaves — and it was the control and power of those in power over these slaves that made possible the building of these temples. . . . Their cities were illustrative of the two extremes of power and dominion on one hand, and the most abject poverty and submission to fear on the other." Modern Greece, its peasantry exploited by absentee landlords, was little better in Gillette's eyes, nor was much of the world that he saw in his travels.

By comparison, the primitive social and economic conditions of the rest of the world put the United States — deplorable as it may have been by Gillettian standards of corporation and cooperation — in the deep shade on any scale of inequity. But Gillette, anchored as he was to his long-held fixed idea, was still on the lookout for ways to bring his vision of progress, of the human drift toward complete equality and centralization, closer to reality. And as he had when his razor company's astounding financial success had first put him in possible conflict with his cherished philosophical notions, he sometimes looked at the Gillette Safety Razor Company as a chosen instrument of that progress.

Gillette did not, of course, impose his ideas on the company itself, though the cooperative store for employees, opened in the wildly inflationary days of 1920 to sell groceries and the like at cost, bore a more than passing resemblance to Gillette's economic goals, and was similar to the operations of the short-lived Twentieth Century Company of 1895–1896. But there is no evidence to suggest that he was more than a spiritual mentor, if even that, behind this venture. Nor did he, after the fashion of some leaders in other industries, seek to foist his political views on his workers. As he strolled past the production lines during his annual visits to the South Boston plant (an employee recalled years later that Gillette looked almost like a policeman in his plain dark suit), he dispensed encouraging words rather than tracts. "Are you happy?" he would ask a startled machine operator or blade inspector. "Keep up the good work," he might say to another worker. Or "Let's be a happy family."

These remarks were hardly calls to revolution, but then, Gillette's idea of revolution did not involve mounting the barricades to hurl paving stones at society's oppressors. Rather, it was a rational, orderly process, and Gillette continued to believe that the razor company, by striving for monopoly, was helping to fulfill human destiny. At the same time, he thought, the company was an agent of progress when it capitalized on the great chain stores that were everywhere supplanting the smaller independent retailers. In this last proposition, at least, he was joined by Frank Fahey, if only as a matter of courtesy. Noting in the spring of 1928 that he had just received a copy of *The Human Drift* that Gillette had sent him, Fahey allowed as how he had "enjoyed immensely looking it over." Quite diplomatically, Fahey went on to say: "That was a long time ago and the subsequent events have followed parallel lines since then, in a great many situations. . . . Chain stores — United, Schulte and Liggett, for instance — began only twenty-two years ago and today they dominate their fields." And to the company's everlasting credit, he added, "I believe we were among the first manufacturers to sense this change years ago and tied our kite to the tails of these large agencies and they have been wonderful factors in our distribution."

Perhaps Fahey was merely humoring Gillette's well-known economic eccentricities, but it was not long before this train of thought suggested some grandiose plans. "I wish the Gillette group (not as a part of razor co.) would start a chain store system," Gillette wrote to Fahey. "It has got the greatest future for profits, and for future amalgamation into a vast controlling factor of industries." This was Gillette the visionary speaking again, impulsively pledging to put a million dollars of his own — "and probably more" — behind such an undertaking. "It must be understood," he explained, "that this business will invade all countries," and that "these chain stores in less than ten years will control most of the industries that supply their products at their source." And in twenty years, he rhapsodized, "practically all of the bigger and most prosperous chain store systems will be consolidated into one vast industry." It was the World Corporation all over again. Fahey's response to the proposal, if any, is unknown.

Gillette did not limit his propounding of grand schemes to mere private letters. Indeed, not long after settling in the Los Angeles area, he had called on the muckraking novelist and political radical Upton Sinclair, in the hope of finding a sympathetic sounding board for his social philosophy. In his autobiography, published in 1962, the long-lived Sinclair noted that he was already familiar with the Gillette corporate scheme, having examined (if not fully read) both *World Corporation* and *Gillette's Social Redemption*. He had come across the books at the Pasadena Public Library, and observed that he was probably "the only person who had ever taken those tomes from the library shelf."

Sinclair also recalled a singular circumstance of his first meeting with Gillette. His secretary was under standing orders never to disturb him while he was working on a book. But one day she entered his inner sanctum bearing a business card, to which was attached a crisp one-hundred-dollar bill. "I looked at the card," said Sinclair, "and saw the name, King C. Gillette, familiar to all men who use a safety razor." Gillette, ushered into the muckraker's office, was pleased to learn that Sinclair was familiar with his plans for worldwide incorporation, and proceeded to elaborate on the scheme. "I discovered that the joy of his life," Sinclair observed, "was to get someone to listen while in his gentle pleading voice he told about his two-tome utopia."

But Gillette wanted more than Sinclair's ear. He had written yet another book and hoped that the facile Sinclair would help put the manuscript into more readable shape. As for the introductory hundred-dollar bill, this was only a symbol of what could be in store. Gillette promised to pay handsomely for Sinclair's editorial services, and he later told Mrs. Sinclair that if she could convince her husband to take on the project, she would never in her life have to be concerned about money. It was an offer that Sinclair could not refuse, though he soon had cause to regret his acceptance. "Mr. Gillette was coming for two mornings every week to tell me his ideas — the same ideas over and over again," Sinclair recalled in his autobiography. Even so, he pressed on, and he was, for all that, quite taken with Gillette's notions. By 1919, he was writing to a fellow socialist, J. G. Phelps Stokes, that "King C. Gillette, the razor man, has a plan for social reconstruction which I think is very remarkable. I have been helping him to get his manuscript into shape and have boiled it down to one hundred and ten typewritten pages."

Later, Sinclair spoke of Gillette's ideas to Henry Ford, whose success as an automobile manufacturer had convinced him that he was also an authority on social and economic matters. The two industrialists agreed to a meeting at Sinclair's home, and on the appointed morning it was impossible for Sinclair to get any work out of his houseboy and the two schoolboys employed to do domestic chores:

"They lined up beside the drive to see the Flivver King and the Razor King come in," Sinclair said. It was not, however, a fruitful session. Ford, lean and spry in Sinclair's description, and Gillette, large and ponderous, ensconced themselves in easy chairs before the fireplace and exchanged their strongly held opinions. Watching them, Sinclair wrote, was "like watching two billiard balls — they hit and then flew apart, and neither made the slightest impression upon the other."

The Gillette-Sinclair editorial collaboration proved somewhat more fruitful than the Gillette-Ford intellectual collision, though Sinclair later complained that Gillette had "scribbled all over" the manuscript. At Sinclair's urging, and with Gillette's promise to supply $25,000 for an extensive advertising campaign, the book — titled *The People's Corporation* — appeared in 1924 with the imprint of the distinguished New York publishing firm of Boni and Liveright. It was a great step upward in Gillette's literary life, for his previous works had all been privately published at his own expense.

Even so, and notwithstanding the fine hand of Upton Sinclair, the book was merely old wine in a new bottle, vintage utopian fare decanted from *The Human Drift*, *World Corporation*, and Melvin Severy's clumsy opera. As Stuart Chase put it in the *Nation*, it was "a working drawing for a new heaven and a new earth, even to the vision of apartment houses fifty stories high, central kitchens feeding a million, and fenceless harvest fields as big as the State of Texas."

Because the author was more famous now than he had been in 1894 or 1910, *The People's Corporation* received somewhat more general notice than had its predecessor volumes, though the increased attention surely did not signal acceptance or approval of his ideas. Stuart Chase, for one, picturing Gillette as a disgruntled stockholder touring the "great world factory," was somewhat amused that "the man who has sold safety razors to hairy Ainos and Russian mujiks takes off his coat, clears the desk, opens the window, gets in a stenographer, and prepares to organize the business of feeding, clothing, sheltering, educating, and amusing the people of this planet." In the end, Chase concluded that Gillette was both sincere and imaginative, but that his proposals were "quite untouched by the realities which guard the road to Utopia." A reviewer in *Outlook* saw Gillette's new world order as merely the latest in a long string of putative promised lands, adding bitingly that it was "the most hideous to date; which is saying much."

The New York *Times*, too, examined the book, and the *Times* reviewer William MacDonald found it an "astounding proposal," one that, despite Gillette's evident earnestness, was difficult to take seriously. Indeed, it was hard to credit someone who was referred to invariably in the press as the "multimillionaire razor manufacturer," but who could write that we "waste our lives in accumulating wealth" and who intoned that the time had come "to ask what has made us the slaves of money getting."

Printers' Ink, while conceding that a man should be permitted to live down his past, took the unkindest cuts of all at what it called Gillette's "dizzy flight . . . into chimerical lands." It was, said this bible of the advertising fraternity, more than a little preposterous — not to mention ungrateful — for a man with King C. Gillette's well-known credentials to claim that "if people really need to buy goods it is quite unnecessary to lure them." Why, the reviewer himself had dashed out to buy his first safety razor (a Gillette, of course) only because he had been enticed by the company's seemingly omnipresent advertising. And what in the world could Gillette be thinking of when he observed with obvious distaste that "the sole purpose of advertising is to make you and me buy A's goods and not B's goods," or that "advertising is part of the game of beating your neighbor"? It was as if Attila the Hun, still on the march, had begun to denounce pillage and speak with the tongue of a pacifist. All in all, the magazine concluded, the People's Corporation urged upon the world by King Gillette was a shaky edifice, one that would surely not "gain a foothold as quickly as did the Gillette Safety Razor Company nor will it exist as long."

Actually, of course, the People's Corporation flourished only in Gillette's wide-ranging mind — which was seldom hobgoblinned by consistency, foolish or otherwise — where it coexisted more or less happily with thoughts of razors, riches, and real estate speculation, of ink cartridges, automobile clutches, and rubber squeezed from rock. And for all that, the persistent utopian vision was not totally removed from the spirit of Gillette's other concerns: his ideal world was not the construct of a humanist social philosopher, but of a world mechanic, a cosmic engineer to whom rational order was the only pearl of great price. There was, therefore, a certain internal symmetry underlying the effusive compliment that Gillette paid in late 1928 to another great engineer, Herbert Hoover, on the occasion of Hoover's election to the presidency of the United States. Wrote Gillette from Palm Springs to Fahey in Boston: "We are going to have the eight most prosperous years in the history of the world provided Hoover lives and his policies [are] carried out. He will be the greatest President ever occupying that high office, not even excepting Washington, Lincoln, or Coolidge. For he combines in his head the soul of Washington, the heart of Lincoln, and the independence and business sagacity of Coolidge. There never has been one like him." (Perhaps Hoover heard of this fulsome praise: he named one of his White House dogs Gillette.)

Gillette had been wrong before, but never quite so spectacularly. And before Hoover's four years in office were out, he would see his company brought low and his stubbornly won personal fortune all but washed away.

6

Cut-out Corners

"Business conditions in America were somewhat varied"

STOCKHOLDERS IN THE Gillette Safety Razor Company received early Christmas presents in 1926. Flush with record earnings, the directors mailed out on December 1 what they termed "an extra Silver Jubilee Dividend" of fifty cents per share to mark the twenty-fifth anniversary of the company's incorporation. As an added flourish, the special payout came by way of distinctive silver-toned checks. The regular one-dollar-per-share dividend checks were of the usual green paper — the color of Gillette's blade packages and also, perhaps more than just coincidentally, the color of money.

In an era of dizzy preoccupation with profits, Gillette had been nothing if not a money-maker. Earnings in the year of jubilee were nearly twice the figure for 1920, and total dividends came to $4.50 per share, or $9 million on the two million shares outstanding. Since earnings had first been reported in the now-distant days of 1906, there had not been a year when the company did not show a profit or pay a dividend, and a toiler at the statistics desk of the daily Boston *News*

Bureau calculated in early 1927 that a farseeing (or lucky) investor who had put a total of $15,717.55 into Gillette stock at critical early junctures would have received over the years dividends to the tune of $328,768.45, and be left holding 13,224 shares with a market value of $1.3 million. It was of such stuff that dreams of the 1920's were made.

But Gillette's financial statements spoke of more than mere fantasy. Unburdened by debt — all expansion had come from earnings — the company had more than $6 million in its bank accounts, and the promise of millions more. When asked about the future, as they frequently were, Gillette executives pointed to the some forty million of their razors that they reckoned were still in service, and observed happily that this still left about 760 million potential male customers in the world. Henry J. Fuller, a Gillette director and a partner in Aldred & Company of New York, was pleased to liken the company to a public utility whose franchise was to furnish continuous streams of blades for use in endless millions of razors. Small wonder that Gillette was a stock-market darling, courted avidly by suitors seeking steady returns and blissful appreciation.

To meet the ever growing demand for its products, the company had surrounded its original South Boston factory with a concourse of buildings that made the Gillette manufacturing complex a jewel of industrial New England. In 1925 alone, work began on two new structures — one of eight stories, the other of nine — that would bring the razor-making capacity to 150,000 a day and boost daily blade production from two million to three million. For those interested in such things, a tour of the sprawling Gillette plant along the Fort Point Channel was a high spot of a visit to Boston. In the winter of 1927, Prince William of Sweden arrived at nearby South Station, where he was met by the company Rolls-Royce — suitably decorated with American and Swedish flags — and whisked off for a look at what happened to all that high-grade steel his country shipped to Boston. The prince, according to the Gillette house organ, "evinced keen interest in the activities of each department, closely scrutinizing our wonderful machinery and marveling at the intricate movements that have been created and developed by Gillette ingenuity." The whole experience, said the visiting Swede, was one of the most impressive features of his extensive American tour.

And yet, just as all was not right beneath the prosperous veneer of the 1920's, there were flaws in Gillette's handsome facade, too — some visible, some yet to be uncovered. Only two weeks after a wondering Prince William had roamed through banks of blademaking machinery, an anonymous resident of Columbus, Ohio, put his finger on one problem. Reading in the Boston *News Bureau* a glowing account of Gillette's banner year just past, he snipped out the article and mailed it back to Boston headquarters. Above the headline, he had scrawled in red pencil: "Have not had a sharp blade for six months."

This was surely a flippant exaggeration. At the same time, after all, other men were happily stroking their cheeks and chins with Gillette blades that had seen weeks, months, and even years of satisfactory service. But Gillette's long honeymoon with the nation's shavers was indeed starting to pall. As Batten, Barton, Durstine & Osborn put it so baldly in a generally rosy report submitted later the same year, "Gillette [was] beginning to carry its share of ill will on the part of the public, the penalty which always goes hand in hand with dominance in industry." The fault was not in the razors, said BBD&O, but "in the blades for which the public is obliged to pay out money constantly." More ominously, the report observed that "a very considerable part of the adult male population of the United States honestly believes that Gillette blades have deteriorated badly." (In fact, there *was* a problem with the new improved razor, leading to an inordinate number of cracked blades. After several modifications, the fault was at last corrected, though not in the millions of razors already sold.)

Actually, blade quality was undiminished, and may even have been better than before. In 1923, company officials were discussing a radical and costly improvement in the grinding, sharpening, and honing process. Chairman John Aldred settled the matter with words that would ring hauntingly through Gillette's executive row some forty years later. "There can be no question," he snapped, "of our knowing how to make a better blade and not making it." With every succeeding year, steps both large and small were taken to assure the matchless keenness of what was proudly known as "the Gillette edge."

But a subtle psychology was at work dulling that vaunted edge. Just as many smokers abuse themselves to the point of cancer or emphysema, constantly switching brands in search of the elusive enjoyment recalled from their early puffs, shavers longed for the comfort and velvety faces that they felt were no longer provided by Gillette blades. But memories grow rosier as time goes on, and custom can stale the infinite quality of even the best of experiences: Gillette's blades were not going downhill; standards of shaving comfort had simply been upgraded and nudged beyond previous levels of satisfaction. And blade-jaded men were beginning to shop around for supposedly better brands.

Gillette was aware of this phenomenon, just as it was painfully conscious of the thickening ranks of competitive blades bidding for the allegiance of the nation's shavers. Indeed, while the later-blooming overseas market continued to grow, domestic sales of Gillette-brand blades had actually started to shrivel, dropping by 15 percent in 1927. As the annual report put it in that year, without going into details, "Business conditions in America were somewhat varied but the foreign business showed steady growth." Put another way, Gillette was in trouble at home.

The company's entry into the less lucrative, cheaper-blade field relieved some of the pressure, but Gillette had enough pride in its name — and in its profits record — to seek more open means of holding a purchase on the market. For a time, spurred largely by the admen at BBD&O, the company intended to salvage one of the trio of notched and new-hued blades projected in early 1927, and introduce a so-called Blue Blade in the spring of 1928 — it is not altogether clear whether the blade as well as the wrapper was to be colored blue. Later that year, the Blue Blade idea was scrapped, and Gillette proceeded with a long-simmering project to introduce a premium-priced, stainless-steel blade. Called Kroman (after the chromium and manganese alloyed with the usual carbon steel), the new blade was slated to sell at a factory price of ninety cents for a package of ten, and to be retailed at a dollar and a half. King Gillette, for one, was strongly opposed to Kroman, which was distinguished from the standard Gillette blade by its triple notchings and orange wrappings. The stainless blade went into production in November, 1928, but Gillette was still telling Fahey in December that the whole notion was a colossal blunder, that the blade was not markedly better than its green-wrapped counterpart, and that "all the advertising in the world will be impotent to convince the masses that it is not a deliberate move simply to get more money for our product." At the very least, wrote Gillette from sunny Palm Springs, the blade should be sold under a separate name, or perhaps gold-plated to make it seem really worth the price. The founder's counsel went unheeded, however, and work continued on the Kroman blade, whose honing and stropping took twice as long as the standard blade's.

At the same time that Gillette had been scouting for ways to parry competitive thrusts from rival blademakers, the company had also been branching into other fields where it could capitalize on its expertise in laying keen edges on metal. In a letter to Pelham in 1921, Henry Sachs had pushed for a product that was somewhat different from the workaday razor. The company should, Sachs suggested, consider making a much larger razor and blade for use in shaving goatskins before tanning. He granted that the idea might seem amusing, but cautioned that "even amusing ideas sometimes develop into business."

As it happened, the company chose not to be amusing, and opted instead for entry into more conventional areas. The first move came in 1920, after a Worcester, Massachusetts, carpet mill had inquired about the best method for resharpening knives used in its operation. An eager Gillette salesman, sniffing a prospect, hurried to the mill and came back with the idea that the throwaway-blade principle could be adapted for making uniform rug pilings. It could be, and was, and by 1924 Gillette was doing a modest but growing business with carpet mills both in the United States and abroad. Impressed, Chairman Aldred called for more such ventures, and the directors authorized management to "take what steps may be necessary in the developing of a diversity factor in the business." By 1927, Gillette was offering lines of twine cutters, paper knives, chiropody chisels, and surgeons' scalpels, all featuring disposable blades.

The scalpels, with their curved cutting edges, posed some special manufacturing problems, but the company was able to call on the aging William Nickerson, still in harness, to design both the handle and the machinery needed for grinding the blades. Later, still another old war-horse, King C. Gillette himself, would do his best on the product's behalf. In mid-December of 1928, while laid up in a Los Angeles osteopathic hospital with high blood pressure and liver problems, he wired Fahey to send him six scalpel sets to pass out to his physicians. He also asked for ladies' razor sets, presumably for presentation to his nurses.

Promising as they may have been in their closely circumscribed fields, the diversified products were pygmies when measured against the blade business that was perforce the backbone of Gillette's prosperity. And as the decade moved to an end, it was becoming apparent that the company's peerless strength was slowly ebbing, that Gillette could no longer claim exclusive ownership of the market that it had created in the first few years of the century.

Perhaps even more telling than the murmurs of consumer dissatisfaction with the Gillette shaving edge were the rumbles of discontent from the trade — wholesalers and retailers whose goodwill is essential for effective distribution — over the Gillette selling policy. In his zeal for ever bigger sales, Pelham had made many special deals with a number of mammoth distributors over the years, putting Gillette goods in their hands at prices considerably lower than those asked of mere run-of-the-market dealers. Usually, these arrangements called for Gillette to pay the preferred customer a rebate for each razor and each package of blades purchased, in exchange for impressive displays of Gillette products in windows and on selling floors. One such agreement, signed in 1924 and running for five years, provided for Gillette to pay thirty-five cents for each new improved razor and four cents a blade package to the large retailing and wholesaling firm of D. A. Schulte, Incorporated. And this came on top of a discount more attractive than that offered to other, smaller dealers. Similar plans were worked out with major firms like Louis K. Liggett and United Cigar Stores.

It was a swift way to pump Gillette goods into the retail pipeline, though at increasing cost to the company. In the fall of 1925, for example, Pelham agreed to supply the Schulte firm with a full ten million basic sets of a razor with a single blade, packed in a pasteboard box. The price was set at a rock-bottom ten cents per set, but after deduction for special allowances Gillette's take was reduced to about a nickel. A similar deal was made at the same time with Palmolive, and it was because of such concessions that Gillette tallied a $204,000 loss on its razor business in the first three months of 1926 alone. Of course, the name of Gillette's game was not razors but blades, and the hefty $5.2 million gross profit on blades during the same three-month period proved once more the wisdom of the company founders' talk of tribute.

Still, such wheeling and dealing with giant customers spoke of a cavalier attitude toward dealers unblessed with the high-volume operations deemed worthy of Gillette's special dispensations, and much of the trade bristled at what was taken as gross mistreatment. And in both retaliation and defense of their own profit margins, increasing numbers of dealers began showing a preference for other blade brands — many of which, despite the league-leading Gillette's spirited offensive, continued to find their way to market, some of them from England. Darwin's, Dunhill, Wexteel, and Wade & Butcher were among the principal brands that joined the welter of blades seeking to edge Gillette from retail shelves.

In response to these attacks, Gillette moved decisively to capture a large segment of the other-branded market for its own, and with goodly results. The Otto Roth and Rubie operations did their work well enough: the Supre-Macy blades sold in large numbers by R. H. Macy, for example, had nettled Gillette, but the company soothed its discomfort by simply underbidding the original supplier and turning out Supre-Macy blades in its own subsidiary workrooms. But other competition just wouldn't go away, and Gillette executives, despite the fact that their basic blade patent had expired long before, continued to disparage makers of the familiar three-hole blades as illicit interlopers and bootleggers reaping what Gillette had sown. To be sure, there were out-and-out counterfeiters who sought to benefit, not only from Gillette's razor, but from its good name as well. The company was rightfully diligent in its pursuit of such offenders, and a druggists' trade publication warned after the breakup of a bogus blade ring in 1927 that "the possession of counterfeit blades is about as dangerous as the possession of counterfeit money," so swift was Gillette to uphold its trademark rights. But the Dunhills and Ever Readys of the world were legitimate competitors, and if their blades fitted Gillette's razors it was no crime but a convenience to consumers, who were, in fairness, entitled to a choice.

For numerous reasons, then, Gillette — the company that had first taught grateful men how to shave themselves a generation before — was now perceived by many as a heavy, a giant that sought by fair means or foul to crush all opposition. It was, perhaps, a harsh perception, but it was one held even by Judge Henry W. Goddard of the United States District Court in New York. In the summer of 1927 he issued a consent decree barring the company from violating the anti-trust laws in its dealings with large and favored customers such as Liggett and United Cigar. Without admitting wrongful practices, Gillette agreed to the order, which Thomas Pelham, as corporate executives so often do on such occasions, said would have "a very salutary effect upon the whole industry."

Perhaps so, but its implications for the Gillette Safety Razor Company were far from favorable, and the handwriting on its boardroom wall said that the company was facing a situation somewhat akin to the 1921 expiration of its basic patent protection. Now, its dominance seemed in danger of expiring, along with its hard-won goodwill. It stood to reason, after all — now that anyone could make and market blades like the Gillette — that someone, somewhere, might well come along with a hotly competitive new blade that would be eagerly embraced by consumers grown tired of the familiar Gillette. Improved manufacturing techniques, too, might give such a competitor an edge on Gillette, and the company knew that machinery more sophisticated than its own was within the grasp of even minor rivals. At the Brooklyn plant of the defunct Handy Razor Company, for example, a Gillette assistant patent counsel, Leo F. Caldwell, had bought at auction in mid-1928 what he described to Pelham as "an unfinished machine that will grind, hone and strop blades in the strip." Perfected and installed on a large scale by others, such advanced equipment would be a serious threat to Gillette, which still relied on the blade-by-blade sharpening method — albeit much refined — first devised by William Nickerson.

Far too much sweat and treasure had been invested in Gillette's great banks of sharpeners for the company to give serious consideration to scrapping its tried-and-true production lines in favor of costly replacements, no matter what the promised improvement in speed and economy. Instead, Gillette continued scouting for a latter-day version of the 1921 new improved razor, a dramatic move that would perpetuate its foremost position in the shaving market. This time around, it turned to a new and improved (or so it hoped) blade. This time, too, Gillette found itself standing head to head with Auto-Strop's Henry Jacques Gaisman, an old adversary who had been popping up in Gillette's affairs with unfailing regularity ever since the patent office and courtroom tiffs that began in 1907.

"A situation which must be given every consideration"

As the New York skyline dropped from view behind the Europe-bound steamer *Olympic* in the spring of 1926, Thomas Pelham and Ralph E. Thompson — who had joined Gillette fresh from MIT in 1909 and worked his way up to be head of manufacturing and a corporate director — were more than a little startled to find that their fellow passengers included Henry Gaisman, leading light of the AutoStrop Safety Razor Company. Much later, it would be said that Gaisman, in his great haste to collar the two Gillette executives, had boarded the luxury liner without ticket or passport. If so, he did not make any display of eagerness. Not until the last day at sea did his conversation get beyond everyday chitchat and down to business. And his business, in any case, was nothing particularly new.

He had, said Gaisman, invented a new kind of razor blade. It was double-edged, to fit the Gillette razor, but it was different from conventional blades. For one thing, the central section was slightly softer than the cutting edges, making it less likely to crack when flexed and tightened in the razor. For another, the holes in the blade were not round, but more or less H-shaped, a feature that would presumably make for a more positive grip by the razor studs — partic-ularly if, as Gaisman proposed, a razor were built whose studs were of the same peculiar shape as the blade's three holes. He hardly needed to point out that the Gillette blade would not fit such a razor, but that his blade would fit the Gillette razor. And since his blade would be demonstrably better than anything else available . . . well, Gillette could just kiss its sweet franchise goodbye.

Gaisman was certain that the invention would be of great interest and value to the world's premier maker of razors and blades, but he was probably not overly surprised when Pelham and Thompson, two of the three most important men in the Gillette organization, showed scant interest. They had, after all, been hearing similar stories from the AutoStrop chieftain off and on since before World War I, and just as regularly rejected his proposals that the two companies should work together in some way to exploit the new blade.

The Gaisman blade idea was not without merit, but his price tag was a bit steep. Having been paid by Eastman Kodak in 1914 the then-record sum of $300,000 for a single invention — he had patented a means of writing on photographs at the time of exposure — Gaisman had hopes of topping this sum in blades. Even when pressed, he was vague about his asking price, but he did say that it fell in the seven-figure range. And lest anyone fail to grasp the magnitude of such a sum, he was quick to point out that it fell somewhere between one million and ten million dollars. He was so certain he was not committing highway robbery that he even suggested calling in Charles Evans Hughes (who would soon join Gillette's legal counsel Louis Brandeis on the United States Supreme Court) to arbitrate a price which Gillette would agree beforehand to pay.

If nothing came of Gaisman's shipboard wooing of Pelham and Thompson, the New Yorker did not cool his courtship. He pressed his cause on Pelham several more times after the three men returned to the United States, and in the fall of 1928 Pelham consented to a rendezvous at the Belmont Hotel, a favorite New York hostelry for visiting Bostonians. There, over a quiet lunch, Gaisman again pleaded his case, pointing out that he had in the meantime been granted a patent for his novel blade. The obvious question now was what Gaisman's next move might be, assuming that Gillette did not come up with the seven-figure asking price that was still the key to the whole proposition. Gaisman's answer was forthright. As the big gun in the blade business, he said, Gillette *should* have the invention. But if the company refused to come to terms, then he would be forced either to sell the idea to someone else or to make the new blade and razor himself. As a matter of fact, he added, AutoStrop had already formed a subsidiary, the Probak Corporation, to do that very thing, should the need arise.

Concerned though he was about the possible Probak blade, Pelham tried hard not to betray any signs of urgency, suggesting merely that if Gaisman were ever in Boston he might be interested in discussing the matter further. Gaisman, too, avoided the appearance of undue anxiety, and it was not until the first day of February, 1929, that he again met with Gillette officials, this time in a suite at the Copley

Plaza Hotel in Boston. (Pelham's brother-in-law was assistant general manager of this establishment, and was frequently provided with special monogrammed razor sets for presentation to valued customers. In return, he saw to it that Gillette people were given favored treatment. Once, he even performed the nearly impossible feat of procuring last-minute rooms for some important Aldred & Company clients who were in town for the Harvard-Yale game. "I had to bribe our office manager to get these by telling him that I would get him some blades," he wrote to Pelham.) The new round of talks went smoothly enough, but things all boiled down to the same old refrain and the same old price. When Pelham said at one point that ten million dollars was a preposterous figure, Gaisman merely smiled and said that he didn't really expect ten million; what he had in mind was more like five million. That, too, was out of the question, and when the session broke up Gaisman announced that while he hated to harm a fine company like Gillette, it appeared that he had little choice but to come out with the new blade on his own.

For the first time in its history, the Gillette blade was facing potentially deadly competition from a worthy rival possessed not only of technical skills, but with established worldwide distribution channels as well. Almost in an instant, the global razor-blade franchise had been thrown up for grabs.

To say that Gillette officials were panicked at the thought of great phalanxes of Probak blades marching through Gillette territory would be to overstate the case. But not by much. Gaisman boarded the train for New York on a Sunday; two days later, Gillette engineers were making drawings of a new razor and blade to meet the Gaisman challenge. A week after that, Pelham and Thompson — Frank Fahey was on a Mediterranean vacation cruise at the time — huddled with the leading New York directors John Aldred and Henry Fuller in Fuller's Fifth Avenue apartment to discuss what Fuller tonelessly described as "a situation which must be given every consideration." All the stops were out now, and development work moved on at a feverish pace.

Firmly wedded to the three-hole blade concept that had worked so well for so long, designers proposed apertures of numerous sizes and shapes, mindful always that the new blade and razor must not be interchangeable with the Probak configuration. Other changes were considered, too. Although the initial idea had been to make the forthcoming blade in the same round-ended shape as the original, Ralph Thompson proposed in March that the new blade's ends be squared, with the corners cut out to remove pressure points that were the cause of much breakage when blades were clamped into razors slightly bent from falls to floors or bathroom sinks. A more subtle advantage of the new shape was that it would give the blade a considerably different appearance and help convince consumers that here was an article that was truly a change from the old model. By early May, a variety of keyhole shapes had been considered for the blade apertures and razor studs, and all had been discarded in favor of a diamond shape that elder statesman King C. Gillette had been partial to when he went over the proposed designs during his annual visit to South Boston.

Meanwhile, still more urgency had entered the blade race. Henry Gaisman had been driving his design and production troops without mercy, and at about the same time that Gillette executives were settling on diamond-shaped apertures, the first of the new Probak blades began infiltrating the market. With the enemy closing in for the kill, Gillette staffers laid into their tasks at an even more feverish pace.

And then, with one of those almost casual decisions that can change the fortunes of even large and well-ordered institutions, the Probak-Gillette competition took a new turn. At the end of May, Pelham and a handful of Gillette executives met to put the final seal of approval on the new razor and blade. It so happened that some of the other models that had been proposed earlier as alternatives were lying on the boardroom table. Almost idly, Pelham started looking them over again. One of them featured on the razor cap a short, horizontal bar that passed through a like-shaped opening in the blade and tightened into a groove atop the toothed razor guard. Why not, Pelham asked, modify this design so that the bar and groove ran the full length of the cap and guard, and make the blade with a long central cut to receive the bar? Leave the three holes — the central one round, the flanking ones square or diamond — but let the long and narrow central slotting be the key element in the blade's design. That way, the blade would still fit the old razor, but just let anyone try to slap one of Henry Gaisman's three-holer Probak blades into the new Gillette razor!

It was, as such snap insights are so popularly believed to be, but so seldom are, a stroke of minor genius, and the new design was adopted within a week. (Just minutes before Pelham's remarks, as the production engineer, Theodore L. Smith, would later note with wonder, everyone in the room had been itching to confirm their bets on the diamond studs.) Its distinctive basic configuration would become the matrix for all future double-edged blades, but its adoption, inspired though it may have been, set the Gillette Safety Razor Company on a collision course with Henry Gaisman, who was yet to have his day.

"*We are not only prepared for any legal controversy, but we invite it*"

In the bitterness to come, it would be maintained by many at Gillette that Gaisman had planted at least two spies in the company's drafting department, and that these agents had purloined drawings and samples of the new Gillette blade. For their part, Probak partisans could be equally insistent that a nameless Gillette official, invited for some undisclosed reason to tour Probak's New York factory, had pocketed some blades and rushed them back to Boston. Whatever the merits of either case — and the drawing-board spy seems more plausible than the light-fingered executive — the fact is that in November, 1929, Henry Gaisman hied himself to the United States Patent Office and applied for a reissue of the 1928 patent under which Probak blades were made. A few weeks earlier, he explained, he had discovered that his attorneys had left a few things out of the original application, and he now wanted to rectify these omissions by making some minor revisions. Before the month was out, Gaisman had done other business in Washington, too, registering as Probak trademarks certain shapes for razor-blade apertures. Three of them were strikingly similar to the pattern chosen the previous spring for the new Gillette blade; another was identical to the Gillette design. It was, at the very least, an astounding coincidence, something akin to a pair of poets who independently address themselves to the same theme and come up with precisely the same sonnet.

No matter what the true source of the revised Probak configuration, the new blades were soon being churned out of AutoStrop's factories at a rapid clip. (Gaisman had for years been making his thicker, stroppable, single-edged Valet blades by the speedy strip method and had smoothly adapted this process to the double-edge Probak.) The blades were cleverly patterned to fit both old and new Gillette razors, as well as the variety of Probak razors, which were just as cleverly constructed so that they would exclude Gillette's blades. In addition, the AutoStrop-Probak blades were specially tempered to give them what seemed to be a marked edge over the famed Gillette edge. And by January, 1930, the first of the new slotted Probaks — stamped conspicuously with three separate patent numbers — were trickling onto the market.

Gillette had planned to throw *its* new products into the breach at about the same time, but had been dogged by manufacturing difficulties throughout the summer and fall. The company's problems were, after all, somewhat larger and more complicated than Probak's — Gillette had to keep spitting out great quantities of the old blade while at the same time tooling up for the smooth changeover to the new. Even with the incessant badgering of top officials, it was not until late February that the first shipments of new Gillette razors and blades left the Boston factory. And along the way, the company's production engineers had abandoned — in the interest of speed — their tentative plans to introduce the faster and more efficient strip method of blade manufacture that Probak used to make its blades and that had so fascinated King C. Gillette fully twenty years before.

At about the same time, Gillette's top executive ranks began to give way when it was found that some of the manufacturing bottlenecks could be chalked up to the unlikely agency of Thomas Pelham, as well as to the engineers. In his single-minded push to move more and more goods, Pelham had worked out so many high-volume, discount razor deals that production capacity that should have been devoted to turning out the new razor was consumed instead by output of special premium goods. Even worse, he had agreed to such low prices that Gillette was losing considerable money on the transactions. Aghast when struck by the full import of the situation, the executive committee gratefully accepted the sixty-seven-year-old Pelham's "retirement" from active service as chief salesman. But Pelham stayed tenaciously on as a vice-president and director of the company, even as Frank Fahey implored big buyers of premium razors to renegotiate their generous contracts and accept less mer- chandise at higher prices.

Though the Pelham problem was the prelude to even greater internal disarray at Gillette, it seemed at the time that the more serious threats were coming from without. Henry Gaisman had been broad- ening the offensive against his much larger rival. Having beaten Gil- lette to market with the new blade, he now began bruiting about the technically correct fact that he had beaten the Boston company to the patent office as well. *His* blades, Gaisman pointed out, were duly patented and so marked; Gillette's blade was stamped only with the problematical "Patents Pending." It required little knowledge of patent law to judge that Gaisman was likely to bring suit; intimately familiar with that arcane field, Gillette's batteries of attorneys advised that Gaisman would do precisely that, though they held that he had a shaky case. In addition, they cautioned that it would be unseemly at the moment, too much like sour grapes, to suggest that Gaisman had appropriated his blade from Gillette's own drawing boards.

Shaky case or not, rumors of an impending high-stakes patent- infringement suit — with Gillette, this time, taking an unaccustomed seat in the defendant's dock — continued to circulate along Wall Street and among Main Street dealers. So, too, did hints that sizable Gillette customers such as United Cigar would be called to answer for alleged misdeeds if they continued to handle the company's wares.

Reeling from an attack on its sales front and detecting clear signs of a coming assault on its patent situation, Gillette was hammered from still another quarter, the stock market. That segment of the brokerage trade whose purview included safety-razor companies had marked in red the fact that Gillette's earnings had declined in 1929 for the first time in nearly two decades, and their alarm was not mollified by the official company explanation that the slump was due to phasing out the old razor and blade and bringing in the new. It seemed to many investment men that Gillette Safety Razor Company shares were losing their allure. With relentless precision, the com- pany's stock edged downward, at a cost in credibility not only in the investment community but among Gillette employees as well. Just two years before, management had magnanimously permitted workers to buy shares on the installment plan at $100 each; at the time, with the stock going in the open market for as much as $125 per share, it seemed like a generous gesture, but many loyal Gillette hands were still making their weekly payments on $100 shares that were now dipping below $90.

At the 40 Wall Street offices of Aldred & Company, the erosion of Gillette's stock was a cause for considerable alarm. In his triple role as major shareholder, "fiscal agent" — for which duty his firm charged a fee of $25,000 a year — and board chairman, John Aldred had a greater stake in Gillette's fortunes than most men did. Indeed, the propensity of the Gillette directorate to declare frequent extra stock dividends had sometimes raised eyebrows in banking circles, where it was known that the largest beneficiary of such largesse would be none other than the Aldred interests themselves. Still, such closed-loop generosity was hardly beyond the pale of 1920's financiering, nor was Aldred's response to the sudden decline in Gillette stock: late in February, he formed a pool of about sixty firms and individuals (among them a number of Gillette directors) to start buying the company's shares in order to shore up their value.

For a time it appeared that Gillette had succeeded in stabilizing its position. The new blade and razor were launched in March to the accompaniment of a nationwide advertising campaign far more lavish than anything Probak could mount. ("Gillette announces the greatest shaving improvement in 28 years," trumpeted the opening page of a five-page spread in the *Saturday Evening Post*.) The stock pool, while it was slow to produce chartable results, was at least in being, and the financial lore of the decade was replete with the wondrous workings of such associations. So confident were Gillette officials that they felt free to break off the merger parleys they had prudently continued to hold with Gaisman — who, equally confident of his own strength, had upped his demand to a 25 percent share of the combined companies. Considering that Gillette was reporting assets of $57.1 million, this did seem a bit excessive coming from a man whose company's assets were a mere $6.4 million.

There remained, of course, the possibility that Gaisman might sue, but in the face of that looming challenge Gillette chose to hurl down a gauntlet of its own. Emboldened, perhaps, by fond memories of past courtroom triumphs and the sure and certain hope of more to come — and at the same time, ironically enough, frightened by a deluge of letters from frantic stockholders seeking assurance that their investment was not about to be trampled by a more powerful patent — Gillette dared Gaisman to commence firing. The Gillette Safety Razor Company, Fahey reminded shareholders in a public letter dated March 18, 1930, had been in business for twenty-eight years, and had a profound respect for patent rights; before coming out with the new razor and blade, the company had made certain that its patent position was sound. "IF ANYONE FEELS THAT OUR COM-PANY HAS INFRINGED HIS PATENT RIGHTS, WE SUGGEST HE COME INTO COURT," Fahey roared on behalf of the board of directors, adding boldly: "WE ARE NOT ONLY PREPARED FOR ANY LEGAL CONTROVERSY, BUT WE INVITE IT." There followed a list of four powerful New York and Boston law firms, all girded to do battle for Gillette.

The challenge was answered soon enough, and when it was, events began unfolding with quickening and (for some participants, at least) sickening speed.

"We had pretty well made up our minds that we would find something, but hoped that we would not"

Four days after Frank Fahey's public request for a courtroom date with anyone aggrieved by the new Gillette razor and blade, a wax-sealed registered letter arrived in South Boston. Signed by Nathan R. Maas, the president of the AutoStrop Safety Razor Company — Chair-man Henry J. Gaisman was above such routine transactions — it was a curt notification that Gillette was infringing AutoStrop's patents on the Probak blade. Unless the alleged infringements were discontinued immediately, the letter concluded, AutoStrop would be "obliged to bring suit In Equity against you for an injunction and accounting." Put in plainer language, it meant that the Gaisman forces were threatening a move that could, if successful, drive Gillette to the wall. At the same time, AutoStrop served similar notice on Gillette's largest customer, the United Cigar Stores Company of America, without whose good graces the Gillette distribution system would be severely squeezed. And United Cigar officials were less impressed with Fahey's claim that such talk was merely a maneuver by "the Auto-Strop people with their Hebrew management" to break down a long-term relationship with two presumably Christian concerns than they were with his later pledge to assume all of United's financial burdens arising out of a court action.

Advised by his attorneys that he stood on firm ground, Fahey had issued an equally curt reply to AutoStrop's stern warning. Gillette was not infringing anyone's patent, said Fahey, and had no intention of curtailing manufacture or sales of the new razor and blade. In effect, he was double-daring AutoStrop to sue, which it obligingly did on April 2. Papers were served on United Cigar a week later.

Gillette and Probak blades continued to pour from factories onto retail shelves, but the focus of battle was now switched from manufacturing and marketing to the legal arena. Lawyers from both sides — the AutoStrop team was captained by a former United States patent commissioner — labored through the spring and summer, carpentering endless arguments in favor of their respective blade apertures and configurations. It was tedious, quibbling work, and Gillette's chief patent counsel was finally moved in mid-August to write to a colleague, "I am leaving this afternoon for a two-week fishing trip in New Brunswick, where I hope to forget all such things as cut-out corners."

As well he might have, for as the pretrial struggle went on, it became increasingly apparent that Gillette's case was perhaps not so ironbound as first assumed. The company could not, after all, really prove that Gaisman had copied its blade, nor could it gainsay a fact that is frequently given considerable weight in patent litigation: the Probak blade, however questionable its antecedents, had reached the market before the Gillette model. As early as May, at least one Gillette attorney was beginning to backslide on his optimism. There was a possibility, he cautioned, that the Gaisman patent claims could be "misconstrued in such a way as to give support to a captious argument of infringement."

Because of the stakes involved, even such embryonic caveats grew weightier as time went by. For AutoStrop was asking for more than merely the withdrawal from the market of Gillette's blade. It also wanted whatever profits the company had made from the new product, and sought on top of that to collect for damages done to its own business as a result of Gillette's alleged horning in on the market. With each mounting sale of a new razor and a package of new blades, the potential cost of an AutoStrop victory grew more staggering, and Gillette determined that it could not gamble its whole future on the coldly impartial decision of a federal judge. Mobilization for legal battle in the fall proceeded, but by mid-June the Gillette director Henry Fuller had begun once more to talk merger with the Gaisman camp. He was, he confessed, somewhat embarrassed to be coming hat in hand to men whose own overtures he had spurned so firmly not six months before.

Indeed, Gillette's position had been sapped considerably since the battle's opening days. AutoStrop stock, buoyed both by the company's performance and by touting from friendly investment houses, had been steadily on the rise since the turn of the year; Gillette stock, despite the best efforts of the Aldred-backed pool operation, had sagged from about $100 down into the $60 range. The market seemed to be saying what both sides knew without being told, that Gillette no longer held the undisputed upper hand in the razor and blade business, and that it was playing a game it simply could not afford to lose. With the tables thus turned, negotiations proceeded apace.

So, too, did contingency plans for a breakdown of talks and a return to bitter hostilities. Just three days after the start of the latest round of consultations, Clifford E. Dunn — the New York attorney who had been so instrumental in upholding the original Gillette patent — was authorized to search out a previous patent that could be purchased by Gillette and used as grounds for a counteraction against AutoStrop. "Any reasonable excuse to start a suit of any kind against them," wrote Dunn to Gillette's chief patent counsel, "would have a beneficial effect on the public at least." Eventually, Dunn did turn up such a patent, granted in 1922 to a William A. Barry of Oklahoma City and winding up — by way of interim owners in Washington, Dallas, and Houston — in the hands of Paul A. Rose of Easton, Maryland, from whom Gillette bought the rights in early September, 1930. But the infringement suit drawn up on the basis of this patent was never filed, for Gillette had by then lurched beyond such claims for courtroom relief.

Within two weeks of settling in once more around the conference table, and after several offers and counterpropositions, Gillette and AutoStrop representatives had ironed out most of their differences and had come to tentative terms. A short time later, aboard John Aldred's chartered yacht *Cyprus* in early July, a bargain was struck: in exchange for 310,000 shares of its common stock, Gillette could walk away with all of AutoStrop and be done with deadly litigation and competition.

The main question remaining seemed to be where the stock to make this life-saving purchase would be coming from: whether the company would issue new shares — on which, of course, additional dividends would have to be paid later — or whether it would, to maintain the per-share payout at the same comfortable levels, buy the necessary stock on the open market. The directors, most of them major Gillette stockholders and, more significantly, members of the still-active Gillette stock pool, chose the second course. On July 10 the board authorized the borrowing of $25 million to carry out the purchases.

Slowly, quietly, so as not to send Gillette stock prices soaring too quickly from the upper 50's to which they had now been driven down, the company began foraging for its own stock. And where the pool had failed, the company succeeded, though not fully by design; as August neared, Gillette was selling at above 80. It was at this point that the company turned naturally enough to the pool (managed, it will be recalled, by Aldred & Company, Gillette's own fiscal agent), whose erstwhile paper loss of some $1.7 million had become a smallish paper profit that was made real when Gillette bought most of the pool's holdings. Coming as it did on the cusp of two vastly different decades, it was a transaction that could be — and would be — seen in a less than favorable light.

Still short the required number of shares, the company tapped a number of Gillette directors, among them King C. Gillette. Failing both in health and fortune, almost desperately seeking to stave off the Depression-born erosion of his real estate baronies, the founder sold 20,000 shares, or close to 40 percent of his remaining holdings. With these buys, the Gillette Company had put together a sheaf of stock certificates thick enough to meet AutoStrop's terms; like a man teetering on the edge of a crumbling precipice, the company had caught its balance and stepped confidently back to solid footing.

Or so it seemed. There remained one critical detail, a matter that had disturbed AutoStrop officials throughout the summer's bargaining.

During the early stages of the merger talks, AutoStrop had relied for its notions of Gillette's financial condition on the minimal accounting contained in its handsome annual reports. Pressed for deeper details, the Gillette men politely but firmly demurred, hinting that further figures were probably not required at that point, and that in any case Gillette was under no obligation to supply them. Put mildly, it seemed a rather odd position to take, and as the deal neared consummation AutoStrop began to have a nagging feeling that all was not as it was said to be. At last Gillette could stall no longer, and submitted its books to scrutiny by independent auditors. By then, as an AutoStrop director would later say, "we had pretty well made up our minds that we would find something, but hoped that we would not."

What they found was a stunning blow to the AutoStrop directors. "The statement didn't look as if it was for the same company," one of them recalled. By their own accounts, at least, the disclosure was also a shock to most Gillette board members as well.

Put briefly — the only merciful way to put a situation that became a catalyst for one of the most complicated litigations ever conducted in the Commonwealth of Massachusetts — Gillette executives had for a number of years been vastly overstating corporate revenues and profits. They had accomplished this feat of bookkeeping legerdemain by recording as completed sales all shipments of blades and razors to overseas subsidiaries, whether or not the goods had actually been sold to dealers. This had been done ostensibly to reduce foreign income-tax payments, and the theory was that things would even out from year to year as sales were completed. In practice, though, the procedure became the key element in flights of bookkeeping fancy that made sales seem to be rising steadily, when in fact overseas warehouses were bulging with unsold — and, with introduction of the new razor and blade, virtually unsalable — merchandise that was carried on home-office books as having already been disposed of at a tidy. profit. More darkly, as it turned out later, the whole exercise seemed also to be a means by which the ruling Gillette triumvirate of Fahey, Pelham, and Thompson assured themselves of fat bonuses, computed as a percentage of reported earnings.

Whatever the motive, Gillette's old figures had lied. By what magnitude and with what effect could be seen in the ledger for 1929, in which year the company generously paid out more in cash dividends than it had truly earned, and then threw in a stock dividend for good measure. Over the entire five-year period examined by the gimlet-eyed accountants, Gillette's earnings had been inflated to the tune of nearly $12 million.

Whatever the rationalizations — it was all "a trifle," said Chairman Aldred at one point — the nearly plighted troth of Gillette and Auto-Strop was broken forthwith, and shattered Gillette directors who had once come hat in hand to Henry Gaisman approached him now on all but bended knee to hear his newest terms. He would still accept Gillette stock as the purchase price, said Gaisman, but it would have to be preferred stock, with first call on dividends. And it must have the same voting power as common stock. In mounting disarray, faced if they refused with a patent suit whose possibly disastrous consequences had only been magnified by weeks of travail, Gillette agreed to the AutoStrop proposition. On October 16, 1930, formal announcement was made of a merger of the two companies, pending stockholder approval, which came little more than a month later.

At least some Gillette shareowners, however, were nursing strong feelings of disapproval, if not of the corporate nuptials, then certainly of what they saw as sordid hanky-panky on the part of trusted company officers and directors. And on October 30 — perhaps fittingly, just a year and a day after the great stock-market crash — a group of minority stockholders filed suit on behalf of the company against its own directors. The charges were many and varied, but they all boiled down to one thing: in pursuit of selfish ends, directors of the Gillette Safety Razor Company had systematically milked the company and those stockholders unfortunate enough to be excluded from the charmed circle of boardroom insiders.

Whatever the merits of the case, many directors took steps that were at least tacit admissions of wrongdoing. Indeed, even before the suit was filed, a singular announcement was made by those who had sold stock to the company from their personal portfolios to round out the lot needed for the initial AutoStrop deal. In view of the precipitous decline in the value of the shares — into the deep 30's by October — they were taking back their stock and returning the money they had received for it. Only King C. Gillette, who had sold 10,000 shares at $80 and 10,000 more at $85, declined to join in this expensively noble gesture. In worse financial shape than anyone knew, he could ill afford to take such a loss, and in any event may well have felt that his signal contributions to the Gillette enterprise were well worth some extraordinary compensation, no matter what the source. A short time later, Frank Fahey and Ralph Thompson turned over checks for $53,318 each, in at least partial reimbursement for bonuses based on bogus earnings. Thomas Pelham, also a major beneficiary of doctored sales and profit figures, did not come up with a check of his own, for reasons made manifest some time later when he appeared in bankruptcy court with liabilities that exceeded assets by $738,483.

Nor did the company forget the hapless employees who had bought and were still dutifully paying for Gillette stock at $100 per share, only to see it slump in market value to $20 and below. To "reestablish the good will and morale" of workers, all money paid in on the ill-fated stock installment plan was refunded with interest.

But well-meaning gestures, no matter how generous or sincere, could not fully atone for past directorial transgressions, at least not in the eyes of the litigious minority stockholders who sought to recover $21 million that they alleged had been lost to the company through sundry peculations. On July 9, 1931, eighteen attorneys stood in a sweltering Boston courtroom for the start of a trial that would not be concluded for more than a year. As coincidence would have it, because of courthouse repairs some of the sessions were held in Young's Hotel, where King C. Gillette and John Joyce had sat down to lunch more than a generation before and made the Gillette Safety Razor Company possible. As such suits invariably are, this one was settled for considerably less than the stupendous sum demanded by the plaintiffs, though the $400,000 repayment that the defendants were at last ordered to make to the company was stiff enough.

The costs were high in other ways, too, perhaps at no time more graphically than on that excruciating December day when John Edward Aldred sat in the witness chair and denied that Gillette stockholders would have been heartsick and angered had they known the true state of their company's financial affairs. And then, as he reviewed a long career in industry and finance, recalling better days of unquestioned trust and honor, the former Gillette chairman's eyes welled with tears and he could not go on.

Indeed, the story unfolded during the proceedings was, as one attorney had promised at the start, "amazing and appalling . . . the story of the downfall of an industry of which New England and particularly Massachusetts were immensely proud."

But if Gillette had fallen from a certain grace, it had not tumbled beyond all redemption. Even in the midst of blossoming scandal, men labored without stint to see that a new and stronger company — chastened by the mistakes and drawing on the strengths of the past — would rise from the wreckage of the old.

And one of the first orders of business would be a changing of the guard.

A Spirit of Confidence

"I have never used a bottle of Listerine in my life"

IN PURSUIT of his social and industrial dreams, King Camp Gillette had frequently written well, at times even eloquently. But now the occasion seemed to call for stilted, copybook business English. "I tender herewith my resignation as President of your company," he wrote in early April, 1931, "to take effect at your pleasure." With those sixteen simple words, signed in a shaky, unsure hand, the ailing founder and namesake of the Gillette Safety Razor Company took his leave, praised by the board of directors and heartily thanked for the "kindly feeling that has continued to exist even though he has had to be away from the Company for so long."

Gillette, weakened by advanced age and declining health, had been foremost among the company's longtime leaders to step aside in the wake of the startling revelations of management misdeeds over the past half decade or more, but he was not the first. And if his time of departure was merely coincidental, dictated more by the ancient human condition than by the rush of contemporary events, the same could hardly be said of other top executives, three of whom sat around their familiar boardroom table on a late November morning in 1930 to hear what Henry Jacques Gaisman had come to say.

With the eyes of King Gillette, John Joyce, and the recently deceased William E. Nickerson observing him from portraits on the boardroom walls, Gaisman must surely have sensed — perhaps even savored — his anomalous position. And if Frank Fahey, Thomas Pelham, and Ralph Thompson had chanced to notice the ornately framed likenesses, the thought would have undoubtedly passed through their minds that they would never be thus honored by the company they had served for so long. Just four days before, on November 18, stockholders of the respective companies had assembled separately and approved the terms of the proposed merger, and Gillette had purchased the assets of AutoStrop. Now Gaisman, head of the far smaller party to the union, sat in the Gillette boardroom as chairman of a newly formed management committee — composed, as he so diplomatically put it, of the "active executives of the business" — with complete authority to conduct the affairs of the combined companies. He had begun the battle with what seemed like fewer battalions, but he came to the conference table as an undisputed corporate conqueror.

Under the circumstances, it could hardly have been otherwise. The accountants' doleful disclosures, coupled with the bitter charges leveled by disgruntled stockholders, had discredited Gillette's top officials and made some form of executive housecleaning a practical necessity as well as a moral imperative. Already, for reasons all too clearly related to Gillette's current poor pass, Pelham was out as the chief of sales, though he stayed on as an officer and director without discernible portfolio. But even this tenuous status was threatened by the New York Stock Exchange. As a requirement for the stock transactions necessary to complete the merger, the Exchange had demanded that both Frank Fahey and Pelham be removed from the Gillette board of directors, either forthwith or at the next annual meeting of stockholders. In the latter event, the Exchange specified that Fahey, the vice-president and general manager, must meanwhile be barred from having anything to do with the company's accounting department.

As bantam-sized men so often are, Fahey and Pelham were stubborn, and refused to budge voluntarily from their director's chairs.

Under the terms of the corporate bylaws, they indeed could not be removed until the next annual meeting (when their names would not be posted for reelection). They did, however, join Chairman Aldred and fellow director and vice-president Ralph Thompson in resigning from the powerful executive committee, and at the same strained board meeting where these welcome resignations were tendered, the old management's influence was diluted still further with the election of five former AutoStrop officials to vice-presidencies of Gillette, their duties plainly overlapping those of the holdovers from the old regime. A more awkward executive line-up is hard to imagine, though the errant legacies from the past may not have been quite so unwelcome as it might seem. They knew, after all, where the bodies were buried, and their lingering presence helped give the immediate post-merger proceedings at least a semblance of continuity.

Having brought to bay the great company at whose heels he had been nipping for a full generation, Henry Gaisman moved carefully but firmly to set Gillette's tumbledown house in order, and at the maiden meeting of his management committee, he made it plain that not all of the ten men who sat with him at the table that day would be sitting there in six months' time. It was hardly necessary for him to specify who these inevitable absentees were to be. Gaisman then proceeded to list some of the manifold problems facing the company: its patent situation was uncertain; manufacturing processes in the Boston plant had been rendered all but obsolete; Gillette blade quality was slipping steadily; consumers were confused about the company's future; many dealers were hostile because of preferential pricing arrangements made with high-volume buyers; large customers such as Schulte and United Cigar were insisting that Gillette abide by contracts that at times required the company to pay out more in special advertising and display allowances than it took in on razor and blade sales; and in general, public confidence in the company and nearly all its works was badly shaken. In the later words of Gerard B. Lambert, who succeeded King Gillette in title and Frank Fahey in function when he assumed the presidency in May, 1931, "Gillette was in a pretty pickle."

Lambert was a socialite son of the founder of the Lambert Pharmacal Company, the manufacturer of Listerine antiseptic. He had learned of the top-level opening at Gillette not long after he returned from the Grand National racing meet in Liverpool, England, where he lost a considerable sum when his horse crossed the finish line minus its jockey. Appropriately enough for a man whose yachting companions frequently included Vanderbilts and the incomparable Bostonian Charles Francis Adams, the word came from his friend George Whitney, a partner in J. P. Morgan & Company and a pillar of the financial establishment. Gillette's directors, Whitney explained, were looking for someone who could move into the tottering company and put it together again, and the house of Morgan had recommended Lambert. With such a sponsor behind him, needless to say, the job was Lambert's not merely for the asking, but almost for the taking.

Though he protested that he knew nothing of razors or blades, the proposition was an intriguing one for the forty-five-year-old Lambert. For personal reasons alone, a sojourn in Boston would work greatly to his advantage — he and his wife had agreed to a divorce, but the only grounds for such action in their home state of New Jersey was desertion. A salvage attempt at Gillette appealed to Lambert for more businesslike reasons, too, for despite his many opportunities to confine himself to the role of gadabout playboy, Lambert was no mere industrial dilettante. He had several solid automotive patents to his credit, and had proved himself a good all-around manager at the family pharmaceutical concern. Even more significantly, he was widely recognized as an advertising man of the first water. Shown in the British medical journal *Lancet* a scientific word for unpleasant breath, he had proceeded to use it to such spectacular advantage in promoting Listerine as a mouthwash that he lived in constant dread that his tombstone might read: "Here lies the body of the Father of Halitosis."

With a fortune made in Listerine, Lambert had retired two years before, but had grown weary of a life of moneyed leisure and was itching to get back to work. Gillette was a challenge he could not refuse. Not long after his talk with George Whitney, Lambert entrained for Boston, took a suite at the exclusive Ritz-Carlton Hotel, and got down to business at the Gillette Safety Razor Company — whose directors were more than a little taken aback when the newly installed president blithely informed them that he shaved with a Schick razor and would most likely continue to do so. Noting their discomfiture at this admission, Lambert remarked jovially, "Don't worry, gentlemen, I have never used a bottle of Listerine in my life."

More than most men in his executive position, the wealthy Lambert could afford such badinage with his employers. He was not in the least beholden to Gillette for his livelihood, and had in fact refused to accept any salary or other remuneration. Rather, he had struck a bargain similar to the one that had so richly rewarded him at Lambert Pharmacal. If and when Gillette stock earned five dollars a share, he said, he would receive from the treasury 20,000 shares; if and when earnings hit six dollars, he would be granted another 20,000 shares. Assuming that the stock would be worth about fifty dollars a share with such an earnings record, Lambert stood to make a cool $2 million; on the other hand, he was risking the possibility that he would get nothing at all for his labors. His bargain was a measure of both his instincts as a gambler and his serene confidence in his own proven abilities, though even the sportsman in him must surely have known that the doldrums of worldwide depression were hardly propitious times in which to start leading a staggering company up the comeback trail.

Still, the unusual arrangement gave him the independence not only prized but frequently demanded by the very rich. He had no power over the directors, but neither did they have much real power over him, and he consistently resisted pressures to make what he regarded as overly optimistic statements about the company's condition and prospects. "As I had no salary," he recalled later, "they could not whip me into line with threats of financial ruin. I was told one day that two of these men were overheard to say that they wished I could be persuaded to take a salary, then perhaps they could do something with me."

Meanwhile, Lambert had been trying his best to do something with a freshly constituted Gillette Safety Razor Company.

*"Don't worry, my dear, only too many men are
careless about shaving"*

Though he often arrived for work behind the wheel of one of his
string of expensive automobiles, Lambert chose for his office a spare,
first-floor room with a no-nonsense rolltop desk and white-painted
brick walls. "When I see the president of a company sitting in Hollywood surroundings," Lambert observed much later, "I sell my stock,
if I have any." And in these simple quarters he set about managing the
affairs of a company that was still in a pickle but undergoing considerable change from the early days of merger six months before.
Henry Gaisman had succeeded John Aldred as chairman of the board,
though Aldred remained a director in deference to his still-consider-
able stockholdings. The old top executive team of Frank Fahey,
Thomas Pelham, and Ralph Thompson had been ousted from both
the board and the company. King C. Gillette, having quit as nominal
president to make room for a very real successor, was still carried on
the rolls as a member of the board, but only out of decent respect for
his name. If there is anything in the life of corporate management that
is comparable to apostolic succession, it had surely been sundered
when the AutoStrop forces carried out their occupation of Gillette.

In the interim, while awaiting the accession of an actual president,
the caretaker management committee had done its best to keep things
under way — and it must be said that even the doomed Fahey, Pelham,
and Thompson, whether from long habit or fond hope of rehabilita-
tion, worked willingly and hard on behalf of the company. Steps were
taken to consolidate the merged companies' sales forces and overseas
facilities, with old AutoStrop hands generally in the lead. A rigorous
economy drive was launched, including even a short-lived rule that
no long-distance telephone calls could be made without permission
from a management committee member. In another money-saving
move, the company shut off the long-standing $25,000 annual sum
paid to Aldred & Company for serving as the Gillette "fiscal agent."
Apparently, it was a service that the company could well do without:
John Aldred was unable later in court to recall anything of real sub-
stance that his firm had ever done to earn its fee.

Action was begun on other fronts, too. As swiftly as possible, the manufacture of Gillette blades was switched from the old single-blade method to the continuous strip process. (Lest the old machinery fall into the hands of cut-rate rivals, at least some of it was committed without ceremony to the briny outer deeps of Boston Harbor.) To help counter a flood of competitive blades, Gillette unleashed a flood of its own. About three million so-called Goodwill razors, many of them old three-stud models converted to take only the new slotted blade, were put on sale in sets with ten blades, all for the price of the blades alone. (So effective was this maneuver that in Maine, where it was first tested, a salesman for Gillette's own Rubie-brand blades went through his territory without booking a single order.) And in light of Gerard Lambert's business background and the long-term prospects for Gillette, the company had made another move, less palpable, perhaps, but surely as significant as the actions taken in the nuts and bolts areas of manufacturing and merchandising. This one came in the more mystic realm of advertising.

At the time of the merger, advertising for the new Gillette razor and blade had ground to a halt. There was little to be gained, after all, from continued bragging about an admittedly substandard product. Nevertheless, buoyed by superior production capacity and memories of past reputation, Gillette continued to outsell the still-advertised Probak by about four to one. But even a dim light, if it is to keep burning and become brighter, cannot be hidden for long under a bushel. By the start of the new year of 1931, Gillette was looking at advertising agency presentations, and by February, Batten, Barton, Durstine & Osborne had been dismissed in favor of Maxon, Incorporated, a Detroit agency which just happened to be the old Auto-Strop agency. It was the start of a long and fruitful association.

Maxon's first campaign theme was not markedly different from previous Gillette advertising, though it did shun the kind of mechanical detail that had sometimes made the product seem to be an engineering marvel to be purchased for much the same technical reasons that a machinist might buy an improved turret lathe. Dealing with the ticklish reality of a blade that was new but not necessarily improved, the copywriters came up with what they called the International Series of ads, which fell back on the old testimonial routine. They were careful, however, to avoid pinpointing the satisfied users, singling out instead the whole world or entire cities as places where Gillette was favored. "World popularity proves its quality," said one, while others specified acceptance in Nome or Nassau, Chicago or Shanghai. All very low-key, a relatively quiet way to keep the Gillette name before the public eye.

The international ads were launched before Gerard Lambert's arrival on the Gillette scene, but the next major campaign, kicked off in the fall of 1931, bore the unmistakable imprint of the man who, with such slogans as "Even your best friend won't tell you," had made halitosis a household word and Listerine the most sought-after cure. Generically, it is an advertising art form known as "social consciousness," and it can be used to promote any number of products, usually by convincing the potential consumer that he will be banished to nether worlds of opprobrium if he does not buy and use the advertised product. In Gillette's case, the combined fine hands of Lambert and Maxon produced a number of classic examples of the type.

"If men only knew," read the headline on one. In the accompanying photograph, a weeping young woman clutched a framed photograph of her husband, while her mother-in-law tenderly consoled her. "Don't worry, my dear," the older woman said, "only too many men are careless about shaving. I know it's a real cross for you to bear and I must admit I'm a bit ashamed of my son. . . . I'll speak to Jim and see what I can do about it. I'm sure he'll shave more carefully and often when he learns how much a growth of stubble distresses you."

Another capitalized on the Depression-era fears of losing a job. Hat clapped firmly on head, brows knitted almost with terror, a thirtyish businessman was clearing off his desk. In the background, wringing her hands and wearing a stunned expression, his secretary looked on. "It wasn't the Depression . . ." the headline said, and then the copy went on to disclose the grim truth: "Of course the manager said, 'It's the Depression. I'm mighty sorry, Bennett, but business is bad and we must cut down. I hate to see you go and wish you all kinds of luck. The cashier has your check.' " Indeed, sales were off and some reduction in force was called for. But why was poor Bennett the one to get the ax? "The plain truth of the matter is simply this — Bennett had become careless in his appearance. He wasn't always particular about shaving." And if he didn't mend his ways, it was apparent that Bennett was in for still more hard knocks. In yet another ad an unnamed character blamed the Depression for his inability to land a job: "It never occurs to him that his untidy appearance has cost him one opportunity after another. He's careless about shaving — frequently leaves a repulsive growth of stubble on his face. Can he expect an employer to overlook this fault?"

Unlucky in love, spurned by his family, rejected by business associates, and buffeted by the winds of depression, the poorly shaved man was painted as a social pariah on the same level with those suffering from untreated halitosis. To whatever extent advertising themes find lodgment in the public brain, the message was clear and insistent: keep yourself clean-shaven or risk losing everything worthwhile.

At the same time, the social-consciousness ads studiously avoided making extravagant claims for the quality of Gillette blades. Rather, their aim was merely to sell the nation's men on the idea of frequent shaving, with the hope that they would think of Gillette when buying blades. "Because Gillette had such a large share of the market," said an advertising department memo of the time, "it was felt that if men shaved more frequently, and consumed more blades, that this company would benefit in greater proportion than other manufacturers in the field." It was a reasonable assumption, though Gillette's proportion was shrinking more with each passing day.

In preparation for the Gillette-AutoStrop merger, both sides had sought legal advice on the antitrust implications of a union of their companies. Working independently, two New York law firms had determined that a merged company would do about 55 percent of the nation's safety-razor blade business, a figure which one firm observed pointedly was less than what Gillette alone had sold during several previous years. And as the deepening Depression made penny-pinching a major tenet of the American creed, more and bigger bites were taken from the market share of the relatively high-priced Gillette blade. Retailers' shelves were rife with a bewildering line-up of cheap, competitive blades, some of them selling for as little as a penny apiece. To President Lambert, it seemed as if "every cellar in America was being used to make off-brand, cheap imitations to fit the Gillette razor."

And no matter what brand of blade they bought, tight-fisted consumers were trying to wring as much service out of them as possible. Resharpening devices — the "dinguses" so wistfully prized by George

Babbitt even in the flush of prosperity — were staples of nearly every pharmacy and variety store, and even those who couldn't afford to buy one benefited from the advice dispensed freely in barbershops and at water coolers. One way to get more life out of a blade, men were told, was to (very carefully) stroke the edge back and forth on the palm of the hand. Another method, more appealing to the faint of heart, was to press the dulled blade firmly against the inside curvature of a dampened water glass, and rub it quickly from side to side.

The keener edges produced by such homely stropping were more apparent in the minds of gullible shavers than to the trained eyes of metallurgists. But what men believe to be true can be as important as what actually is true, and the fact was that vast numbers of men were convinced that their bathroom water tumblers could turn out a sharper blade than could all of Gillette's vaunted machinery. And no amount of advertising featuring the tribulations of seedy characters with stubbly cheeks and chins would really convince them otherwise. What was needed, Lambert knew, was a product that was not only new but looked it, and an advertising campaign that transcended bromidic fantasy and became credible. The trail to this double-barreled goal led not only to what even today is probably the most-remembered Gillette product, but also to a series of advertisements that have seldom if ever been matched when it comes to leveling with the American consumer.

"After you have confessed, people are very tolerant"

HERE ARE
THE INSIDE FACTS
— A STATEMENT BY
THE GILLETTE SAFETY RAZOR COMPANY

The Gillette Safety Razor Company in fairness to its millions of customers feels called upon to make a confession and a statement that are undoubtedly unique in the annals of American business. It is with deep regret and no little embarrassment that we do this in order to tell you frankly what actually happened a year ago when we introduced a new Gillette razor and blade.

What had actually happened, the ad went on to say — and it was almost certainly a unique voluntary confession of monumental business bungling — was that Gillette, in its great haste to introduce a new and better blade and razor, had overtaxed its equipment and come out with a disappointing product unworthy of the Gillette name. To make amends, the company had sought for and found a superior manufacturing process which it had purchased at great price. (Under the circumstances, a certain gilding of the true Gillette-AutoStrop situation is surely forgivable.) Now, the Gillette blade was *really* an improvement, "built by an entirely new process, a marvelous blade that gives cleaner, cooler shaves than you ever before have known."

According to Gerard Lambert's much-later recollection, the germ of the so-called confession advertising lay in his belief that "there is no joy so sublime, with the possible exception of the ecstasies of sex, that equals the admission by someone that you are right." Millions of men felt that Gillette had palmed off a bad blade, so Lambert sat down with a pencil and a piece of yellow foolscap and dashed off an ad telling them that they were right and that Gillette had been wrong. Then he hoped for the best.

The ads were given a trial run in the summer of 1931 in two of the "test towns" that Lambert had set up soon after his arrival in South Boston. Tried out with good results during his Listerine days, test towns were paired cities of ten thousand or so population which were used to assess the relative effectiveness of various advertising and promotion approaches. By running a certain campaign in some towns but not in others, and then checking prestocked dealer shelves for comparative sales, it was possible to determine with fair accuracy the drawing power of a given program. Ever since they were introduced, test towns have remained a key element in Gillette's marketing strategy.

Luckily for Lambert — a number of people both within and without the company held that it was suicidal to admit error on so grand a scale — the ads seemed to work, and further test-town operations proved that the first success had been no fluke. Then in January, 1932, the ultimate method to their frequently alleged madness was disclosed when confession ads running in Cleveland appeared with a small, inconspicuous announcement at the bottom. The deluxe Kroman blade — which had at last appeared as a premium-priced article in the new slotted shape — was being withrawn from production, said the simple, boxed announcement. In its place, Gillette was now offering something dubbed the Blue Super-Blade, hailed as "positively the sharpest blade we have ever manufactured." Soon enough, the new bluish blade with matching wrappers would supersede the long-familiar Gillette green and become the company's standard product.

The idea for a colored blade, by Lambert's probably exaggerated account, had come to him as a way to convince shavers that the company's newest blade offering was truly a departure from the old familiar steely model. And when he was convinced that the newly installed strip machinery could indeed produce a superior blade, Lambert said, he took a company engineer to lunch at the nearby railroad-station restaurant and asked if it were possible to color razor blades blue. Told that it was possible to make a blade in nearly any color he wanted — a thin coat of lacquer would do the trick — Lambert asked to see some samples and was so impressed with the results that his production lines were soon switching over to blue blades. Whatever its paternity (and it may well have owed something to the proposed "Blue Blade" of several years before), the Blue Super-Blade was well received in test towns and was eased into national distribution by early 1932, though it continued to be sold side by side with the green-wrapped blade.

As a gauge of the new blade's appeal, and as a measure of the confessional advertising campaign's effectiveness, Lambert often liked to tell the story of six Wall Streeters who had gathered one night for dinner and a discussion of some of the stocks they were following. When talk got around to Gillette, one broker began lambasting Lambert for his arrant foolishness in telling the world of his company's blunder. Everyone at the table, of course, had seen the ad at issue, and most agreed with their fuming companion's assessment of the whole affair — until one of them asked how many of the assembled diners had been moved to buy Blue Super-Blades. They had to a man, and the evening ended with an agreement that there was yet some life to the old Gillette Safety Razor Company. "After you have confessed," Lambert observed later, "people are very tolerant."

While Gillette blades were getting better in the eyes of New York stockbrokers and the rest of the public as well, the same could not be said for the state of the national economy. And if the new blades were marketplace successes, they hardly ran off with the field. Sinking more deeply into the sloughs of the Depression, most men continued — by necessity if not by choice — to favor the plethora of bargain-basement blades whose cheerful cries of "50 for 49¢" were considerably more appealing than Gillette's more somber asking price of a dime per blade. The company's sober campaign to convince consumers that the higher-quality Blue Super-Blade was actually a better per-shave bargain fell on the same deaf ears that usually greet counterappeals to penny-wise reason, and to an extent undreamed of in previous days of plenty, Gillette's cheap-blade subsidiary companies found themselves in growing competition with the parent corporation. On occasion, this intramural rivalry took an almost ludicrous turn. A meticulous consumer test organization, for instance, reported to its subscribers that Tuxedo brand blades were superior to Gillette's Blue Blade, when in fact Tuxedos were Blue Blade seconds deemed unfit to wear the Gillette label.

The name change from the tongue-tripping Blue Super-Blade to the snappier Blue Blade had come shortly after the product went into large-scale distribution. Other blademakers, knowing as always a good thing when they saw it, appropriated the blue color for themselves, blunting Gillette's selling edge with a rash of identically hued blades and wrappers. After a few brief rounds of legal hair-splitting, Gillette managed to establish its rights to the term Blue Blade, limiting competitors to such usages as Blue Zilch Blade — but not Zilch Blue Blade. In a business where brand names can carry much weight, it was no small victory.

Though it ran circles around its unfortunate green-wrapped predecessor — which was, however, kept in the Gillette line-up until the eve of World War II — the Blue Blade was unable to counter the Depression-born frugality that continued to nourish the proliferating penny blades. None of these brands grew large enough individually to challenge Gillette's market leadership, but there were enough of them

— perhaps as many as three thousand were on the market at one point — to clamp an effective lid on the more expensive Blue Blade's volume and cap the company's bid for a return to the hands-down dominance of old.

To lessen this pressure, Gillette trotted out a number of advertising strategies, but only to small avail. The claims of per-shave economy flopped, and so did a later campaign that shunned appeals to reason in favor of blatant scare tactics. "They'll never sell me cheap razor blades again," vowed a resolute, lantern-jawed shaver in a Blue Blade ad that went on to warn: "Look out! Constant irritation from cheap, inferior blades often brings on: rash, boils, eczema, pimples, folliculitis, running sores and even malicious growths!" Another ad of this type quoted an unnamed "eminent dermatologist" who advised that "in effect, shaving is a surgical operation," and went on to caution the reader: "It is clearly established that faulty shaving [that is, shaving with non-Gillette blades] is a serious menace to skin health."

Not all ads in this series — known even within the company as the scare campaign — were quite so clinical, or quite so scary. "May I ask you a frank question, Joe?" said a swell in evening dress to his companion over cigarettes and coffee. "I suppose I shouldn't ask you this, Joe," he went on, "but the question has been on my mind for some time."

"That's all right, Harry. What's the question?"

"Well, Joe, you've developed a peculiar habit in the last few weeks and I'd like to know what it's all about." Joe's peculiar habit turned out to be that he constantly ran his hand across his face, a quirk that Harry found disconcerting when carrying on a conversation. "What's the matter with your face, anyway?" he asked his close friend.

"To tell you the truth, Harry," Joe replied, "I really haven't given it much thought. But as a matter of fact, now that you mention it, I wonder if I may be headed for some really serious trouble. I'm having a little difficulty shaving. I guess that's why you catch me running my hand across my face." Poor Joe — he shaved with such a nondescript razor blade that he couldn't even remember the brand name, and was truly thankful when Harry put him on to Blue Blades.

Called the "Frankie and Johnny" series by Gillette admen, this approach did not last for long. It was scrapped along with the rest of the scare campaign when research showed that consumers weren't believing it, and when word came that the Federal Trade Commission had taken an interest in some of the more extravagant medical claims.

(In a later antitrust suit that was dismissed for lack of evidence of monopoly, former officials of Gillette's cheap-blade Otto Roth subsidiary — which had absorbed the old Rubie sales operation — would testify that the quality of their private-label product was sometimes keyed to these high-pitched campaigns against so-called gyp blades. From time to time, they said, word would come down from Boston to remove the stroppers from the machinery that turned out many of the brands competing with the Blue Blade. Presumably, disgruntled users of these intentionally inferior blades would hearken to Gillette's dire warnings and make the switch to the more expensive and profitable Blue Blades. True or not, it was a tale that was hardly calculated to inspire public confidence in the company.)

Although stumbling in the advertising arena, Gillette engaged the competition on other fronts. In the summer of 1933 the company brought out under its own name the two-for-ten-cents Truflex blade. A short time later, bowing lower to cut-rate competitors, Gillette broke long-standing policy and slashed suggested retail prices fully in half. Shavers could now buy Blue Blades — or Probak or AutoStrop Valet blades, both of which had remained on the market — at five for twenty-five cents or ten for forty-nine cents. A short time later, following again the lead of rivals, Gillette began putting up its standard products in two-blade packages selling for a dime. For the first time in its history, the company had committed itself to competition on the basis of price rather than patent protection, though Gillette attorneys continued to do what they could to maintain the company's patent rights (they eventually lost on appeal a critical case that would have given Gillette exclusive rights to blades with cut-out corners).

At the same time that it was wooing shavers with lower-priced blades, Gillette was also trying to court dealers whose affections were still alienated by the special treatment accorded big-volume buyers, a practice that had continued even after the general housecleaning brought on by the merger with AutoStrop. Full-page ads in the trade press denounced the chaos reigning in the blade business and announced the so-called Gillette Protected Profit Plan to end the disorder. The newly set retail prices, the ads claimed, matched the lowest level at which price cutters had sold Gillette products. Dealer prices had been adjusted accordingly, and set to allow retailers enough return to cover their overhead plus a 5 percent profit. Gillette urged dealers to stick to the suggested retail price, and added, "If chaos returns and again destroys your blade profits — the fault will rest with the non-cooperating dealers of America." Not long afterward, Gillette showed that it meant business by shutting off supplies to fifty-seven New York dealers who refused to go along with the retail price structure.

Even so, it was a poorly kept secret that Gillette's own selling prices to distributors remained highly flexible and that quantity buyers were still offered discounts unavailable to smaller dealers. A standing cynicism in the trade was that the company was far more diligent in maintaining standard retail prices than in assuring that all its dealers were given the same fair and even break. None of these latter-day special arrangements, however, came near the proportions of a Pelham-era contract with United Cigar, which would have obligated Gillette through 1937 to pay United more in display allowances than United was paying for blades. Untenable or not, it was still a legal obligation, and when Gillette was forced to break the agreement it had wound up 1931 by paying United a $1.9 million cash settlement.

Such esoteric goings-on were of small moment to American shavers, whose major concerns did not generally include retail profit margins. And with quality much improved, with Gillette's prices more in line with the competition's — and an even cheaper Probak Junior blade was introduced in 1934 at four for a dime — the company returned to social-consciousness themes for its central advertising thrust for the mainstay Blue Blade. Again, jobs and wifely affection were put at hazard by those who were careless about shaving. "I didn't get the job," a crestfallen man announced to his worried wife in an ad that played the all-too-familiar chords of Depression-era concerns: "He'd counted on landing the job — but he missed out. Again he'll have to 'stall' the landlord, the grocer and all the rest. One thing stood between him and a weekly pay check. His wife is somewhat reluctant to tell him. He doesn't realize that a fresh, close shave is important in getting and holding a job." In another ad in this series, the wife was far from reluctant to tell her slovenly spouse what she thought of his shaving practices. "Once more and I'm through," she announced on their return from a social affair. "You've disgraced me for the last time! I'm sick and tired of going out in the evening with you when you haven't shaved since morning. . . . I'm sure there's a razor blade that will remove your whiskers without hurting your face, and it's up to you to find it."

Even the most effective advertising approaches can grow cloying in time, and by 1936 Gillette had switched to the testimonial technique — with a slightly different twist. Instead of merely plugging Gillette's wares as satisfied users, a number of well-known figures were brought to Boston and shown through the plant, and then wrote of the wonders of what they saw along the production lines. Said Lowell Thomas: "In my wanderings around the world this is just about the most astounding spectacle I have observed in modern industry." Lou Gehrig of the New York Yankees was so impressed that he commented, "I nominate the Gillette Blade for all-time Clean-up King." Melvin Purvis, a former G-man, noted that "familiar as I am with the microscope I was greatly impressed with Gillette's constant use of this scientific instrument to assure perfection in the finished product." Clem McCarthy, Grantland Rice, Robert ("Believe It or Not") Ripley, and George Gershwin were among the other notables who appeared in this series.

The following year, the company was off on still another tack, this time with cartoon ads stressing the importance of shunning "misfit" blades in favor of the genuine Gillette — and sometimes featuring talking razors and blades. "How many times have I told you not to have my eggs well done?" barked a man to his wife. Said his razor, hovering conveniently near the breakfast table: "I feel sorry for his wife. If only she'd slip a Gillette blade into his Gillette razor he'd be lots pleasanter to live with." In 1938, the testimonial was back in favor, with the likes of Paul Whiteman, Blackstone the Magician, and Jack Dempsey (billed as the "wire-haired terror") singing — or snarling — the Blue Blade's praises.

There had been many changes, but through them all, through confessions and colored blades, through folliculitis, stubble-caused job losses and testimonials and talking razors, one thing remained solidly the same: the timeless picture and signature of King C. Gillette still appeared on every blade wrapper. "No package contains genuine Blue Blades unless it carries the portrait of King C. Gillette," some of the company's ads had warned when the first competitors had

The photograph, taken in 1906. Printed on tens of billions of blade wrappers, it would make King C. Gillette the best-known man in the world.

Dissect My Razor

The "GILLETTE"

Observe its convenience—its perfection in every detail.
Figure out how much time and money you can save by adopting the "Gillette" habit.

You will then know why over two million men are proclaiming the superiority of the "Gillette."

BECAUSE it gives you a clean, comfortable, safe shave in three to five minutes—no matter how inexperienced you are.

BECAUSE the harshest beard, though on the tenderest skin, willingly yields to the soft, easy action of the keen "Gillette" blade.

No Stropping, No Honing.

BECAUSE the holder lasts a lifetime.

BECAUSE its blades are so inexpensive that when dull you throw them away as you would an old pen.

King C. Gillette

The Gillette Safety Razor Set consists of a triple silver-plated holder, 12 double-edged flexible blades—24 keen edges, packed in a velvet lined leather case, and the price is $5.00.

Combination Sets from $6.50 to $50.00

Ask your dealer for the "Gillette" to-day. If substitutes are offered, refuse them, and write us at once for our booklet and free trial offer.

GILLETTE SALES COMPANY

206 Times Building   206 Kimball Building   206 Stock Exchange Building
New York   Boston   Chicago

Gillette Safety Razor
NO STROPPING NO HONING

VUE EXTÉRIEURE DE L'USINE

Overseas manufacturing operations began in this modest Paris bicycle-seat factory in 1905.

Though he sometimes ridiculed the whole philosophy of advertising, Gillette was not shy about pushing his razor.

By the eve of World War I, the Gillette razor was a worldwide standard. This German ad appeared before the outbreak of hostilities.

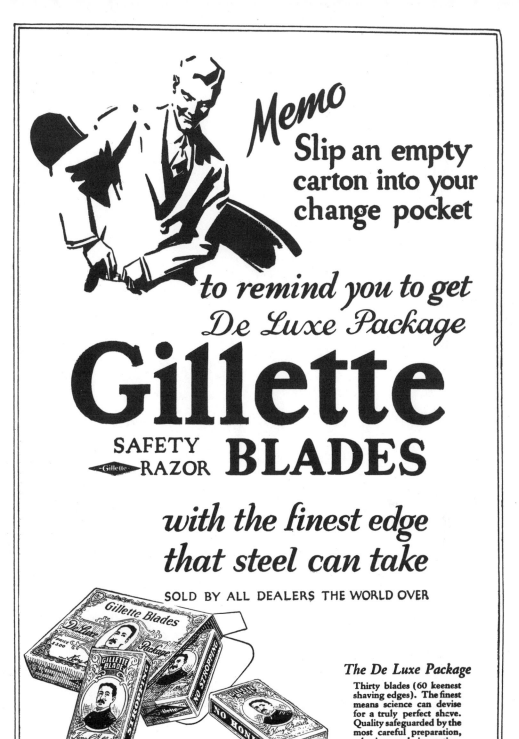

Memo Slip an empty carton into your change pocket

to remind you to get
De Luxe Package

Gillette

SAFETY —Gillette— RAZOR **BLADES**

with the finest edge
that steel can take

SOLD BY ALL DEALERS THE WORLD OVER

The De Luxe Package

Thirty blades (60 keenest shaving edges). The finest means science can devise for a truly perfect shave. Quality safeguarded by the most careful preparation, selection and inspection.

Returning doughboys were convinced Gillette users, and much of the company's advertising in the 1920's simply reminded shavers to keep enough blades on hand.

A generation before this 1923 cartoon, a boy's first shave could be a major bloodletting. The Gillette had done away with much of the danger. *Courtesy of the I.H.T. Corporation*

In the early 1920's, long since retired from active service with the razor company, an aging King Gillette fed pigeons in the Piazza del San Marco in Venice. With him was Alfred A. Gaipa, the company's man in Italy. *Courtesy of Alfred A. Gaipa*

Several years before the Probak debacle of 1930, Gillette's directors were in a relaxed mood. Left to right: Channing M. Wells, Philip Stockton, John Aldred, Frank Fahey, William A. Gaston, Henry Fuller (middle), William Nickerson, Thomas Pelham, Robert C. Morse, Maurice Curran, and Ralph Thompson. *Courtesy of Maurice J. Curran III*

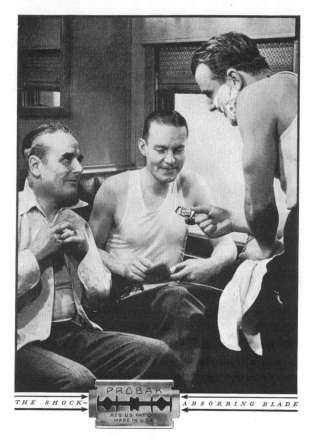

THE SHOCK- ←PROBAK→ ABSORBING BLADE
REG. U.S. PAT. OFF.
MADE IN U.S.A.

MAN after MAN
passed the good news along

FROM the moment of its introduction Probak made friends and held them. Man-talk swept this double-edge blade to spectacular popularity. Shock-absorber construction and automatic machine manufacture set a new standard of shaving comfort. Prove this on our guarantee. If every shave isn't a revelation in comfort return the package to your dealer and get your money—$1 for 10, 50c for 5.

For Gillette and
Probak Razors

PROBAK BLADES

The Probak blade was a strong challenger
to Gillette's decades of dominance.

WE MADE A MISTAKE

—A STATEMENT BY THE GILLETTE SAFETY RAZOR COMPANY

THE Gillette Safety Razor Company feels called upon to make a confession and a statement that are undoubtedly unique in the annals of American business. It is with deep regret and no little embarrassment that we do this in order to tell you frankly what actually happened when we introduced a new Gillette razor and blade.

Soon after this was done, we found that, although the great majority was pleased, some users complained quality was not up to standard.

We learned why. Our equipment had not been equal to the task of producing millions of blades at high speed without a certain variation in quality that affected a small portion of our output. As a result some blades that left the factory were not as good as you had a right to expect. Immediately we directed our principal effort toward the achievement of uniformity. Everything within our power was done to end variation. More than this—impossible as it seemed of accomplishment at the time—we set out to develop or find a better production process, having as a major requirement the elimination of varying quality.

We discovered and purchased for our exclusive use and at the cost of millions of dollars a manufacturing process that was amazingly superior to our own.

By this method, modern and automatic, millions of blades can be made at top speed without variation in quality.

We incorporated refinements of our own invention and installed the new machinery, throwing out all of our old equipment.

Now we announce today's Gillette blades, made by the new management. The usual superlatives have no place in this sincere statement of ours, so we will let the quality of the blades speak for itself. The green Gillette package remains unchanged, but the blades are new in every respect, quality, performance, and method of manufacture.

You can try today's Gillette blades without risking a cent. If you don't agree they are superior, return the package and your dealer will refund your money. **Our reputation depends upon the proof of these claims. Being absolutely certain of the quality of these Gillette blades, we do not hesitate to make this statement over our signature.**

The Gillette Blue Super-Blade

The $2 Kroman De Luxe blade has been withdrawn from production. We offer the Blue Super-Blade as its successor. This sensational blade is far superior to the Kroman and costs considerably less. You pay only a few cents more than for the regular blade and get unmatched shaving comfort. **Its extraordinary shaving performance will convince you that the Blue Blade is the sharpest ever produced.** A blue color has been applied to the blade for easy identification. It is contained in a blue package, Cellophane wrapped.

GILLETTE SAFETY RAZOR CO.
BOSTON, MASSACHUSETTS

In 1932, a repentant Gillette confessed to rushing out with an inferior blade, and announced the Blue Super-Blade's debut.

Baseball Commissioner Kenesaw Mountain Landis (seated, left) and Gillette president Joseph P. Spang, Jr., signed the contract for broadcast rights to the 1939 World Series. It was the start of Gillette's long association with the sports world.

begun coloring *their* blades blue in the summer of 1932. But by then Gillette was dead, spared only by his final illness from the ultimate insult and ignominy of being dragged, a nearly broken man, into a courtroom by the company whose world-renowned trademark was his own face and name.

"*Management looks forward to 1939 with a spirit of confidence*"

Gerard Lambert, to the manner born (as a Princeton undergraduate, he was said to have a $30,000 annual income), was often praised for his foresight in selling off his considerable holdings in the family pharmaceutical company for a reported $25 million just ahead of the stock-market crash. King Gillette, sprung from far humbler surroundings than his successor at the Gillette Safety Razor Company, was neither so prescient nor as lucky. Obituary writers would refer out of habit to his millions, but he was well on the way to losing the fortune he had so confidently anticipated in the first flush of innovation in 1895. The advancing Depression caught him heavily mortgaged in real estate of declining value, his remaining razor-company shares in the icy hands of bankers whose paramount interest was to sell them off in a falling market to cover delinquent loans. Accepting a faulty economic system for what it was, the old socialist was taking a beating in the capitalist game.

Gillette had seen the coming of an end, but it was his own rather than prosperity's — he believed, after all, in Herbert Hoover. Just two weeks before the great Wall Street debacle of 1929, he wrote to Frank Fahey from Nice, confirming that he had indeed instructed his personal attorney, Walter S. Hilborn — son of the old Gillette backer Jacob Heilborn-Hilborn — to sell 15,000 shares of Gillette Company stock. He was, Gillette explained to Fahey, burdened with mortgages and loans amounting to $2 million, on which annual interest alone came to $120,000. Nearing seventy-five and in ill health, Gillette needed no foreknowledge of the Depression to write that "it would be good business to realize sufficient to clean up all this borrowed money and owe no one a dollar in the world." By his own reckoning, this would leave him with $6 million worth of prime California real estate, free and clear, plus his remaining 35,000 shares of Gillette stock. It was surely the sort of thing that Gillette had had in mind so long ago when he had written to his wife: "I have got it; our fortune is made."

But some fortunes seem made to be lost. Fahey and John Aldred, mindful of what the investment community — not to mention other stockholders — would think if the founder-president dumped 15,000 of his company's shares, managed to dissuade Gillette and Hilborn from the proposed sale. And soon enough, the bottom fell out of the national economy and the razor company alike, and not even the pool-inflated proceeds of Gillette's 20,000-share sale to the company could brace his sagging finances. The permanent prosperity that Gillette had so recently envisioned was turning instead to personal disaster, and by the spring of 1932, seeking a human agency to blame for conditions almost beyond the control of mortal power, Gillette went to court and charged that Hilborn had mismanaged the Gillette fortune to the tune of a million-dollar loss. In ironic symmetry, the son of the man who had helped make Gillette's dream of fortune possible was now blamed for the nightmare that it had become.

Meanwhile, back in South Boston, plans were being made for yet another court case, one that could bear the unlikely citation of *Gillette Safety Razor Company* v. *King C. Gillette*. The directors, sensing correctly that the minority stockholders would soon be victorious in their prolonged suit for recovery of financial damages rung up during preparation for the AutoStrop merger, determined to sue Gillette for whatever his proportional share of the cost might be. Only in late June did the board decide against such action, reasoning that it might make the company look bad in the eyes of faithful customers who strongly associated Gillette the man with Gillette the razor blade.

There were to be few more such reprieves for King Gillette or for his heirs, and within five years the wealth that the inventor had gained from his razor would be largely gone, disposed of by banks or foreclosed by mortgage holders. The Pershing Square parcel, bought for nearly $1.5 million in 1924 as a show of faith in Los Angeles's boundless future, was liquidated to cover taxes and interest, leaving only $17,500, which went to settle other debts. The other downtown property shared a similar fate, but with even less return. Piece by piece, it was sold off in a steadily drooping market to cover what seemed to be ever mounting obligations. Little if anything was saved, even to the furnishings and artworks that the Gillettes had collected with such care during decades of world travel. The desert place at Calabasas went, too. Built at a cost of some $500,000, it was ordered sold by creditors and brought less than $150,000.

It had been there, in that neo-Spanish southern California rancho home, that King Camp Gillette had died quietly in his sleep at three o'clock on the morning of July 9, 1932, his wife and son at his side. Known by sight and name to most of the world's population, the inventor of the disposable safety-razor blade had achieved a kind of immortality granted to few men, but only at the Boston *Evening Transcript,* where obituaries were works of consummate art, did anyone have the wit to observe that the inventor of the system of world corporation had died with his greatest ambition unfulfilled.

If the advancing Depression had been cruel to the Gillette fortune, it had hardly been kind to the razor company. Gerard Lambert's long-shot bet that he could pump earnings up to five dollars a share never did pay off, and when the restless yachtsman moved on to other things in 1934 — the divorce that had figured in his decision to come to Boston was at last final — he left without having taken a cent of Gillette money. Twice offered a salary when fellow directors saw that his gamble was hopeless, Lambert twice refused, and also declined compensation for his briefly continued service as chairman of the executive committee. Even when given the chance, a gentleman gamester does not withdraw his wagers, especially when he doesn't need the money. Later, Lambert took a dollar-a-year job with the Federal Housing Administration, where he displayed a striking affinity to the utopian King Gillette by building at his own expense a pilot public-housing project to prove the feasibility of profitless dwelling units that could be rented for as little as five dollars a room.

Lambert was succeeded in the Gillette presidency by the conventionally salaried Samuel C. Stampleman, a former AutoStrop executive whose luck was no better than Lambert's. Gillette and the national economy had both slipped too far for rapid comebacks, and Gillette's progress was in any case slowed considerably by the packs of penny-a-blade competitors nipping at its heels. With its sprawling factories and the necessity for maintaining a national advertising program, the cost to Gillette of doing business was considerably higher than it was to the horde of small, low-overhead operators with no really long-term commitment as blade marketers, and the Boston company's financial performance fell painfully short of the standards set in the prosperous past. Profits crept up at a sluggish pace from a dolorous $3.6 million in 1933 to nearly $5 million in 1936, and then slid back to $4.5 million the following year. In 1938, a bad time for the whole country, they plunged down to $2.9 million, less than Gillette had paid out in cash dividends in 1921. With deadpan understatement, Stampleman informed stockholders in his annual report, "Results as reported for 1938 were disappointing."

Still, Gillette was doing more than merely treading water, and even during the dismal days of the Depression the company had been making moves that would provide additional strength in the better times that only the most dedicated pessimist could doubt were sure to come. Overseas, especially, Gillette hardly conducted itself after the fashion of a company without hope for a brighter future. The company's foreign position had been bolstered considerably by the AutoStrop union; in Brazil, Gillette took over the AutoStrop plant in Rio de Janeiro and began spinning out ribbons of blades for the promising South American market. In England, the old Gillette Company's first foreign outpost, Gillette Safety Razor, Limited, and the Auto-Strop Safety Razor Company were combined to form Gillette Industries, Limited, under the able chairmanship of AutoStrop's Canadian-born Ernest (later Sir Ernest) H. Cooper. As in Boston, the strip method replaced the old single-blade means of manufacture, and as in Boston, too, much of the outmoded machinery was barged out to sea and heaved overboard. A new plant was opened in Paris in 1934; two years later an expanding Gillette Industries completed a factory building whose green-topped 150-foot tower is still a landmark in West London. The Berlin subsidiary, still doing business as Roth-Büchner, moved into new quarters in 1938.

It was more than mere window dressing, this flurry of worldwide activity. Domestic difficulties aside, Gillette was still something of an international standard, and its products were sold openly in every country in the world except Soviet Russia — and even there, a certain amount of under-the-table trade was carried on for the benefit of high officials whose beards were more comfortably removed with capitalist tools. Even more critically, the profits gleaned by its international arms kept the company afloat at a time when cutthroat competition at home might otherwise have proved fatal. Over half of the earnings in 1935 came from overseas, where production and advertising costs were generally lower than at home, and by 1937 the foreign contribution reached two-thirds. In rock-bottom 1938, nearly all of the company's profits were provided by foreign operations, stark testimony to the long-ago wisdom and vision of King Gillette, without whose hurried intervention the directors would have given up all foreign rights to the razor and blade in exchange for a mess of paltry royalties that would have helped little in these parlous times.

The times may have been hard and uncertain, but Gillette continued to move ahead with product innovation, too, though not always with happy results. Among the winners was the one-piece Aristocrat razor, its open-and-shut top resembling tandem trap doors. It remains the standard design for double-edge razors. First introduced widely in 1935 — and based in very small part on two patents taken out by the multitalented Gerard Lambert — the razor sold for four dollars, but by 1937 another version of the same principle was offered for just ninety-eight cents. In 1936, Gillette made the first of what would prove to be many moves out of the hardware line when it launched the straightforwardly named Gillette Brushless Shaving Cream, whose main selling point was that it was "made with costly peanut oil." The next new product, the so-called Thin Gillette blade introduced in 1938, was more in keeping with the company's traditional goods, and at a price of four for a dime was meant to strengthen Gillette's position in the cheap-blade field.

Competition was also behind a short-lived line of electric shavers that went on sale in time for the 1938 Christmas season. Fearing that the growing popularity of this relatively new appliance might make serious inroads in the blade market, Gillette had determined to fight fire with fire, even though it would, in effect, be undercutting its own main-line business. A year later, the company ventured even further into electric territory with Kumpakt, a lower-priced shaver whose name had been appropriated from an old AutoStrop dollar razor set. It proved to be barren ground, and with electric-shaver

sales falling nationwide, Gillette withdrew from the arena in 1940 —
the same year in which it augmented its more fertile shaving-soap
line with a lather cream — to concentrate on razors and blades.

But even here, in the field that it had created and knew best, Gillette
continued to slip, until its once-lavish share of the domestic market
had been shorn to 20 percent and less. Small wonder, with earnings
for 1938 at the lowest level since the pre–World War I year (for the
United States, at least) of 1915, that Samuel Stampleman had conceded disappointment over the company's performance. What is
really to be wondered at is that Stampleman, who had recently moved
up to the chairmanship, could then go on to say that "management
looks forward to 1939 with a spirit of confidence."

He could not know it, of course, but 1938 was also a prewar year.
And Gillette's seemingly beleaguered managers were not the only
ones who were sanguine about the future. Adolf Hitler — whose half-
brother Alois, we are told by the biographer John Toland, once sold
razor blades (though not, apparently, for Gillette) — was also supremely confident as he looked forward to 1939, and in the fall of that
landmark year his Panzer armies plunged across Poland. Warsaw fell
by late September, and early in the next month Hitler was switching
his gaze from the east to the west, and plotting epochal conquests
that would in time make all of Europe a battlefield.

In the still-neutral United States, however, life and commerce went
on almost as usual, protected by widespread indifference and a broad
ocean from the building Continental conflict. And for Gillette, fortune was about to take a new turn on a field far different from
Europe's bloodied ground.

Look Sharp, Feel Sharp, Be Sharp

*"Joe DiMaggio just hit a home run four hundred feet
over the center-field fence"*

FROM THE START, it was a classic pitchers' duel, the two squads stalemated much as the French and German divisions that faced each other in grim irresolution across the Maginot Line. The Reds took a one-run lead in the fourth, when Ival Goodman drew Charley Ruffing's only walk of the day, stole second, and then scampered home on Frank McCormick's left-field single. The Cincinnati advantage was short-lived, however, and the Yankees tied things up in the fifth on a Wally Berger throwing blunder that let Joe "Flash" Gordon hurtle across the plate untouched by catcher Ernie Lombardi's frantic tag. It was spellbinding baseball from then on — no hits, no runs, no errors for either side — until the last of the ninth, when New York rookie Charlie "King Kong" Keller smashed a one-out triple to deep center, with Joe DiMaggio limbering up in the on-deck circle. Many of the fans who had gathered in Yankee Stadium on that early October afternoon booed when the Reds pitcher, Paul Derringer, gave DiMaggio a strategic base on balls, but they needn't have bothered; the next man up, catcher Bill Dickey, came through with a game-winning tap to center field. The opening round of the 1939 World Series was over, played out before a cheering crowd that didn't much care that banners were flying and church bells were pealing in Germany that day to hail the stunning victory over Polish arms, and that Adolf Hitler was preparing to enter a prostrate Warsaw at the head of his conquering Wehrmacht.

In New York, the day was perfect for baseball. Leaden clouds that had threatened the Bronx through the night and early morning had largely burned off by the 1:30 P.M. game time, and the temperature moved up to a comfortable enough sixty-two degrees. Dorothy Arnold, Joe DiMaggio's fiancée, arrived early, so as not to miss any of the preliminary activities that included the usual antics of baseball comic Al Schacht. Other notables, among them Governor Herbert Lehman of New York, Mayor Fiorello H. La Guardia, and Postmaster General James A. Farley, made it to their seats just in time to see the baseball commissioner, Kenesaw Mountain Landis, consecrate the proceedings with a toss of the first ball. All told, 58,541 men, women, and children were gathered together in the waning autumnal sunlight to observe the defending champion New York Yankees and the Cincinnati Reds begin the seasonal conclusion of a game that President Herbert Hoover once said has had "a greater impact on American life than any other institution" except religion.

Thanks to the Gillette Safety Razor Company, tens of millions of other devotees were there, too, plugged in to the airwaves and listening to the veteran sports announcers Red Barber and Bob Elson bark out the play-by-play descriptions, relieved at the microphones by commentaries from the likes of Grantland Rice, Lowell Thomas, and Gabriel Heatter. Across the nation, 179 radio stations carried the broadcast, as did two stations in the Territory of Hawaii. Canadians who cared about their southern neighbor's national pastime had a line-up of thirty-four stations carrying the game, and the French and German soldiers on the solidifying Western Front in Europe must have been somewhat mystified when they tuned in on the shortwave broadcast by General Electric station WGY. It was all with the compliments of Gillette, Red Barber told the international radio audience, and added: "They're bringing you a swell ball game, and if you pick up that Tech razor tonight with a Gillette Blue Blade, it will bring you a swell shave tomorrow morning and every morning."

Gillette was no stranger to the sports world, or to radio, either. Baseball players had done testimonials for the razor as long ago as 1910, when the immortal Honus Wagner was credited with (or blamed for) saying: "I shave with a Gillette. I know of nothing that could induce me to change the system." The company had gone to a national radio hookup in 1929, with a weekly musical-variety show "planned to satisfy the tastes of practically every group of radio listeners" and featuring an instrumental group dubbed the Ten Gallant Blades and vocal harmony by the Five Young Gay Blades, all backed up by Director Sam Lanin and the Gillette Blades Ensemble. For those whose tastes ran to piano duets, the Original Double Edges sat by at their keyboards, and the National Broadcasting Company announcer Graham McNamee fleshed out the half-hour presentation with a five-minute sports review.

Even in those relatively pioneering days on the airwaves, Gillette had a firm understanding of radio's uses as a commercial vehicle, and plotted its own involvement accordingly. "Because the value of radio as an advertising medium is in direct proportion to its entertainment value," a company advertising staffer explained to employees in the house organ, "you will notice that we are careful not to burden our listeners with too much commercialism." He added that in a day when stations could be changed or radios turned off with the merest flick of a finger, wise advertisers were well advised not to be heavy-handed, and Gillette relied primarily on short, pointed messages and a catchy theme song, "We Are the Blades," to get its message across.

The Depression and the abortive new 1930-model razor blade tuned Gillette out of big-time radio, but the company took another stab at it in 1935, lacing its hopes this time to the world heavyweight boxing champion Max Baer. A hands-down favorite to whip challenger James Braddock in the June title bout, Baer seemed ready-made as a way to reach the male shaving public, and Gillette sponsored not only the match itself, but also a weekly detective drama starring the fighter as one Lucky Smith. Numerous prizes — including free ringside seats and railroad fare to New York — were offered in connection with the promotion, and to extract top mileage from the whole affair,

Gillette carefully scheduled the thirteen-week Lucky Smith series to straddle the main event in Madison Square Garden. Unfortunately for both Baer and Gillette, the champion's luck ran out when he stepped on the canvas, and Braddock's surprise victory left Gillette with six more weeks to sponsor a radio show starring a defeated world champion. Making the best of a bad situation, Gillette whipped up a nationwide contest to name Baer's dog. No matter that Baer didn't really own a dog; he wasn't Jewish, either, yet he hyped the box-office take when fighting in New York City by pinning a Star of David on his trunks.

For the record, the winning name was Livermore Gay Blade, in honor of Baer's California hometown, his propensity for nightclubbing ("gay" in those more innocent times did not signify sexual preference), and, of course, the razor-blade manufacturer that sponsored the competition. But it wasn't the quality of the entries that impressed Gillette — it was the quantity. Over 250,000 of them, each accompanied by a Blue Blade wrapper, poured into the mailroom in South Boston, evidence enough that sports events and related promotions had the kind of pulling power needed by a company whose product was used mainly by men.

Still, athletics hardly keynoted Gillette's next sally into network radio — it was a variety show called "Community Sing," whose most durable legacy was the introduction of its host, Milton Berle, as a broadcast personality. In time, the irrepressible Berle would go on to be known as Mr. Television, and he was not the only one to use "Community Sing" as a springboard to bigger things. Gillette, too, would graduate from sponsorship of the pedestrian variety show and launch a string of successes far more memorable than Uncle Miltie. Known as the "Gillette Cavalcade of Sports," the program would become possibly the best-known continuing feature on radio and television, forging an unbreakable link between Gillette, the sports world, and the American public. And it all began with that long-ago 1939 World Series, still redolent of the American Dream and the heroes who had helped sustain it in years past.

Crosley Field in Cincinnati was jammed to the rafters for the third game of the series, and in the third inning the whole nation and then some could hear the authoritative cadences of Bob Elson:

Here's Joe DiMaggio up. First pitch to Joe is a curve ball. Missed the outside corner knee-high for a ball, ball one. Left fielder Berger playing very deep for Joe. . . . Joe DiMaggio batting with the tying run on first base for the Yankees. The next pitch [*Crack!*] — he hits a long fly ball, way back into center field, way back, back, back — it's a home run, over the center-field fence! Joe DiMaggio just hit a home run four hundred feet over the center-field fence, out over the car tracks, and the Yankees lead in this ball game now by a score of four to three."

Gillette did not, of course, underwrite such excitement as a mere public service, and it wasn't long before Red Barber chimed in. "Fans," he said, "the improved Gillette Blue Blade in the revolutionary new Gillette Tech razor is an unbeatable shaving combination. Prepare your face with Gillette Brushless Cream, and you get absolute tops in shaving speed and comfort."

For the record, the Yankees were an unbeatable combination, too. Bill Dickey followed DiMaggio to the plate and was thrown out on an easy infield grounder, but New York went on to win the game by a score of 7 to 3. As Red Barber once said when describing the progress of a masterfully pitched slowball, it was "almost as easy as that Gillette Tech going to work."

"From shaving pigs to shaving people"

Still hailed as a stroke of almost unparalleled advertising genius, Gillette's long-lived "Cavalcade of Sports" was conceived in New York during a lunch-table conversation between the Gillette advertising manager, A. Craig Smith, and the head of the Mutual Broadcasting System. Smith, a somewhat eccentric advertising wizard who had jumped to the company from its ad agency several years before, would guide Gillette's extensive advertising programs for nearly three decades. Now, almost casually, he was about to have the idea that would be the keystone of the company's growth for a full generation.

It was the spring of 1939, and the sixteen major-league baseball teams had come up from their training camps to begin the long season of campaigning. The New York Yankees had mowed down the Chicago Cubs for a four-game World Series sweep in 1938, and were heavily favored to score a repeat performance over the next National League challenger. In a Depression-plagued decade, the easy rhythms of baseball had captured the national imagination as never before, and it was only natural that talk among friends and business associates should turn to a game that had been transfixing crowds from Yankee Stadium in New York to Wrigley Field in Chicago.

It was only natural, too, that the subject of radio advertising should arise and that the Mutual man should mention the possibility of Gillette's sponsoring World Series coverage over his network. World Series broadcasts were nothing new. Starting in 1934, the Ford Motor Company had sponsored them for three years running, paying the big leagues $100,000 a season for the exclusive privilege. Ford dropped out in 1937 — forfeiting its $100,000 option in the process — because national interest seemed scant for another parochial New York Yankees–New York Giants contest, and no other advertiser had felt big enough or bold enough to rush in where Ford had balked. But there was something about a Gillette–World Series combination that seemed to fit as snugly as a Bob Feller fastball in a well-oiled catcher's mitt. Nearly all men shaved, after all, and nearly all men were baseball fans, at least when things got down to the World Series wire and it became almost obligatory to glue one's ear to a radio for the duration.

The prospect of untold millions of potential customers enthralled by a play-by-play description interspersed with pitches for razors and blades was an inviting one to Smith, though he knew it would be a costly enterprise. Just how costly, he learned some weeks later. Told that the asking price for exclusive sponsorship of the series was still $100,000, he figured that announcers' fees, broadcasting expenses, and other incidental costs would bring the tab to more than $200,000, or about 13 percent of the whole year's advertising budget. Put another way, if the Yankees played true to form and took the series in four games, Gillette stood to spend about one-eighth of a 365-day advertising allotment in eight or so hours of afternoon broadcasting time. Confronted with such odds, even the savants at Gillette's own ad agency counseled against the move.

A year before, with advertising funds pared to the bone in response to financial emaciation, such seeming prodigality would have been beyond all rational consideration. But since then Gillette had got a new president who had fleshed out the ad budget and put a World Series connection within at least the realm of daring possibility.

Boston-born and Harvard-educated — though he failed to graduate with his class of 1915 — Joseph Peter Spang, Jr., once summed up his life by quipping that he had progressed "from shaving pigs to shaving people." Indeed, his first job at Swift & Company had been to slice the bristles from freshly slaughtered hogs, though his college background and incisive mind quickly earned him a series of more elevated positions. During World War I, he served as a flight instructor in the Army Signal Corps Balloon Service, stationed at Fort Omaha, Nebraska; in later years, he was proud to recall that he had also been editor of the post's weekly newspaper, the *Omaha Gas Bag*. After being mustered out of the military, Spang returned to Swift, where he made a name for himself as a tough marketing official and an able assistant to the company's top executives; by 1930, he was rewarded with the vice-presidency in charge of sales. Like many displaced Bostonians, however, Spang longed to return to his native city, and in 1938 he was more than willing to listen to the proposition laid out for him by Gillette directors Philip Stockton and William A. Barron, Jr. Stockton, who was chairman of the executive committee of the powerful First National Bank of Boston, had served on the Gillette board since the Aldred & Company takeover in 1917, and had emerged more or less unscathed from the scandal involving the company's financial affairs. Barron, a wealthy friend of Spang's from Harvard days, shared Spang's interest in football and track, and in 1914 had set a world indoor record for the 440-yard dash. He had been elected to the board only in 1936, and was a partner in the highly respected investment firm of White, Weld & Company. Together, the two men represented what may be called the Boston wing of the directorate, as opposed to the New York faction, consisting of the old AutoStrop group. Their proposal to Spang was simple enough: the president of Gillette, Samuel C. Stampleman, was growing tired of seemingly hopeless battles, and yearned for peaceful superannuation in the Florida sun. If Spang would sign on as executive vice-president, he would be moved up to the presidency as soon as he learned his way around the blade business, and would then be given a free hand in a field far more challenging than selling pork bellies and sides of beef.

It is said that Spang took six months to make up his mind, carefully testing Gillette's products against those of the competition. If so, he must have found Blue Blades to his liking, for he moved to Gillette as arranged in the fall of 1938. A swift learner, Spang was named president by December, and for nearly two decades he would introduce himself to strangers with a crisp "I'm Joe Spang of Gillette." Former President Stampleman moved up to the chairmanship vacated by the retiring Henry Gaisman, and at the same time John Aldred, who had first heard of the Gillette Safety Razor Company from John Joyce not long after the turn of the century, retired too. With the two prime antagonists of the old Gillette-versus-AutoStrop days departed from the scene, the company seemed truly ready, if only in the symbolic sense, to begin a new ball game.

Spang not only learned quickly, he could also act at a rapid clip, once he had determined what needed to be done. And from his first few weeks in South Boston, he had noted several areas where Gillette was in sore need of improvement. For one thing, the vaunted "Protected Profit Plan," launched with such fanfare in 1933 and proclaimed as a spearhead in the wave of fair-trade laws that were passed throughout the nation during the 1930's, was still regarded as a gloomy joke by much of the trade. Big-volume buyers continued to enjoy special discounts, meaning that selected dealers were getting considerably more profit protection than their smaller competitors. Within months after settling into the president's chair, Spang decreed that from then on all customers would be charged the same price, with absolutely no exceptions allowed.

Blade quality also, though much improved over the past few years, did not yet measure up to Spang's exacting standards, so he ordered a speedup in the installation of a new grinding, honing, and stropping method that allowed for close inspection at each step. Developed largely in the British plant, the process made for a markedly keener blade, and would lead eventually to the adoption of one of Gillette's most famous commercial taglines: "The sharpest edges ever honed." Assured of a virtually unequaled product, Gillette salesmen could now talk quality with little fear of contradiction, and leave prices to take care of themselves.

Spang also took steps to assure that top-management men in Boston could talk more freely among themselves, and with the company president. He did this by instituting a so-called open-door policy, which became so pervasive that, according to Gillette folklore, Spang ordered the removal of all executive-office doors. In fact, most doors stayed on their hinges, though all of them — including Spang's — remained open most of the time. Encouraged to forgo formality, staffers could nip problems before they got out of hand, and also had ready access to the chief executive. Some of them, though, the ones who were called on Spang's carpet for a vociferous dressing-down over poor performance, must have longed for a closed door and walls more substantial than the glass that lined Gillette's unpretentious executive row.

With management taking a new turn, with price and quality straightened out, Spang could turn to the problem of getting his message to the all-important consumer, and the World Series seemed ideally suited to his purpose. Sports-minded as he was, Spang knew that every male baseball fan — or follower of nearly any sport, for that matter — was a potential Gillette customer, and he liked the idea of sponsoring the World Series even if Maxon did argue against it (Maxon was plumping instead for a reprise of a 1937 football score-prediction contest that had tallied only minor results on its first go-round). The problem was that Spang was still a relative tyro in the razor and blade business, and had little inkling of what kind of sales results to expect from such an undertaking. If the company went with the World Series, the touted item would be a special set, consisting of the Tech model razor — a three-piecer and the first Gillette razor without a comb-tooth guard — and five Blue Blades, all for just forty-nine cents. Spang's main question was straightforward: how many such sets, hurriedly done up in World Series wrappers, could the company sell if it took the big plunge?

Asked for an answer at a special meeting, Sales Manager G. Herbert Marcy whipped out a pencil and went to work on a scratch pad. After a few minutes of diligent scribbling, he looked up and announced, "We'll sell a million." Told that this was more than enough to turn a profit, Spang gave the go-ahead signal, and on August 1 he sat down with Commissioner of Baseball Landis and signed a contract for exclusive World Series broadcasting rights. Baseball made an effortless $100,000 on the deal, and professional sports would never be the same again. Neither would Gillette: when the cheering was over — and the Yankees, as their fans had hoped and Gillette had feared, took the series in four quick games — the company had sold not one million, but two and a half million razor sets.

Only later did Spang guess that the optimistic Marcy, having no solid bench marks of his own by which to measure possible sales, had merely doodled on his pad and all but pulled the one-million-razors figure out of the air.

It took no fancy computation, either, to conclude that broadcast sports could be a bonanza for Gillette, and the company quickly rounded up other major events to follow the World Series lead. The Orange Bowl and the Sugar Bowl fell into line for New Year's Day of 1940, and in May the nation's horse-race fans tuned in to the Kentucky Derby and heard Ted Husing shout out Gallahadion's upset victory over the runaway favorite, Bimelech, along with more reserved pronouncements on the superiority of Gillette razors and blades. Another Gillette-sponsored World Series went out over the airwaves in the fall, and this time the pin-striped Yankees got their comeuppance, Cincinnati had its day, and Gillette got its full money's worth. Edged out of the American League pennant race by Detroit, Yankee players who did not make it to the ball parks sat back and listened to the radio like everyone else, as the Reds topped the Tigers in a 2-to-1, seventh-game squeaker. Next came the professional-football championship game in December (Bears 73, Redskins 0), and then the East-West All-Star football contest to kick off the first day of 1941. For Gillette, a whole new future was unfolding.

At about the same time that Gillette's advertising team was first batting around the possibility of World Series sponsorship, a company attorney was drafting a careful letter to James E. Kelby of Los Angeles. Kelby, an aged lawyer who was minding the residue of Mrs. King C. Gillette's assets, had written to the company some months before to advise that the founder's widow was rapidly sinking below the borderline of genteel poverty, living mainly on the kindness of family and friends, and an income of one hundred dollars a month from a trust established by her brother's will. Nor could she turn for help to her son. King Gaines Gillette, wrote Kelby, was "without income from any source whatever, and may be said to be floating with •

the tide." So much for what dynastic dreams King Camp Gillette may have harbored; his whole estate was "a colossal wreck . . . gone with the wind."

Without Atlanta Gillette's knowledge, Kelby had subtly suggested that the company, though under no legal obligation to do so, might come to her aid with some sort of pension. A lawyer of the flowery old school, he conjured up King Gillette's inventive genius: "Still do not the mystic chords of memory stretch back to the creation of Gillette Safety Razor Company?" he asked. "Rob not life of its sentimentality; for without it it is death." Now it had fallen to a Boston attorney to prepare a possible response to Kelby's plea on Atlanta Gillette's behalf. He wrote:

> Our management has considered at length your suggestion that it make some cash payments to her, possibly in the nature of pension payments.
>
> The management deeply regrets Mrs. Gillette's situation as indicated in your letter. While it would like to make some provision for affording her some relief, it feels, under all the conditions and after discussing the matter with counsel, that it should not authorize the use of funds of the Company for this purpose.

And there the matter might have ended, except that the letter was never mailed. Advised that the company had the legal authority to pension its founder's widow, and certainly mindful of the public embarrassment that might follow if word got out that Mrs. King C. Gillette's impoverishment was known but ignored by the company established and personified by her late husband, management had a quick change of heart. On April 18, 1939, the executive committee voted to pay Atlanta Gillette two hundred dollars a month "for her comfort, maintenance, and support."

Informed of the action, Kelby responded in his florid style: "May the Divine Law of Compensation, frequently referred to by Emerson, not only overtake, but abide with, your corporation and its chivalrous Executive Committee." For her part, Mrs. Gillette was more restrained, though hardly less grateful. She thanked the company from the bottom of her heart, she wrote, and as a token of her appreciation she sent a rug, custom-made for her husband in Spain during the couple's last European trip. Woven into the design were a large Gillette razor and blade. It was, she said, one of the few remnants of the once-vast King Gillette estate, and she believed that "the most fitting place it could be used is in an office of the company he founded."

The company founded by King C. Gillette continued to comfort his widow until she died in 1951 — which happened to coincide with the fiftieth anniversary of Gillette's first incorporation. It was a notable year in other ways, too. Surely lofted more by managerial and marketing skill than by any divine law of compensation, the company's annual sales were soaring past the $100 million mark, and Gillette had made a name for itself as one of the fastest-growing and most profitable enterprises in the world. The once-anemic blademaker had risen far from the down-and-out days of the late 1930's, with sports and Joe Spang still leading the way.

"Look sharp, feel sharp, be sharp"

Until it became show business in the late 1960's, boxing was a sport as captivating and legitimate in its own brutal way as football or baseball. And few bouts fired the public imagination as much as the one in which Billy Conn first came up from Pittsburgh to challenge the heavyweight champion, Joe Louis. On June 18, 1941, at the Polo Grounds in New York, the two met in combat, and even though Louis outweighed his opponent by twenty-five pounds and was heavily favored to win, Conn was given a good fighting chance against the champion whose race and relentless punches had earned him such nicknames as Brown Bomber and Dark Destroyer.

By the twelfth round, Conn was clearly leading in points and seemed well on the way to seizing the title from the man who had held the highest crown in boxing since whipping Jim Braddock four years and eighteen battles before. Closing in for the kill, Conn rocked Louis back on his heels with a full-arm left hook to the jaw; only a clinch kept Louis from falling and Conn from delivering his coup de grâce.

Conn smelled victory when the bell rang to start the next round. Moving quickly to the attack, throwing rapid-fire lefts and rights to Louis's jaw, the challenger brought the roaring crowd to its feet as he galvanized Louis into desperate retaliation. Almost from nowhere, the champion's punishing right hand shot through Conn's defenses and caught him squarely on the jaw, buckling his knees and sending him into a backward sway. Gloves cupped to his face, Conn warded off as best he could a rain of blows that shifted savagely to the body; then came the almost unopposed right-hand smash to the jaw that crumpled Conn to the canvas and broke his championship dream with just two seconds left in his unlucky thirteenth round. Back home in Pittsburgh, Mary Jane Conn collapsed beside her radio as Referee Eddie Joseph stood over her fallen brother and counted him out.

Across America, the millions of other fight fans who had tuned in to the epic match were not quite so stricken by the outcome, and were able to hear the closing commercial for Gillette's new Tech razor, a one-piece version that sold with five Blue Blades for just ninety-eight cents. And if his victory was a major milestone in Joe Louis's long career in the ring, its radio sponsorship marked a critical turn in Gillette's fortunes, too. After the Baer-Braddock debacle of six years before, after turning to the World Series, the Kentucky Derby, and football bowl games to beam its messages to America's sports fans, the company had come back to ringside. For nearly a generation to come, on radio and later on television, Gillette and boxing would become almost synonymous, and tuning in to Friday night fights would become part of the weekly ritual of tens of millions of men.

In the beginning, Gillette's wide-ranging sports broadcasts were not tied together by any common name, but by the summer of 1941 the programs had been dubbed the "Sports Cavalcade." By the end of the year, this name had been refined to "Gillette Cavalcade of Sports," a title that is written indelibly in the mind of nearly every American born before the early 1950's.

The close of 1941 was hardly a propitious time to be launching long-range commercial plans and projects, however, particularly when they involved large-volume precision products made of high-grade steel. Even before the Japanese attack on Pearl Harbor and Adolf Hitler's declaration of war, the United States had instituted military conscription, and observers at the Joe Louis–Billy Conn battle at the Polo Grounds had noted that the audience was liberally peppered with young men in navy blue and olive drab. Soon enough, these same young men would be joined in uniform by millions more, their whole generation committed to a global conflict with stakes far different from mere sports championships.

American industry was likewise pressed into war service, both voluntarily and by government direction. Already Gillette had gotten into vital ordnance work in a small way; then in 1942 the War Production Board ordered that razors could be made only for military use and limited export sales, and blade production was pegged at just four-fifths of the 1941 total, with most of the output bound for service in the armed forces. The company got into warwork in a more direct way, too, becoming a subcontractor for the Bendix Aviation Corporation and producing fuel control units for aircraft carburetors. By the end of the war, the Gillette-made product had been built into more than a third of the thousands of aircraft engines thrown by the United States into the struggle against the Axis powers — to the growing wonder of Adolf Hitler, who had been assured by Air Marshal Hermann Göring that "the Americans cannot build airplanes. They are very good at refrigerators and razor blades."

Gillette had been in conflict with Hitler even before the United States entered the war. In 1940 the treasurer, Stafford Johnson, returned from a visit to Berlin with word that the Nazi government wanted Gillette to oust Chairman Stampleman, or at least reduce the number of Jews on its board. Otherwise, Gillette would face expropriation of its German razor and blade factory. Among the directors, William Barron was the most outspoken. The company, he insisted, should not allow Hitler to handpick its board members. Even so, two of the four Jewish directors decided not to stand for reelection at the next meeting of the shareholders. But Stampleman, who stayed at his post, was as impressed by Barron's show of support and determination as Göring was with the quality of Gillette blades, which the company continued to produce throughout the war.

Indeed, though more than 70 percent of its man-hours went into war production, Gillette's main business was still shaving, and before the final instruments of surrender were signed, the company had turned out a whopping 20 million razors and 1.5 billion blades for use by soldiers, sailors, airmen, and marines. On a far grander scale than had been dreamed of during World War I, Gillette had been given an opportunity to introduce men to its product and to daily shaving.

With blades stacked high in quartermaster depots from North Africa and England to Australia and the Pacific islands, supplies on the home front were of course limited, and Gillette tailored much of its advertising accordingly. Starting in the fall of 1942, radio commercials, window displays, and ads in newspapers and magazines frequently included tips on how to get the most out of what few blades were available. Among them: wash the face well with soap, lather thoroughly, and shake the blade dry rather than wipe it on a towel, which might dull the edge. The ads also called attention to the marks **|** and **||** at either end of each of the blade's two edges, put there so shavers could tell the edges apart and get maximum use from each. "Buy Sparingly, Use Thriftily" were Gillette watchwords in those spartan days, and in an age of newly aroused interest in conservation, these tips still stand, as do the distinguishing marks at the edges of many of Gillette's double-edged blades.

Later, as World War II shortages grew chronic and retail clerks tired of answering customer gripes with the standard reply ("Don't you know there's a *war* on?"), Gillette staged a contest in which harried salespeople could suggest alternative retorts. Nearly three hundred winners were named, though the winning entries were not disclosed — possibly because they were little better than some of the suggestions offered by the company itself. "The Gillette razor is 1-A in this war and every one is drafted for the armed services," was one. And customers seeking a whole carton of blades to tide them over the war years were to be dissuaded by a smiling clerk who advised: "Sorry, sir — soldiers and sailors come first. That means only one package to a customer."

Soldiers and sailors did come first in Gillette's wartime scheme of things, and their blades even came to them in a different color. Guarding against civilian black-marketeering of military blade production — and seeking in advance to thwart a postwar glut of surplus blades indistinguishable from the home-market product — Gillette turned out a special khaki version of the Blue Blade. Identical in every other way to the standard article, it also came in a khaki-hued package that lacked the distinctive King C. Gillette portrait. All seemed well until word got back to South Boston that the nation's far-flung fighting men were grousing because they weren't getting the same thing provided for the home folks. Told that the blades were indeed just Blues of another color, many men continued to gripe. "But why the hell can't we get the same blades with the old man's picture on the package?" they would ask.

If the Gillette blade with King C. Gillette's portrait was prized overseas, it was coveted at home, too, and a frequent consumer complaint toward the end of the war was that there were enough razor blades to be had, but that there weren't enough genuine *Gillette* razor blades. By keeping up its standards of high quality, the company had been able to prove its blade better than most and recapture much of the old luster that had been lost over the previous decade and before.

Gillette's repute was not hurt, either, by its continued, heavy advertising campaigns. Even during the leanest of the war years, when few razors and blades were available to the civilian market, Gillette kept faith with the nation's sports fans — and also maintained a priceless string of exclusive coverage options against the postwar years when blades could be run off in never-ending streams. Sponsorship of the World Series, the Kentucky Derby, and football bowl games continued unabated throughout the war, and Gillette even expanded its sports repertoire by adding the All-Star Game in 1943 and the Cotton Bowl in 1944. Boxing, too, remained a staple in the "Gillette Cavalcade of Sports," which brought to wartime listening audiences the contests between such stalwarts as Allie Stolz and Chalky Wright, Lulu Constantino and Al Guido, Johnny Greco and Cleo Shans.

In 1944, Gillette brought boxing to a new and different kind of audience as well, when it began experimenting in New York City with weekly televised bouts. The audience was small — no more than six thousand television sets were in use at the time, mostly in barrooms — but the promise was almost beyond calculation. As President Spang observed with breathtaking understatement in his annual report to stockholders for that year, "Knowledge gained here should prove valuable in time to come when television receivers are in more general use and our merchandise is in full supply."

Later, as Spang's prescient guess came true and television aerials sprouted from America's rooftops like runaway weeds, Gillette's maiden video venture did indeed prove its boundless value. For the moment, though, radio was still king of the national airwaves, and in the fall of 1944, as troops of the American First Army were moving toward the Ardennes and an unanticipated engagement with fifteen last-ditch German divisions, Gillette optimistically announced what was called its "postwar" radio fight schedule of fifty-two bouts a year: a fight every Friday night. Also televised on a limited basis, the weekly matches were to reach more and more home screens as transmission cables snaked across the land, and before the famous Friday night fights signed off for good twenty years later, they could claim to be the longest continuing program on television.

When the fighting finally stopped in Europe and the Pacific, Gillette was well primed to face a postwar era in fact as well as in commercial fancy. Despite wartime restrictions, sales and profits had moved up smartly during the years of conflict, and in the first full year of peace sales topped the $50 million mark, more than double the figure for 1942. The $10.5 million profit record in 1946 was not yet up to the glory days of the late 1920's, but it was twice as much as the performance of 1945 and three times heftier than that of 1942. Equally important news from the fiscal front was the increase in earned surplus to $14.8 million, more than double the amount posted in 1942. Moving into a time of peace and expected prosperity, Gillette had totally repainted its once-grim financial picture.

Nor were the company's accountants the only ones to bear bright tidings. Researchers had developed a razor-blade dispenser that did away with paper wrappings and promised to help thwart the strong competition from the Schick injector razor ("Push pull, click click, change blades that quick") and keep Gillette well ahead of the other would-be rivals that had survived the war years. Its advertising men had concocted the felicitous and long-lived "Look sharp, feel sharp, be sharp" theme — after first assuring themselves that the slogan's "sharpness" did not conjure up images of rapacity — that in the 1946 World Series radio broadcast would first be counterpointed with the insistent F♯, A♯, and C♯ gongs that still chime in the head of anyone who remembers hearing the phrase. And on the production lines, engineers had continued to fine-tune great banks of machinery to ensure that Gillette's blades did indeed have "the sharpest edges ever honed."

Market-research staffers also had been hard at work, outlining expansive new borders for Gillette's postwar world. By 1950, they said, the company could be selling a billion blades a year in the United

States alone — more than double the 1940 record — a figure that would bring the Gillette market share to at least 35 percent. Distant as this goal was from the prewar level of some 18 percent, President Spang believed, not only that such heights could be scaled, but that the climb might be made in an even shorter time. All he needed was a hardy leader to set the pace, and by early 1946 Spang had enlisted the services of Boone Gross, a hard-driving, no-nonsense West Pointer (Class of 1926) who had served two years in the Army Corps of Engineers before resigning his commission to join the Motor Wheel Corporation in his hometown of Lansing, Michigan. After dipping his feet in nearly every area of the business, Gross had settled on merchandising, and in 1935 he moved on to Hiram Walker, Incorporated, as assistant sales manager. Four years later, he was named general sales manager of the subsidiary distributor, Gooderham & Worts, and soon was president as well. After time out for wartime service as a colonel in army ordnance, Gross had barely returned to his peacetime executive chair when he heard of the new post at Gillette, and in early 1946 he signed on at the razor company as general sales manager. His marching orders from Spang were simple enough: sell a billion blades by 1950 or be drummed out of the company.

Gross, whose given name honors maternal descent from Daniel Boone, was not one to shrink from such a challenge, nor did he suffer gladly those who would not or could not follow his battle plans. Within six months — cracking some heads and raising hackles along the way — Gross had revamped the Gillette sales organization along semimilitary lines, splitting the country into eighteen districts under the command of three decentralized divisions. Like generals in the field, division managers were responsible for the performance of their troops, whose ranks Gross greatly increased when he tripled the size of the sales force.

He changed the accepted sales doctrine, too. Before, salesmen had believed that they were selling razor blades, but Gross told them otherwise. What they were selling, he said — and dealers were soon bombarded with the same message — was a profit opportunity, a high-margin article that moved fast and took up little shelf space.

Whatever Gillette was selling, customers bought it. By 1947, three years ahead of schedule and stepping out to the gongs of "Look sharp, feel sharp, be sharp," Gross and his men had battered down the billion-blade barrier and had driven their company's market share up to about 40 percent. Spang must have seen the early victory coming: he rewarded his sales manager in the spring with a vice-presidency.

The all-important sales drive in the hands of a tough and able taskmaster, Spang and Chairman William Barron (Samuel Stample-man retired from his post in 1946) had also taken time to look beyond the miles of shaving edges moving out of Gillette's loading docks. And the coming billion-blade year notwithstanding, what they saw in their wide-angle survey of the company was not totally encouraging, at least not to growth-minded businessmen. For the shaving market, no matter how lucrative it might be, was tightly tied to growth in the adult male population. The birthrate during the Depression had dropped considerably, and it would be a long time before the bumper crop of war babies reached shaving age. Beyond that, it was obvious that an essentially one-product company was dangerously vulnerable to straight-on competition as well as to unforeseen developments — the unlikely return to general fashion of full beards, for example, or the introduction of a completely harmless and easy-to-use chemical prep-aration for whisker removal.*

If Gillette was to protect its flanks and keep on growing — and corporate growth was almost a moral imperative in the full flush of American postwar prosperity — some new avenue of expansion was obviously in order. Spang and Barron passed the word to their fellow directors, who quietly began scouting the countryside for promising prospects. By the fall of 1947, one of them came upon a young entre-preneur from Saint Paul, Minnesota, the garrulous and rambunctious Richard Neison "Wishbone" Harris, who had been presiding not long before over a rickety assembly line where his meager work force

---

* Despite enduring rumors, Gillette does not have formulas for such chemical shaves hidden away in top-secret South Boston vaults, though the company prudently investigates all such possibilities. The problem is that hair and skin are of similar organic composition, and any potion that would remove whiskers would continue to do its work on sensitive skin layers as well. Even so, the stories persist, and along with them tales of perpetual light bulbs, tires, and batteries, and gasoline engines capable of delivering a hundred miles to the gallon — all of which are allegedly known to the leaders of their respective industries, but suppressed because they would put an end to profitable markets. Some people believe in perpetual motion machines, too.

used rubber mallets to pound oversized corks into small bottles filled with a compound called ammonium thioglycolate. Labeled and boxed in a kit with a couple of other equally inexpensive ingredients, the bottles had been packed in secondhand shipping crates and dispatched to dealers who scoffed at first but later prayed for more. Now, just three years after the product's humble beginnings, it had caught on much more rapidly than King C. Gillette's original razor and blade. American women were buying more than a million of the home permanent-wave kits a month, and "Which Twin Has the Toni?" was a national guessing game and catch phrase. Skyrocketing almost from nowhere, Wishbone Harris's little Toni Company had grown to be one of the country's leading radio advertisers.

Toni had also caught the roving eyes of large, established companies with merger on their minds, and by the time Gillette arrived on the scene, Wishbone Harris had already shaken hands on an imminent deal with the giant Procter & Gamble.

"What a dilemma! All my assets are tied up in cash"

Women have been braiding, curling, waving, and frizzing their hair almost from the time their men first began to scrape off whiskers with sharpened flints. But artificial curls were only temporary adornments, and it wasn't until the early nineteenth century that wigmakers learned to make them permanent by dipping rolled hair in boiling water or strong alkaline solutions. Fine for inanimate wigs, such processes could hardly be used on human heads, and the French hairdresser Marcel Grateau caused quite a stir among women in the 1870's when he introduced a hot curling iron whose handiwork would last for several days.

The first "permanent" waves were achieved in 1906 by the British hairdresser Charles Nessler, who used borax solutions and electrically heated irons. His treatments took as long as twelve hours to complete and cost the equivalent of a thousand American dollars — in Nessler's first year of operation he had only eighteen customers, some of whom were dismayed to find that their expensive coiffures were permanent only to the extent that they lasted until the growth of new hair.

In shortened form and at greatly reduced prices, Nessler introduced his techniques in the United States in 1915, and the American hair-waving industry was firmly established by the 1920's. For women, the beauty parlor became the social center that the pre-Gillette barbershop had been for men, particularly after the development of cold-wave techniques brought the price of many permanents down to ten dollars or less.

After coming out of Yale in 1936 and returning to his native Saint Paul, R. Neison "Wishbone" Harris (his nickname came from a singular childhood fondness for that part of the chicken, and he sometimes styled himself formally as R. N. W. Harris) cast about for a growth industry to get into, and chose the beauty business. With $5,000 borrowed from his father, he bought into a small beauty-shop supply company called Noma, Incorporated — not to be confused with the much better known maker of Christmas tree lights. Its name came from its chemically activated curling pads that required no machines to generate curl-setting heat. By the war years, Noma had moved to cold-wave preparations that needed no heat from any source, and Harris was somewhat surprised when he learned later that his cousin Milton Harris, a Washington-based consultant who had helped in formulating cold-wave solutions, had also been working for the Gillette Safety Razor Company: he was trying to track down the ever-elusive chemical shave.

At about the same time, Neison Harris was struck with an idea quite similar to King C. Gillette's notions about quick home shaves with disposable razor blades. Women spent a lot of time sitting around in beauty salons, he thought, and even with prices edging downward, they spent a lot of money there, too. What was needed, he decided, was a good, cheap way to do permanent waving at home.

It was hardly an original idea. Since the early 1930's, in fact, numerous home-permanent kits had gone to market, but with little lasting impact. Most of them took about eight hours to do their curling, to the accompaniment of sulfurous odors that made users long for the good old days under the hands of a chattering beautician. Repeat sales were almost nonexistent, and it was not uncommon for manufacturers to introduce a product for a brief time, quietly withdraw it from the market, and then after a decent interval bring out the same formulation under a different name. Much better setting compounds for both domestic and commercial application had been developed just before the war, but kits for home use had somehow failed to catch the public fancy.

Harris's first entry in this sleeping market was a failure. Called Rol-Wav, it sold for just twenty-five cents — and women wouldn't buy it because they figured that anything so cheap couldn't be much good. Instead, they preferred other brands, selling in the range of fifty-nine cents to two dollars. Harris's path was now clear: he would bring out a better product at a higher price.

Switching from Rol-Wav's rank sulfite to a gentler and somewhat less offensive thioglycolate, Harris put together a kit consisting of fiber curlers, waving lotion, and a neutralizer to set the curls. A friend suggested Toni as a name for the product, and was somewhat surprised when Harris, graduate that he was of a tony Ivy League university, said he had never heard the word. Set straight, Harris decided that Toni was an ideal trademark for his product, and by the summer of 1944 he was pounding the hot pavements of Minneapolis and Saint Paul trying to convince skeptical drugstore owners that Toni was somehow different from all the other home-permanent kits gathering dust on their shelves. Finally, after many turndowns and cold stares, he offered to put fifty-four dollars' worth of Toni kits in a druggist's hands, buy fifty-four dollars' worth of advertising, and take the consequences. If the kits sold, the druggist would give Harris his asking price and pocket the profits; if they flopped, Harris was out fifty-four dollars. Either way, the merchant couldn't lose, and the persuasive Harris closed his first sale.

He had also launched a fabulously successful company. The dealer sold all his Toni kits and ordered more, and other druggists in the Twin Cities area did likewise. The following year, Harris expanded distribution throughout the Midwest and beyond, and by the end of 1945 Toni had run away with something like 35 percent of a rapidly growing market, far outpacing competitors who did not work so hard or wish upon the same stars as Neison Harris. Swamped, Harris called for help from his older brother, Irving, who took over advertising and administration. From then on, Toni was nothing but upward-bound.

It was Irving Harris, one memorable night in 1946, who had a brainstorm that really sent Toni soaring. For no particular reason, the idea of twins popped into his mind, followed by the thought that perhaps the company could use twins for comparative advertising. One would have a Toni permanent, the other would sport a beauty-parlor wave; consumers would be asked to guess which was which. After a few rounds of tinkering and testing, he refined the concept and came up with the memorable slogan, "Which Twin Has the Toni?"

At first, suitable sets of twins seemed so hard to come by that Toni's advertising agency wanted to scrap the whole idea. But the brothers Harris knew a good thing when they saw it, and persevered. By April, 1947, readers of the *Ladies' Home Journal* were treated to photographs of Consuelo and Gloria O'Connor, and invited to determine which one had a Toni. The correct answer was Consuelo, on the left, but what mattered even more was that the phrase was almost immediately seized upon by cartoonists, radio gagsters, and punsters everywhere. Every time the line was used, no matter how egregious the variation (nurse to two Italian fathers in a maternity-ward waiting room: "Which Tony has the twins?"), the idea of Toni home permanents was imbedded in more minds — without taking a cent from the company's advertising budget. It was a publicity man's dream, and Toni was soon flooded with so many pairs of applicants that the company had to hire a full-time twin-screener. Hollywood fell under the spell, too: Rosalind Russell and Loretta Young showed up together at the 1948 Hollywood Press Photographers' Ball costumed as slinky Toni twins, and their pictures were featured in five movie magazines read by millions of potential Toni users.

Radio listeners were also pelted with the Toni gospel. It is likely, in fact, that the Toni twins might never have made their debut if not for the effectiveness of the company's first venture into broadcasting the virtues of its wares. Beginning in mid-1946, Toni sponsored a West Coast show called "Meet the Missus," on which women were picked at random from the studio audience and asked to tell listeners of their experiences with Toni kits. Conducted live and with no coaching — and with no provision for squelching a possibly disparaging comment — this on-the-air testimonial technique was a remarkable demonstration of Toni's faith in its product. Happily, the faith was well founded, and the interviewees proved invariably to be satisfied customers. Sales in the listening area soared, and similar interviews were soon being conducted on national programs. By the fall of 1947,

Toni had taken on the sponsorship of such shows as the soap opera "This Is Nora Drake" and the seemingly perpetual "Breakfast Club," a morning variety show that had the loyal ears of millions of women.

Toni had truly arrived. As it zoomed through 1947 it was selling a million kits a month and heading for annual sales of $20 million. This was a long way from the seat-of-the-pants beginning of just three years before, and there were days when the ebullient Wishbone Harris was hard pressed to take the whole thing seriously. Some time later, when the company had become even more successful, a *Life* magazine writer observed that even then, the rapid progress of the enterprise struck the founder as funny, and that "he infects his entire staff with the idea that their business is somehow a vast joke."

Potential competitors — among them some of America's cosmetics giants — did not think Toni's runaway success was particularly funny, nor did Wishbone Harris, either, when he thought seriously about its consequences. Like Gillette, Toni was subject to all the pitfalls that lie in the path of a one-product company, and the Harris brothers, as majority owners of Toni, were laying up fortunes that could not be tapped to any large degree without payment of horrendous personal income taxes. For both business and private reasons, some changes seemed in order at the ballooning Toni Company.

One way out of the tax bind was a public stock offering that would also enable the Harrises to sock some of their holdings into other, more diversified investments. But even the fastest-growing corporations need seasoning before throwing their shares on the open market, and investment advisors counseled a delay before going public. The other way to solve the problem was to sell out to a large, established company, a transaction that would minimize taxes and put Toni under a protective corporate umbrella.

Choosing the latter course, Toni struck up talks with Lever Brothers in early 1947, and came to a $7.5 million understanding by spring. When this deal foundered, Procter & Gamble stepped in, only to find that the Harrises' asking price was rising steadily with every passing week of record sales volume. Following much dickering on both sides, Toni struck a bargain that would have brought its owners a total of some $18 million. But Procter & Gamble negotiators, having all but closed the deal, held off into November on making ironclad commitments.

Gillette, meanwhile, had been making a quiet study of the burgeoning home-permanent market, examining the products and prospects of half a dozen entries in the field. Although the products were judged to be virtually identical, Toni's sales lead made it far and away the hottest candidate for a purchase bid. Unfortunately, when Neison Harris was told of Gillette's interest, he replied that he had gone too far with Procter & Gamble, and was in no position to break away for talks with still another suitor.

Harris had first been approached on Gillette's behalf by a partner in the Chicago investment banking house of A. G. Becker & Company, whose chairman, David B. Stern, had been a Gillette director since the AutoStrop merger. Indeed, Stern had represented AutoStrop's Henry Gaisman during many of the touchy talks leading up to the union of the two razor-blade companies, and had a more than passing interest in Gillette's fortunes. Stern kept up the pressure on Toni, and Harris, assured by his attorney that he was not yet bound to any agreement with Procter & Gamble, agreed to meet with a delegation from Gillette. First in New York, later in a drawn-out session with President Spang and Chairman Barron at the Palmer House in Chicago, Harris worked out a deal whereby the Gillette Safety Razor Company would purchase the Toni Company on much the same terms as those offered by Procter & Gamble. "We had our contract with Procter & Gamble all drawn," Harris recalled later, "so we just struck out Procter and put in Gillette." When it was all over, Gillette agreed to pay the Harrises $12 million up front for their stock and net worth, plus another $8 million as a percentage of future Toni profits.

To celebrate the occasion, David Stern invited his fellow negotiators to dinner at a private club, and Neison Harris, recalling the evening years afterward, said that "I must have had a quart of whiskey, but you never would have known it. Because I was, believe me, cold sober at that point."

Spang and Barron must have been sobered on the train back to Boston, too, for Harris had imposed a rigid condition to the sales proposal. Weary of dilatory dealing — but still entertaining the Procter & Gamble offer — he had wanted a firm and final go-ahead signal from Gillette's directorate within twenty-four hours. Bad flying weather allowed a day of grace, but on the morning of December 12 the president and chairman faced their fellow board members and asked for almost instant approval of a $20 million transaction. Assisting them in their presentation was the attorney Carl J. Gilbert, from Gillette's old-line Boston law firm of Ropes, Gray, Best, Coolidge & Rugg, who explained Toni's complex patent and trademark position and detailed the financial terms. It was an impressive performance, and the directors quickly gave unanimous assent to the purchase; not long afterward, they also hired Carl Gilbert as the company treasurer.

By the second day of the new year, Gillette had consummated its first — but hardly its last — acquisition outside the standby shaving field, and the almost breathless Harris brothers were presented their shares of the first payment. It is said that Wishbone Harris, never at a loss for the ready quip, stared for a moment at his check for nearly $6 million and then remarked, "What a dilemma! All my assets are tied up in cash."

The Harrises did not take the money and run, however. As part of the agreement with their new parent company, the two were elected to the Gillette board of directors and stayed on at Toni to run the show almost as before, though headquarters were moved from their native Saint Paul to the more central Chicago. But this slightly closer proximity to the main office did not yet mean that executives in Boston were getting set to keep strict tabs on the management of their booming new subsidiary. Indeed, Neison Harris noted long afterward that things were little changed at Toni after the takeover by Gillette. Delegates from the parent company — among them Carl Gilbert, obviously a rising star — started off by paying periodic visits, but they seldom issued directives and the visits grew less frequent as time went by. It was President Spang's feeling, and Harris's, too, that little could be gained by poking too many fingers in a well-baked pie. "I think that as long as you have management that is making money and knows the business," Harris has said in looking back on the experience, "you had better keep your hands off of them and let them enjoy it."

Harris knew his business, and his money-making talents seemed considerable. In the first year of the Gillette-Toni marriage, corporate sales zoomed from $59.5 million to $85.9 million; profits took a jump from $20.4 million to $25.6 million.

Overseas markets beckoned, too, and with Gillette's worldwide distribution system to build on, Toni made a strong bid to wrap up the foreign market for home-permanent kits. But Toni did not have quite the same worldwide appeal as razors and blades. Six sets of Toni twins were well received on a 1948 promotional tour of the British Isles — "It was really a little like traveling with royalty," a Gillette Industries, Limited, official recalled later. "Everywhere we went, there were motorcades, receptions, and mayoral welcomes. We also sold a lot of product." But in France and other Continental nations where almost weekly visits to a friendly neighborhood beauty parlor were part of the feminine social routine, Toni was viewed with considerably less enthusiasm. In the French city of Lyon, Toni was test-marketed after the construction of a small manufacturing plant in France, but irate hairdressers picketed retail shops that sold the home-permanent kits, and opponents in the French National Assembly trotted out a bald woman who maintained that her hair had fallen out after an application of Toni's waving lotion. Following the passage of restrictive legislation, Toni marketers concluded that the better part of valor was to go along with the Gallic temperament: the French plant was shuttered and Toni quietly withdrew from the market.

Nor did Latin America prove to be the bonanza that some had foreseen — Toni's instruction sheets were simple enough, but even when translated into faultless Spanish they could not penetrate the gauze of illiteracy enfolding many would-be South American customers.

With its main chance clearly in the United States, Toni continued its concerted efforts to gain the affections of American women. Half a dozen sets of the now-famous twins set out in 1949 on a 25,000-mile nationwide tour, ostensibly to seek still more twins to join the Toni stable, but also to carry the home-waving message far and wide. Getting a leg up on the competition, Toni introduced in the same year the industry's first one-piece plastic curler, known irreverently as the chicken bone, and in 1950 the company greatly expanded its advertising coverage by moving into television with sponsorship of the highly popular "Arthur Godfrey and His Friends." The following year, Toni sought to broaden its attack on the hair-care market with three new products: White Rain lotion shampoo, Prom home permanent, and Tonette, a permanent-wave kit for young girls who had, presumably, been converted to the home permanent wave by playing with the popular Toni dolls brought out not long before by the craze-conscious Ideal Novelty and Toy Company.

No matter what their age or how they had been put on to Toni, the company's female customers soon proved to be a far different breed from the male customers that the Gillette Safety Razor Company was accustomed to dealing with. When it comes to grooming products, women are not generally such creatures of plodding habit as men are, and are more prone to heed advertising's siren songs and switch to newly introduced products. Cosmetics marketers have always capitalized on this tendency, which is praised by its beneficiaries as evidence of the venturesome female spirit, but blamed by its victims on fickleness and brand disloyalty. For whatever reasons, Toni was quickly hit with stiff competition in a market that soon seemed almost saturated, and it would be several years before sales would again match the peak of $24 million in 1948.

New products, skillful marketing, and advertising helped the Toni Company maintain the dominant position in its field, but at a mounting price. In 1952, advertising budgets and the costs of free samples came to about $10 million, or close to one-third of that year's record sales. (By comparison, the advertising costs of Gillette's razors and blades seldom topped 20 percent of sales.) There was some consolation, however, in the knowledge that rivals were also spending heavily in their bids for a generous slice of the pie, and Harris had been cheered in 1950 when he estimated that Procter & Gamble was laying out so much to advertise its Lilt home-permanent kits that it could have saved $1.50 on each package by merely passing them out free of charge on street corners. Deftly wielded, advertising can be a two-edged sword that at one and the same time captures markets and forces competitors to bleed their own treasuries — a strategy that King C. Gillette would surely have appreciated and approved.

No matter what skirmishes Toni was engaged in, of course, Gillette still had an almost invincible weapon in its razor blades, whose continuing successes more than offset spasmodic movement in the hair-care field. Leaping from the springboard of 2.3 billion blades in 1947, the company had gone on to soar ever higher, reaching the stratospheric 3.4 billion mark by 1950. And then in the same year—

appropriately enough, on the day after Christmas — Gillette ensured perpetuation of its sales spiral and farsightedly scored one of the greatest coups in the history of American advertising.

"How're Ya Fixed for Blades?"

Clown prince Milton Berle, erstwhile host of Gillette's old "Community Sing" radio program, had shown postwar America the power of television as an entertainment medium, and consumers had responded by purchasing television sets in phenomenal numbers. There were perhaps sixteen thousand sets in service at the start of 1947; by 1950 the number had topped ten million. Television also showed its strength as a commercial medium, with gross advertising revenues bounding from less than $9 million in 1948 to about $100 million just two years later.

Gillette, with its early entry into television as a sponsor of New York boxing matches, had slipped in on the ground floor, and stood second only to the Ford Motor Company as a sponsor of sporting events. Ford sought to steal a march on Gillette with a 1947 offer to pay $1 million for rights to televise the World Series games for the next ten years, but the czar of baseball, Albert B. "Happy" Chandler, rejected that long-term proposition in favor of stepped-up, year-to-year contracts. For openers, Chandler wanted $100,000 for the 1947 series, but that was more than either Gillette or Ford was willing to pay for an audience far smaller than the radio audience. Together, the two companies agreed to put up $30,000 each for dual sponsorship rights, but Liebman Breweries, Incorporated, of Brooklyn agreed to meet Chandler's terms and beat them out. Then four days before the start of the series, Chandler suddenly spurned the Liebman deal, explaining that "it would not be good public relations for baseball to have the series sponsored by the producer of an alcoholic beverage," and signed up Ford and Gillette for $65,000.

The following year, in part because Ford's expertly filmed commercials had outshone Gillette's own radio-style sales pitches, the razor company decided to do the series alone. This time, though, the price tag was $175,000, for the cost of broadcasting rights was rising right along with the rapidly growing number of television viewers. And during the World Series contest between the Boston Braves and the Cleveland Indians, Gillette increased this number still further when it installed, at a cost of about $25,000, a hundred open-air television sets on Boston Common. Some fifteen thousand fans a day were enthralled by the video action; the stunt drew national press coverage and Mayor James Michael Curley publicly thanked Gillette for its civic generosity.

Television, once a novelty with an uncertain future, had become an important commercial medium. By 1950, the cost of an exclusive World Series franchise had risen so steeply that Gillette, under a first-refusal agreement that gave the company the right to the series if it matched the highest competitive bid, had to come up with $800,000 to cover the top offer from Chevrolet.

Gillette found itself riding on a rapidly accelerating escalator, and some kind of continuity and stability were clearly in order. Already, in 1949, the company had nailed down long-term radio rights, agreeing to pay $1.4 million for exclusive World Series and All-Star Game sponsorship through 1956. But at the time the radio deal was closed, Happy Chandler had still been reluctant to make a similar commitment for the increasingly lucrative television rights. By mid-1950, however, he had changed his tune — his employment contract had not been renewed, and he may have wanted to make a big splash with one of his last official acts as head of big-league baseball. In any event, he and Gillette's top officials came to terms and signed a pact giving the razor company exclusive television rights to both the World Series and the All-Star contests through 1956.

At a million dollars a year, it was the highest price ever paid for athletic events, and Warren Giles, president of the Cincinnati Reds, was concerned that Gillette might have been taken to the cleaners on the deal. "It looks like a lot of money to me," he said, "and I hope they get their value out of it. It will probably take six years to tell whether it's a good deal or a bad deal." But Fred Saigh, the president of the Saint Louis Cardinals, had a less cloudy crystal ball: "Television is in its infancy," he said. "Television rights worth a million dollars today may be worth several million two or three years from now." So sure was Saigh that Gillette had come out ahead that he offered to buy the company's contract for a quick $7 million. "I'd be willing to take my chances on doubling my money," he said.

Gillette, of course, wanted no part of such a proposal, and it was soon apparent that Saigh's bet would have been a sure thing. The ranks of television sets — and the numbers of potential customers watching big-time sporting events — had more than tripled by the time the World Series contract expired, and when it came time to wangle a new deal with the now-wiser heads of baseball, the best Gillette could do was a five-year pact at more than $3 million a year. When *that* contract ran out, Gillette had to agree to a $20 million ante to sponsor World Series and All-Star games for the next five years. Later, as the price of televised sporting events ballooned still further, only the huge broadcasting networks could take them on, parceling out precious commercial seconds to panting advertisers — Gillette among them. They would pay more for a minute of commercial time than Gillette had once paid for sole sponsorship of the entire World Series.

Meanwhile, Gillette and the nation's television sports fans were in for a long, exclusive love affair that spanned the continent for the first time when the Pacific was linked to the Atlantic by coaxial cable in the fall of 1951.

"Good afternoon, baseball fans everywhere," said Russ Hodges at the opening game of the World Series between the Yankees and the Giants. "This is Gillette's fifth consecutive telecast of baseball's annual championship classic and the first year that these thrilling games will be seen by millions of folks on the West Coast. So welcome to our audience, all you fans in the San Francisco, Los Angeles, and San Diego areas. And a hearty greeting to our other brand-new audience in Salt Lake City, Utah." Already, the audience was probably worth more than what Gillette had paid for it, and Hodges was quick to remind his tens of millions of viewers of the company's close ties to sports of all kinds. "Because so many of you sports fans are also Gillette fans," he said, "we broadcast and telecast major boxing, racing, and football events as they occur throughout the sports calendar. So folks, remember — for the tops in sports, tune in Gillette's 'Cavalcade of Sports' the year around." And then, with the storied playing field of Yankee Stadium as a backdrop, the familiar diamond-and-arrow trademark selected so long ago by King C. Gillette himself flashed on millions of flickering television screens scattered across America.

The musical introduction to the 1951 World Series games was the old standby "Take Me Out to the Ball Game" — an appropriate enough tune, to be sure, but one that lacked the kind of product identification inherent in the well-known Pepsi-Cola jingle that frequently jangled Gillette's nerves when marching bands blasted it free of charge over the airwaves during half-time ceremonies at Gillette-sponsored football games. By the following fall, though, Gillette was ready to unleash a stirring musical rendition of its own, one that would shortly become so closely associated with sports that it is still played on television talk programs when famous boxers or ball players stride on stage. It was, of course, the "Look Sharp March" ("To *look* sharp, ev'ry *time* you shave / To *feel* sharp, and be on the ball . . ."), composed by Mahlon Merrick, the leader of the Jack Benny Orchestra, and chosen out of a field of several dozen contenders.

The selection process took place on the highest corporate level, engaging the attention of both Boone Gross, by then the president of Gillette, and A. Craig Smith, vice-president in charge of advertising. Smith had been the prime mover behind Gillette's World Series acquisition in 1939, and largely responsible for developing the whole "Cavalcade of Sports." Their happy choice was given a more than merely commercial blessing a little more than a year later when the durable Arthur Fiedler and the Boston Pops played the march on a Christmas-night television special — sponsored, of course, by Gillette. The conductor also led his men through the bars of the snappy "How're Ya Fixed for Blades?" Forever after, both numbers have been standbys of high school and college bands, many of whose members are too young to recall that the original purpose of the tunes was to help sell razor blades.

The same World Series broadcast that saw the debut of the "Look Sharp March" and "How're Ya Fixed for Blades?" also marked the first flight of yet another long-lived Gillette advertising standby, an animated-cartoon parrot named Sharpie. It was Sharpie's mission to remind men to buy fresh blades before the last edge grew dull, and he did so in a raucous voice while capering across the television screen in light superimposition, so as not to block the sports fan's view of the playing field or boxing ring. First sprung on unsuspecting fellow executives by the ever-imaginative Craig Smith, Sharpie quickly became a widely recognized symbol of Gillette, and if his face was not quite so well known as King Gillette's, he was almost as familiar as Bugs Bunny or Porky Pig.

Television opened up versatile new advertising avenues for Gillette, but it also posed some problems, particularly during the so-called golden age, when television, including most commercials, was presented to the public live and uncuttable. In those early days, ladder-toting carpenters sometimes ambled in front of cameras during a drama program's most emotional scene, or a recently dispatched "murder victim," unaware that he was still in range of millions of home viewers, would rise to his feet and brush off his clothes. Advertisers, too, had their sheepish moments — consider Betty Furness and the perverse Westinghouse refrigerator door — and Gillette was not immune to such bumbling. The clincher came between rounds of a Friday night fight in the late 1940's, when the all-seeing, live-camera eye zoomed in on a pair of disembodied hands manipulating a Gillette Super Speed razor and a Blue Blade dispenser. "Twist, it's open," the announcer said breezily, and twist, the hands flipped the razor open. "Zip, a new blade," and the glinting Blue Blade was deftly slipped into position. "Twist, it's closed," and twist . . . twist . . . *twist*, it wouldn't close, and the cameraman mercifully averted his lens from the struggling hands and gaping razor. Early the next Monday morning, Gillette's advertising staffers made a quick decision to switch from live action to film.

Filmed commercials allowed for much more flexibility, and by the early 1950's Gillette was relying heavily on the testimonial approach that had been used for so long both in print and on radio. The Yankee pitcher Vic Raschi was the first baseball star to step before the cameras for Gillette's $500 endorsement fee, and as the years went on, the list of ballplayers who shaved on camera read almost like an All-Star roster. Bob Feller, Warren Spahn, Roy Campanella, Willie Mays, Maury Wills, Pee Wee Reese, and Elston Howard were among the members of Gillette's video shaving team, and it became a bit of baseball folklore that a player hadn't really made it out of the bush leagues until he had been signed up as a Gillette pitchman. And small boys of any age will be gratified to know that the stalwarts who endorsed Gillette's razors and blades actually used the products regularly — Gillette saw to that by stocking major-league locker rooms with ample supplies of its wares.

It wasn't always easy to extract usable commercial footage from men who were aces on the playing field but became mumbling amateurs when they stepped on camera. Speaking parts were held to the barest minimum ("It's a cinch, Mel," said Whitey Ford when Mel Allen asked about shaving the Gillette Super Speed way), but it often took many run-throughs before Gillette's admen were satisfied. Once, after the tenth abortive take of a shaving session, Yankee infielder Moose Skowron — one of the few college-educated big-leaguers of the time — turned to the Gillette staffers and said sympathetically, "Geez, you guys must get tired working with dumbbells like us."

There were other unexpected problems as well. Years before it became fashionable, Gillette featured Negroes in television commercials, and stood by its guns even in the face of complaints from some southern broadcasters. Occasionally, there were technical difficulties, too, such as the bright sunny day when the ad scenario called for Willie Mays to make a spectacular leaping catch and then, when he hit the ground, to be joined by a nimble announcer who would relate the black outfielder's athletic grace to easy shaving. As it happened, the white announcer was uncommonly fair-skinned, and the cameraman's light meters told him that the juxtaposition of the black and white faces would produce faulty film exposures. After a hasty consultation, the resourceful Gillette man determined that the only way to salvage the scene was to ask Mays to lighten his face with make-up. Somewhat amused by the whole thing, Mays agreed, and the shooting proceeded as planned.

The Gillette Company, too, had put on a different face, splitting its corporate organization in 1952 into a parent company with three major divisions — the seminal Gillette Safety Razor Company, Toni, and an Eastern Hemisphere division headed by the largely autonomous Gillette Industries, Limited, of Great Britain. Joseph Spang — with Vice-President Carl Gilbert close by his side — stepped up to the presidency, leaving Boone Gross in charge of the razor company and Neison Harris as head of Toni. Spang and Gilbert were thereby free to survey the big picture and plot future strategy. It was a move that led

Fortune to observe not long afterward that the company had "finally decided to take off its tight shoes and get into something more suitable for the longer, faster race it would run in the future."

Of course, Gillette already had a running start in that race, not only at home but also overseas, where the company had been picking up many pieces in the wake of the disruptive ravages of World War II. In the troubled years that lay ahead, Gillette's foreign bounty would give proof once more of the clarity of vision that had inspired King C. Gillette to see the great international promise of his company.

9

A Remarkable New Stainless Blade

"If you succeed, you are a genius"

"BERLIN IS TERRIBLY BATTERED, almost beyond comprehension or description," President Spang had written after a European trip in the summer of 1946. "As a graphic comparison it is just as though you walked in New York from Central Park to the Battery and found not a single building standing." Happily, Spang found that the factory of Gillette's Roth-Büchner subsidiary, adjacent to Tempelhof Airport, was one of the few structures left relatively unscathed by Anglo-American bombers and Russian artillery. But the plant was only a shell of its prewar self. Much of the machinery had been removed by the Russians and transported hundreds of miles into Poland, where it was eventually abandoned and allowed to rust away; inside, a handful of workers busied themselves not at blademaking, but at resharpening used blades that were occasionally wrapped in pieces of newspaper when supplies of wax paper waned. Most of the recycled blades were of the Rotbart brand, which was Gillette's mainstay in Germany, but new edges were also put on any brand that happened to appear. For a time, the company ran a resharpening service for fastidious customers whose lots of blades would be tagged to ensure that shavers would get back the same blades they had brought in. And while all this piecework was going on, the plant also served as a billet for three companies of soldiers from the United States army of occupation. "The officers invited us to lunch in our own building," Spang noted, "which was a rather novel experience."

It had hardly been the only novel experience for Gillette executives sifting through the physical and economic rubble of war-wrecked Europe, where the company's regular business had been at a virtual standstill since 1940. And it would be several years before Gillette's European affairs were back on a humming peacetime footing.

Even before V-E Day, the London plant had started the switch from making war materiel to turning out razors and blades, and within about eighteen months production was almost double the prewar level. The Paris factory, intact but poorly maintained during the German occupation, took a bit longer to bring up to snuff, and it was not until 1948 that the plant in West Berlin was back in full operation – and even then it was running at a greatly reduced rate. Meanwhile, to help keep a grip on the Continental market – and biding its time through France's postwar political uncertainty – Gillette had opened up a Swiss plant in late 1946.

But it was not enough merely to make blades. They also had to be sold, which was no mean feat in a time of postwar economic chaos, when monetary values fluctuated wildly and all but a few currencies were of questionable mettle. Consequently, company officials turned to what was termed compensation trading, a practice better known both before and since as barter. Gillette Industries, headed now by T. Carleton Harrison – who had come to Gillette with the 1931 Auto-Strop merger and tightened his old-school ties with wartime service as a Royal Army brigadier – embarked on rounds of free-wheeling trading that would have done credit to those early Boston seafarer-merchants who plied the globe dealing in everything from tea and spices to beeswax and indigo. Produce and commodities were much more easily converted to hard cash than was soft currency, so Gillette blades were swapped for asparagus, tomatoes, and strawberries from northern Italy; blades were shipped to Austria and Czechoslovakia in exchange for lumber and glass. Blades were traded for wine, which was in turn traded for Chilean copper, which was sold for cash in the United States.

These were stopgap measures, to be sure, but they worked, and the Gillette foot was firmly replanted in the postwar European door. By 1951, the London operation was shipping $5.5 million in profits back to Boston, totting up fully a third of Gillette's total profit for the year. And 60 percent of this contribution came from export sales outside the British Isles. Sales subsidiaries were operating again in nearly every nation, and to keep up the stream of razors and blades, the British manufacturing facilities were expanded in 1948 and again in 1952. By the latter year, too, Gillette had outgrown its refurbished Paris plant and bought land for a new facility on the border of the city. Then the French government, just beginning an ambitious program to industrialize the southern provinces, intervened and asked Gillette to consider relocating the factory. Offered a selection of six possible sites, company officials chose the idyllic lakeside Alpine town of Annecy, not far from the international airport at Geneva. Chairman Spang — like most American businessmen, he was unable to speak a foreign language — pleased and startled those who gathered for the new facility's dedication ceremony by delivering a speech in painfully rehearsed French.

The Eastern Hemisphere was not the only postwar foreign market beckoning Gillette. There was also Latin America, where the company had managed to do a limited amount of business even during the war years. Indeed, Gillette had opened up a plant in Argentina in early 1942, having stepped in to fill a void left by hastily departed German blademakers. By 1947, this plant had raised Gillette's share of the Argentine blade market from about 12 percent to more than 50 percent. In Brazil, Gillette had built a new factory in 1943, and though hampered at first by a squeeze on raw materials, annual sales were topping a million dollars by the first full year of peace. In both Argentina and Brazil, however, stiff government regulations kept a cap on greater expansion, and also constricted the flow of profits back to the parent company.

Mexico, too, was a lush Gillette market. Supplied by goods from the United States and Canadian plants, the sales subsidiary there boosted its performance by 400 percent between 1946 and 1948, thanks largely to radio sponsorship of a popular Monday night sports program and such straightforward slogans as *"Use la auténtica Gillette azul, no raspa"* ("Use the authentic Gillette Blue Blade, it doesn't scratch"). And somewhat later, Gillette's famous stateside admonition would move south of the border as Mexican men were advised to *"Luzca elegante, siéntase elegante, sea elegante."*

To get an even better hold on the Mexican blade market — and to revamp and expand Gillette operations in all of Latin America — Spang picked the new treasurer, Carl Gilbert, fresh from working out details of the Toni merger. One does not graduate from the University of Virginia and the Harvard Law School, and then go on to a partnership in an old-line Boston law firm, without acquiring a goodly ration of self-possession and polish, and Gilbert quickly proved to be an ideal Gillette ambassador. Gaining the good graces and warm support of the Mexican finance minister, he was able to smooth the ways and get a Gillette blade plant built and in good working order by 1949.

Meanwhile, Gilbert had been on another mission as well, this one to Panama. To strengthen the Panamanian economy, the authorities were considering the creation of a duty-free zone, thereby making it more attractive for foreign companies to operate Panamanian warehousing and manufacturing facilities. For Gillette, it was a tailor-made arrangement, and the diplomatic Gilbert was on the scene even before the enactment of the law. He was so much in evidence, in fact, that the act establishing the free zone was called by some "the Gillette law." The Gillette Export Corporation, set up in Panama on a small scale in 1951, was to be the nucleus of much of Gillette's later growth in South America and the Caribbean.

Flying home from London after his European visit in 1946 — his outbound ocean crossing had been aboard the *Queen Mary*, and regular commercial flights had begun just two weeks before — Joseph Spang was struck by the world-shrinking prospects of aviation. "What particularly impressed me on the overseas flight," he noted not long afterward, "was the annihilation of time through air travel in the conduct of future business." Even with stops in Shannon and Gander, he was catching up on Gillette's domestic situation in the New York office just twenty-one hours after waving goodbye to his British colleagues at Heathrow Airport. Though overshadowed later by jet propulsion, Spang's hours-long trip was surely a startling accomplishment when measured against the days it took to span oceans by steamship or continents by train. The laying out of wide-ranging civil air lanes seemed to bode well indeed for a company with Gillette's global interests, and in both hemispheres the blade business produced increasing returns, even if the foreign contributions fluctuated considerably because of currency devaluations. By the early 1950's Gillette's foreign operations were accounting for more than 40 percent of total profits, up from just 30 percent in 1949.

Meanwhile, headquarters was still haunted — on the domestic side, at least — by the old specter of being essentially a one-product company. To be sure, the Toni acquisition had broadened Gillette's base beyond blades and razors, but the move from removing male whiskers to washing and curling female hair was hardly enough to qualify Gillette as a truly multidimensional enterprise. If anything, the whimsical vagaries of female fashion made Toni's products even more vulnerable than the standby blades, and there were already nagging signs that tightly curled hair was on its way out of style, leaving Toni to fight even harder for its lead in a steadily shrinking market.

The way around this bind was clear enough: the company's only course was to diversify its wares, bring out new products to outpace competitors and spread the risks of business. But if the strategy was clear, it was by no means easy to carry out, and the road ahead was planted with many unmarked pitfalls for both the corporation and its managers. As Boone Gross, by then the president of a company that was poised unwittingly at the edge of potential disaster, remarked some years later to a group of financial analysts, new-product introduction is high in both risk and potential reward. And the judgment of the marketplace leaves little room for appeal. "If you succeed," said Gross, "you are a genius; if you lose, you are a bum." The managing of new products, he added, "really separates the men from the boys in the marketing field."

As early as 1950, following a year of sales and profit slump at Toni, Gillette's marketing men had reconnoitered the underarm deodorant field as a possible avenue for broadening Toni's scope. For a time, some thought was given to outright purchase of the well-known 5-Day deodorant pads, or of Stopette, a popular squeeze-spray product of the day. Gillette also toyed with the idea of bringing out an entirely new brand, and company wordsmiths drew up a list of hundreds of possible names — among them the likes of No-O-Dor, O-Do, King's Breath, Sprayno, Scram, and Flit. But nothing much came of either alternative, and the deodorant project was left to simmer.

Next on the new-product agenda was lipstick. Women in the late 1940's and early 1950's had flocked to buy heavily promoted lipsticks put out by such companies as Coty, Hazel Bishop, and Revlon, and it seemed reasonable to assume that Toni, with its advertising clout and well-known name, could also be a winner in this lucrative but hotly competitive field. Following two years of careful marketing planning and consumer testing, the Toni entry in the lipstick sweepstakes, dubbed Viv, made its national debut in early 1954 to the accompaniment of heavy advertising in women's magazines and on the top-rated "Arthur Godfrey and His Friends" television show. Almost immediately, Viv was off and running at a gratifying pace. In the first few months, factory sales hit a respectable $3 million.

Unfortunately, this sum was exceeded by the product and advertising costs, a state of affairs that is not wholly uncommon when new products are launched with a big promotional push. The assumption is, of course, that sales will continue their momentum and soar into the profit stratosphere. Viv, however, was not fated to achieve such altitude. In 1955, its first full calendar year on the shelves, the product remained locked at a $3 million annual sales level; at the same time, cost of goods and advertising went on climbing, reaching almost $4 million. Meanwhile, Viv's archrivals at Revlon had hardly been sitting on their hands. Not only did they manage to buy the "exclusive" Viv formula from the contract manufacturer that made the product for Toni, but they had also, in the summer of 1955, scored an unexpected television victory: after a string of lackluster video ventures, Revlon signed on as sponsor of a low-cost summer replacement show called "The $64,000 Question." The high-stakes quiz program became a national sensation, and from then on the life was gone from Toni's Viv, and the lipstick line was discreetly dropped. Sadder, but presumably wiser, Boone Gross observed a few years later that Viv's main shortcoming was that it was "more or less a 'me too' product," differing little from the competition.

Yet another "me too" product came out of the Gillette laboratories in 1954, but the company hardly made any spectacular claims for it. Indeed, it was mentioned almost as an afterthought in advertisements for razors and blades, and Gillette cheerfully conceded that its own new product was no better than anyone else's. "Have you tried the new instant lather shaving cream?" asked one ad. Millions of shavers were using the new aerosol item, the ad continued, and sales were still on the rise after having tripled in the past year. Readers were advised that Gillette just happened to make an instant lather called Foamy, but "if stores near you aren't yet supplied, try another brand." It was a far cry from the days when Gillette ads had warned of loathsome diseases that could be caused by competitive blades.

For that matter, Foamy had shortcomings of its own, as Chairman William Barron discovered when he first used the can presented to him by the company's hopeful marketing men. The container turned out to be overpressurized, and when Barron pressed the nozzle to dole out a dollop of lather, he wound up spraying his whole bathroom with shaving cream.

Both Viv and Foamy had been developed within the company, in research laboratories that were becoming more and more comprehensive, but even as the two products were making their various ways to the marketplace, Gillette was making plans to diversify by yet another route. Taking a cue from the Toni experience, the company was about to buy a going concern whose product was strikingly similar in concept to King C. Gillette's razor with disposable blades.

"Fantastic, atomic era, miraculous pen"

Laszlo Joszef Biro is hardly a household name, yet there is probably not an office or a home in the industrialized world where the fruit of his inventive mind is not in daily use. For it was Biro, a Hungarian by birth, who patented the first really workable ball-point pen. As a newspaper proofreader in Paris, he had snagged and spoiled many a conventional pen point while marking corrections on newsprint, and in the late 1930's he at last developed a new kind of pen that fed a viscous ink around a tiny ball bearing clutched in a minuscule socket.

Shortly before the war, Biro moved to Buenos Aires, where he set up shop to manufacture his pens.

The ball-point became popular in Britain, where it caught the eye of Royal Air Force and United States Army Air Corps officers whose high-flying air crews needed a writing instrument that would operate for long periods of time without refilling, and would not leak, or at least would not leak as copiously as fountain pens, at unpressurized high altitudes. Pressed into combat service, ball-point pens joined a host of other war-born military products for which there was a pent-up peacetime demand. When the first ball-point pens — made by the Reynolds International Pen Company and priced at $12.50 each — went on public sale in New York in the fall of 1945, thousands of eager customers lined up outside Gimbels to get their hands on what full-page newspaper ads had billed as the "fantastic, atomic era, miraculous pen." In a single week, the Manhattan department store sold thirty thousand of the Reynolds pens, which were guaranteed to write under water.

Inevitably, the country was soon flooded with ball-points from a variety of manufacturers and at a wide range of prices. By 1948, consumers could choose between pens selling all the way from twenty-five cents to twenty-five dollars. But no matter what their price tags, these pioneering pens generally had several quirks in common. Their malodorous ink was subject to unexpected leakage, both on writing surfaces and in the user's pocket; put to paper, the ink readily smeared and faded; performance was so poor that ball-points were said to be the only pens that could turn out eight carbon copies without producing an original, and wags had it that the Reynolds pen worked better under water than it did on paper.

Others did more than just crack jokes about ball-points. Bankers refused to accept checks written with the pens, pointing out that forgers could literally lift off ball-pointed signatures and transfer them to other checks. Lawyers were cautioned that legal documents signed with ball-points would become invalid if, as was highly likely, the signatures faded and disappeared. Teachers, weary of smears and smudge marks, barred the pens from the classroom. By 1949, it appeared that the pencil, inkwell, and fountain pen were good bets to hold their own against the upstart ball-point.

Patrick Joseph Frawley, Jr., thought otherwise. An unpredictable twenty-five-year-old who had nevertheless followed in his father's footsteps and built up a thriving import-export business in San Francisco, Frawley had also been lending money to a company that made parts for ball-point pens. When the company couldn't pay its notes, Frawley took over the business, determined to make a fortune in pens with disposable refills. His first move was to find a chemist who had a formula for a nonfading, nontransferable ink. But even with a truly superior product, Frawley had a hard time convincing dealers that his pens would sell to consumers made cynical by unhappy experiences with some of the other brands that glutted the market. To clear this barrier, salesmen gave retailers a sample pen for a week's trial, and then came back with a dozen pens that were to be paid for only if sold. Meanwhile, Frawley had cajoled two San Francisco banks into honoring checks written with his aptly named Paper Mate pens, enabling him to advertise loudly that his ball-point was the only one that was "banker-approved."

The buying public approved, too, and after capturing the local market, Frawley went national. Sales in 1951 topped $1 million; the following year, volume was more than $9 million. To much of the public, Paper Mate had become the overnight, indelible standard for ball-point pens.

Paper Mate's rapid success and momentum were noted with interest by the Toni president, Neison Harris, who saw in Frawley and in Paper Mate many elements of his own accomplishments as a late starter but runaway leader in the home-permanent field. Beyond that, Harris also saw that Paper Mate and Gillette could make an ideal match because their merchandising and distribution techniques were similar. In late 1952, he suggested to Gillette's top officials that Frawley's company would be a likely prospect for acquisition, reckoning that the price tag would come to about $650,000. At the time, Gillette was considering with various degrees of serious interest a number of other merger possibilities — among them a cigarette-lighter manufacturer, a photographic film company, and a brewery — and Paper Mate did not seem compellingly attractive. Nor was there much more interest in the proposition when Harris laid it out again about a year later — this time with a tab that had jumped to more than $2 million. As with Toni years before, the asking price accelerated with every week of rising sales.

Finally, in mid-1955, Frawley advised Harris that he was about to sell his company to Eversharp, Incorporated, in a deal that had been hatched at a Beverly Hills bar with the Canadian financier R. Howard Webster and the former world heavyweight champion Gene Tunney, who held controlling interest in Eversharp — which also owned, in addition to its pen division, the Schick injector razor and blade line. For Frawley, the deal was an enticing one, calling for $8 million in cash and stock, plus $1 million a year for ten years. Even so, the mercurial Paper Mate founder had his doubts, and confided to Harris that he didn't really want to sell out to Eversharp. As an alternative, he proposed to let Neison Harris have a half interest in Paper Mate for $1.5 million, and to make him chief executive officer of the company.

A year or two before, Harris might not have entertained any such offer. But things had changed. Joe Spang, while still holding the title of Gillette president, was easing himself into retirement, leaving company affairs more and more to Vice-President Carl Gilbert and to Boone Gross, the head of the razor division (one of the two, it was clear, would be Spang's successor). Harris did not have the same rapport with these two executives that he had with Spang, and rightly or wrongly, he felt that his counsel was not as valued as it once had been. Years later, he told of a visit to corporate headquarters not long before Frawley made his offer. "Suddenly," he said, "everybody disappeared and they had a meeting. And I just sat around all afternoon twiddling my thumbs."

Spang was in Europe at the time, so Harris called Carl Gilbert to tell him of Frawley's proposition and of his own inclination to leave Toni and Gillette to join Paper Mate. He was so stunned by Gilbert's response, he recalled later, that he asked him to repeat it. Why, Gilbert asked, doesn't Gillette buy Paper Mate? "Carl," Harris replied evenly, "you know I've been talking for two years about this."

With top-management approval of his pet project — Boone Gross, too, favored the Paper Mate purchase — Harris determined to stick with Gillette, and negotiations with Frawley proceeded apace. Spang, who was returning from his overseas trip, this time by ship, was met at dockside by Neison Harris, who filled him in on the final details. With characteristic dispatch, Spang gave his seal of approval even before he had retrieved his luggage. By September 30, 1955, the deal was closed, and Gillette had acquired the nation's hottest maker of ball-point pens and refills. In return, Pat Frawley received a cool $15.5 million in cash.

As Neison Harris had done when Gillette bought out his Toni Company, Frawley stayed on as president of the company he had built; unlike Harris, Frawley was not elected a director of the parent corporation. If he had been, his would surely have been the shortest term of service on record. Within three months, he was gone, in a departure that surprised no one. A temperamental individualist whose erratic traits were often magnified by a drinking problem, which he would later discuss in public with startling frequency and frankness, Frawley was hardly the kind to take to the ordered ways of a large and tightly structured corporation. Much later, *Fortune* observed that it was "difficult" to conceive of Frawley fitting into the Gillette scheme of things; a more appropriate word might have been "impossible."

Succeeding Frawley as head of Paper Mate was none other than Neison Harris, who later left Toni in the hands of Vice-President Stuart K. Hensley, who had joined the company as a salesman after World War II naval service. Harris's first order of business in his new post was to oversee the unraveling of the labyrinthine maze of separate companies and facilities, scattered from California to New York and Puerto Rico, that comprised the Paper Mate enterprise. Frawley, meanwhile, had gone on to promote an abortive cartridge-loaded camera idea, and though he had signed a routine agreement not to compete with Gillette in the writing-instrument field until at least 1960, the Boston company would be hearing from him again much sooner than that, and closer to home, too.

Not long after Neison Harris picked up the reins at Paper Mate, there was a major management change at Gillette's corporate headquarters, as well. It was hardly unexpected, having been foretold — not to say decreed — some months before by Joseph Spang, whose long and successful tenure as president had earned him extraordinary powers to call the corporate shots. Meeting with his fellow directors in the latter part of 1955, Spang informed them that when Chairman William Barron retired the following March, he, Spang, would move up to the chairmanship, and that the presidency would then be filled by Carl Gilbert. Gilbert, in turn, would become chairman when Spang retired from the post two years thence, and Boone Gross would assume the presidency of the parent company.

Spang's prescription was to be fulfilled to the letter, and in choosing Gilbert as his successor he had disclosed his perception of the kind of company that Gillette had become. In Spang's eyes, the parent concern was largely a holding company, almost a staff operation, that needed at its helm a coordinator and administrator rather than a go-getting marketer and idea man. Indeed, with sales bobbing past the $200 million level in 1956 (they would sink somewhat in the next two years, however, mainly because of an economic recession that peaked in 1958), and with two major subsidiaries under its belt, Gillette could reasonably be judged ready for a time of consolidation.

It was not yet ready for complacency, though, and in 1957, the final year of Spang's active service, the company broke new ground for itself with several new products. And as always, the results were mixed. The standard rule of thumb in the marketing fraternity has it, after all, that something like 80 percent of new-product ideas turn out to be failures. Hush, a women's underarm cream deodorant put out by the Toni division, was among the casualties. Despite a heavy advertising push, it was unable to break the competitive hold of established leaders in the field, and Hush was quietly withdrawn from the market. Also from Toni came Adorn, an aerosol hair spray that had been in the works for more than four years. Billed as "Self-Styling Adorn," it compensated for Hush's disappointing performance by quickly capturing and holding the top spot among women's hair sprays. It also helped make up for some of the slack in Toni home-permanent kit sales as straighter hair styles continued as a growing fashion trend.

Venturing even further away from its traditional product areas, Gillette also formed in 1957 a proprietary drug division known as Gillette Laboratories, whose inaugural offering was a cough syrup called Thorexin. As expected, this new undertaking got off to a slow start, but management was firm in its assurances that the drug market held "interesting possibilities" for Gillette.

For all the attention paid to hair sprays, deodorants, ball-points, and cough medicines, razors and blades remained the kings of the Gillette roost. By the mid-1950's, the company's share of the total blade market in the United States had moved up to the 65 percent range, and the safety-razor division was accounting for something like three-quarters of total corporate sales. When it came to profits, the division's contribution was quite a bit higher than that, underscoring beyond doubt the nature of Gillette's primary business.

To assure the continued good health of its flagship operation, Gillette was unstinting in its advertising efforts, and was active, too, in launching and promoting new products to catch the fancy of the shaving population. In 1955, the company came out with a line of razors in three weights — light, medium, and heavy — for men who wanted to match the heft of their razor to the toughness of their beards. A year later, test-marketing began for a premium-priced, adjustable razor that enabled users to choose the closeness of a shave by turning a dial that changed the exposure and angle of the blade. (Though highly refined, this was not exactly a novel feature. The first 1903-model Gillette had also been billed as adjustable, and users were advised that they could get a closer shave by slightly loosening the razor's handle.) Introduced nationally at $1.95 in 1959, the adjustable Gillette razor quickly established a new standard for shaving equipment.

And in the same year, Gillette began setting still another new shaving standard, one that would shortly prove to be both a blessing and a bane.

"*A new blade so good it's hard to describe*"

The scenario is right out of a publicity man's wildest dreams. The President of the United States, about to embark on an eleven-nation tour to reassure world leaders of his country's abiding interest in global peace, has invited congressional leaders to the White House for a breakfast briefing. As the high-powered group moves from the state dining room to an adjoining lobby to meet with an eager press corps, the Chief Executive is seen in earnest conversation with the Speaker of the House of Representatives. Is he making a last-ditch plea for bipartisan support of his foreign mission? Is he telling of some critical development in the Kremlin? No, the President is extolling the merits of a new kind of razor blade.

Actually, it was not so wild a dream after all. According to the New York *Times*, this is precisely what happened when President Dwight D. Eisenhower huddled over the morning meal with key legislative figures on November 30, 1959. The Speaker of the House, of course, was the powerful Sam Rayburn; the razor blade, while not plugged by name in the *Times* account, was beyond all shadows of doubt the Gillette Super Blue Blade. And it would not be long before millions of Americans would be sharing their President's enthusiasm for this truly revolutionary shaving product.

Though quality had been consistently upgraded and maintained, Gillette had not launched a wholly new blade since the budget-priced Thins went to market in 1938. By the middle 1950's, however, it was becoming apparent that the old products would not be enough to maintain Gillette's lead in a market that seemed to be undergoing subtle and not-so-subtle changes. For one thing, electric shavers — or dry shavers, as they are sometimes called — were making disquieting headway, surging in sales from $45 million in 1950 to $125 million in 1956. Even the murkiest crystal ball disclosed that if this trend continued without a strong countering response from Gillette, wet shaving would eventually be on the wane. For another thing, after years without really vigorous competition on its own side of the wet- versus dry-shaving fence, Gillette saw alarming signs that it was about to face a challenge from none other than the feisty Patrick Frawley, late of Paper Mate, who signed on in January, 1958, as president of Eversharp, Incorporated. Frawley's noncompetitive agreement with Gillette covered only writing instruments, not razors and blades, and Eversharp had conveniently sold off its pen business a little more than a week before Frawley's arrival. The company had held on to the Schick safety-razor division, however, and it was there that Frawley was expected to make his mark.

He did so in fairly short order, fulfilling Gillette's worst fears. Frawley opened up with a withering barrage of advertising fire that by unmistakable inference ridiculed the Gillette adjustable razor as a perilous utensil given to slashing a shaver's face as readily as cutting off his whiskers. Magazine ads were followed by similarly disparaging television commercials, one of which featured a Schick pitchman hacking at heavyweight Ingemar Johansson's boxing glove with a double-edged safety razor and leaving behind a gaping gash.

"Look!" he said. "If that can happen to this glove, think what could happen to your face."

"No thanks!" Johansson replied in thickly accented English.

Another commercial showed a double-edged razor and blade doing their allegedly vicious work on a football. Whether in print or over the airwaves, the message was that such facial carnage could be avoided by using the Schick injector razor, billed as "so *safe* you can shave in the shower!"

The Schick assault got under way in mid-1959, and Gillette's immediate — and largely unavailing — response was to fire off testy letters of complaint and to dispatch executives to publication offices to explain why Gillette felt the ads were misleading and unfair. It is said that even President Gross joined in this behind-the-scenes counterattack, stomping into the office of a startled television-network official to demonstrate that a football could, indeed, be shaved the Gillette way without leaving behind a single nick. Meanwhile, Gillette was doing some behind-the-scenes work of another kind, quietly putting the final touches on a new technology that would in time change the whole nature of the razor-blade business, and of the company itself.

It had all begun several years before, when Gillette researchers, as part of a continuous program to explore possible new products and make improvements on old ones, had tried putting a variety of chemical coatings on standard blades. Edges treated with one particular compound gave such demonstrably superior shaves that work proceeded to develop a way to apply the coating — a silicone that seemed to reduce the blade's cutting pressure against skin and whiskers — on high-volume production lines as well as in the laboratory. Under a shroud of secrecy that would have done credit to an advanced nuclear project, Gillette technicians and engineers had developed the required mass manufacturing techniques by the fall of 1959, even as Schick was mounting its heated challenge to the Gillette blade and adjustable razor.

The company's marketing men had been at work, too, determining how best to position the new blade in relation to existing Gillette products, and how to advertise it to the public. Some plumped for selling the blade under an entirely new brand name, at double the price of the Blue Blade. Others thought that it should simply be substituted quietly for the regular Blue, with no increase in price. The compromise decision was to sell the blade at a premium price — seven cents, versus five cents for the old Blue Blade — and to call it the Super Blue Blade.

Only those who came of shaving age before the introduction of coated edges can appreciate just how super the new Gillette blade really was and what a quantum improvement it marked in terms of comfort and ease. Indeed, one company executive maintained at the time that the Super Blue was probably the most revolutionary shaving development since King Gillette introduced his disposable blades in 1903.

Unfortunately, all manner of everyday products were — and still are, for that matter — billing themselves as super, fantastic, stupendous, and a whole lexicon of other hucksterish superlatives. Now Gillette, ready to come out with something *really* superior, had to contend with public cynicism that was in part of its own making. Vincent C. Ziegler, who had come up through the Gillette sales management ranks to succeed Boone Gross as president of the safety-razor division in 1958, put the problem this way not long after the Super Blue Blade was launched: "Over the years the language has been so beggared by extravagance that superlatives have lost their impact. We ourselves," he observed in a refreshing burst of candor, "have not been overly modest in advertising our Blue Blades. Now we have a radical improvement. What do we do?"

As one of his first maneuvers, Ziegler sought to win over the advertising copywriters, by nature a jaded lot, who would be handling the introductory campaign. Arranging an early morning meeting with the staff of the Gillette agency — which was still, as it had been since the AutoStrop merger, the Detroit-based Maxon, Incorporated — Ziegler requested that the men show up unshaven, explaining that he wanted them to try out a new product. It is a measure of their good-humored cynicism that when the earnest Ziegler strode into the conference room on the appointed day, he found the walls papered with drawings of Fidel Castro and a host of other notable whisker-wearers, and his advertising men sporting false beards and mustaches. "It was a hilarious meeting until we got down to the point where they actually shaved," Ziegler observed later, "and the result was of course electric."

The strategy chosen for springing the Super Blue Blade on the public seemed anything but electric, however. Mindful that raucous tub-thumping on the blade's behalf was likely to be greeted with shrugs and yawns from consumers whose credulity when it came to advertising claims had long since been strained, Gillette opted instead for a quiet, straightforward approach that was startlingly similar to the technique of a generation before, when the company had frankly confessed its error in turning out an inferior blade. Now, though the all-type format was virtually the same, the message was quite the opposite.

"Gillette Offers a New Blade So Good It's Hard to Describe," was the stark headline on an early 1960 advertisement, which went on to claim that some men using the Super Blue had to check to make sure there really was a blade in their razors. But shavers satisfied with their plain Blue Blades were advised not to bother switching to the super version, though Gillette offered two free blades to anyone wanting to give them a try. Taking deft aim at both Schick and the dry-shaving industry, the ad confidently guaranteed the best shave ever, "regardless of what shaving method you have used in the past." In television commercials, too, the approach was quiet and low-key, with authoritative endorsements from the respected journalists Earl Wilson, Cedric Adams, Frank Conniff, and Quentin Reynolds. (Later, of course, less-polished athletes were called on to say a few words about the blades. "Hey Harmon, Harmon Killebrew," Curt Gowdy shouted in one television spot. "Have *you* tried the new Gillette Super Blue Blade?" In the best tradition of John McGraw and Honus Wagner, Killebrew replied, "Yes, Curt, a guy gave me a pack and I never knew shaving could be so quick and easy.")

If the introductory advertising for the Super Blue Blade seemed something less than galvanic, the same could hardly be said of consumer response and sales results. Some of the early ads had spoken of Gillette's conviction that the blade would be "one of the most talked-about improvements in shaving history," as it surely was. Dwight Eisenhower, after all, had already told Sam Rayburn about it, and many other opinion leaders who were supplied with free samples were equally voluble when it came to singing the Super Blue's praises. Other free samples — accompanied by new adjustable razors — mailed out to householders in selected cities generated letters of praise the like of which had not been seen since the early part of the century, when straight-edge users discovered King Gillette's first razors and blades. In some of them, the writers said that they had at last been moved to retire the old three-piecers they had been issued in World War I when they were doughboys. And one satisfied user spoke with both praise and prophecy when he noted, "We always think things are refined to the utmost, and then along comes something better."

As the Super Blue Blade gained national distribution, sales climbed at a phenomenal rate. By July, 1960, a little more than six months after the official introduction of the blades, Vincent Ziegler was saying that volume had exceeded even his most optimistic projections by more than 50 percent, with Super Blues accounting for something like a quarter of the company's total blade sales. And no end seemed in sight. Premium price aside, the superior quality of the new silicone-coated Super Blue was making it the most popular razor blade in the country, leading Gillette to new pinnacles of market dominance. The company closed 1961 with a seemingly unbreakable grip on more than 70 percent of the total blade trade; in the double-edged field — comprising about three-quarters of the market, and the only area where Gillette was competing — the Boston company could claim near-total command, with some 90 percent of the market. In the same year, the pace-setting and profitable Super Blue Blade outsold the old Blue and Thin blades combined. As President Gross put it at the time, "It hurts to lose business on any of your brands, but if you have got to lose it, it's very pleasant to do so to a more profitable brand of your own."

As Super Blue Blades went, so went the fortunes of the parent company, though both the Toni and Paper Mate divisions had turned their respective corners by 1962 and were contributing a relatively comfortable ration of profits. Sales, which had dropped for two years running from the 1956 record of $200.7 million, had rebounded to $209 million by 1959 — the last pre–Super Blue year — and then, fueled by the new blade, soared still higher. The tally for 1960 was $224.7 million; 1961 saw a jump to $253.5 million. And in what would prove to be the watershed year of 1962, sales volume hit $276 million. Profits, too, posted healthy annual increases — the 1960 figure was up by $6 million over the previous year — and Gillette's 16 percent net return in 1962 made it beyond doubt the most profitable major company in America.

The Super Blue bet had paid off handsomely, almost in spades. Buffeted first by marketplace vagaries and then by the impact of the coated blade edge, sales of dry shavers had plateaued and then fallen. A rival double-edged blade thrown into the market by Patrick Frawley's Schick had made hardly a mark on the overall sales charts. Gillette was, as *Business Week* put it some years later, "gliding along as smoothly as a Super Blue Blade through hot-lathered peach fuzz."

"A remarkable new stainless blade"

One day in mid-1962, a store on Madison Avenue in Manhattan opened for business with a single razor blade displayed in a show window. Beside it was a neatly lettered sign that announced: "Limited Supply, Fifteen Cents Each." By the end of the day, both blade and sign were gone. At about the same time, New York disk jockey Gene Klavan told his fans about the new razor blade he had been using. "I'm a one-blade-a-shave guy," he said enthusiastically, "and I got twelve shaves with it."

Klavan was not talking about the Gillette Super Blue Blade, nor were hordes of New Yorkers besieging shopkeepers to get their hands on some superkeen new edge from the world's leading maker of razors and blades. The blade they were after, the blade that literally millions of men seemed to be talking about that season, was made by a small British firm called Wilkinson Sword, Limited, whose main products were carriage-trade garden tools — among them a triple-edged implement dubbed the "swoe" (sword-hoe) and claimed to be the first improvement in the lowly hoe since biblical times. Now, it seemed to many that Wilkinson had stolen a march on Gillette and come up with a significant improvement in razor blades, too.

Wilkinson was no stranger to sharpening steel. Founded as a firm of swordsmiths in 1772, the company had turned out blades flashed by British troopers on the plains of Waterloo. The doomed horsemen of the Light Brigade had waved Wilkinson swords as they galloped into the valley of death at Balaclava; the company's wares had also been wielded during the Boer War at Omdurman, the last great cavalry charge in history.

The sword's steady demise as a workaday combat weapon had led Wilkinson to change the thrust of its business. The company went on producing limited numbers of swords for presentation and ceremonial purposes, but in 1890 its skilled cutlers began turning out straight razors; in 1898, Wilkinson came out with a safety razor similar to the American Star model that had inspired King Gillette to develop his disposable blade. (By ironic coincidence, it was at the unrelated Boston hardware store of A. J. Wilkinson & Company that Gillette had bought the tools and materials to craft the first metal models of his invention.) Later, as Gillette's blades caught on in England, Wilkinson capitalized on the boom by making stroppers to resharpen used blades, and in 1908 the company tried unsuccessfully to trademark "Gilledge" as a stropper brand name. But not even a self-stropping razor put on the market in the late 1920's enabled Wilkinson to make significant advances in the shaving market so heavily dominated by Gillette, and during World War II the company dropped out of the race and concentrated on keen-edged commando knives. Then in 1954, Wilkinson began to take a look at the mass market for disposable razor blades.

Most blades, including Gillette's, were made at that time of carbon steel, and grew dull fairly rapidly under the twin assaults of mechanical damage and corrosion. In the main, shavers had accepted this breakdown with good grace, regarding a blade change after every third or fourth shave as a part of the human condition. It was possible, of course, to make longer-lived blades of corrosion-resistant stainless steel, as Gillette itself had done in the late 1920's with the Kroman blade. But blademen paid a price for the longevity of stainless steel, which is slightly softer than its carbon counterpart and contains vexatious particles called large carbides. During the sharpening process, some of these carbides rip out, leaving behind a microscopically jagged edge. Such blades would last longer than blades made from carbon steel, but they would not give as smooth and comfortable a shave. It was for that reason that Gillette had withdrawn the old Kroman blade after a brief span on the market.

Despite the shortcomings of stainless-steel blades, some men were willing to sacrifice comfort for durability, and a handful of small companies continued to crank out limited quantities of the blades. Wilkinson approached one of them, in the world-renowned German steel town of Solingen, and arranged to make blades of the same high-quality Swedish steel in England. Sharpened one at a time — much as Gillette blades had been before the introduction of the strip process in 1931 — the first Wilkinson blades went on sale in 1956.

To say the least, it was a tiny enterprise. Together with its German associates, Wilkinson was turning out fewer than two million blades a year, at a time when Gillette's own worldwide annual production was well over five *billion* blades. The product did, however, gain a limited reputation for relatively good quality and a long life, and by 1958 Wilkinson began switching to the faster and more efficient strip method of manufacture. Then, in 1960, Wilkinson got an unwitting helping hand from Gillette.

Arguing against introduction of the premium-priced, stainless-steel Kroman blade in 1928, King C. Gillette had suggested with a hint of sarcasm that the blade should be gold-plated to make it seem worth the extra cost. Wilkinson did not appropriate that idea, but its chairman, Denys Randolph, later told members of the Royal Society of Arts that his company took another, somewhat similar cue from Gillette. Inspired by the chemical film that Gillette had applied to its Super Blue Blades, Wilkinson's researchers developed a coating of their own. Put on the edges of stainless-steel blades, a compound with the tongue-twisting name of polytetrafluorethylene was more durable than silicone and masked the characteristic rough edges, thus making possible a product that not only gave a comfortable shave, but lasted two, three, and even five times longer than even the best of carbon-steel blades. Wilkinson called the new blade the Super Sword-Edge, and it would almost in a twinkling change the whole complexion of the razor-blade business.

The first of the Super Sword-Edges went to market in England in the fall of 1961, and their success was nothing short of phenomenal.

Introduced into the United States on a limited scale early the next year — they were at first used primarily as a premium to promote the sale of Wilkinson's garden tools — the blades quickly became a minor sensation, their appeal only heightened by a shortage of supply due to Wilkinson's limited production capacity. Men who just months before had marveled at the smoothness of Gillette's Super Blue Blades were now bragging about the rare British blade that seemed equally smooth and was good for perhaps a dozen and more shaves. A mere seven million of the blades found their way to the American market during all of 1962 — at a time when American shavers were consuming better than three billion blades annually — but before the year was out there was probably not a man in the country who had not at least heard of the amazing Wilkinson Super Sword-Edge.

The president of Gillette's high-flying safety-razor division had first heard of the Wilkinson blade when the initial uncoated version trickled into the British market in 1956, and the subsequent appearance of the coated Super Sword-Edge did not particularly astound him. Indeed, as far back as 1958, when Gillette researchers had first applied the thin film that made for an incomparably smoother shave, Vincent Ziegler had summoned his top aides to inform them that a Pandora's box was about to be flung open in the shaving field. Previously, he said, Gillette had been primarily in the metals-fabricating business, but the advent of blade coatings had thrust the company into the chemical business as well. And given the proper coating, even a mediocre rival blade could conceivably pass muster with enough shavers to cut into Gillette's towering market share. Advancing technology had made the company more vulnerable to potential competition than ever before.

As in the past, the answer lay in diversification, and by the fall of 1959 Gillette executives were poring over a report from the Opinion Research Corporation of Princeton, New Jersey. The main thrust of the study, entitled *The Gillette Image as Related to Possible New Products*, reinforced what a number of Gillette marketing men had believed for some time — that consumers did not necessarily look at Gillette as exclusively a razor and blade operation. Rather, the company was perceived as a source of men's grooming products of all sorts. Armed with this insight, Gillette was already in the midst of breaking new product ground when the Wilkinson challenge was mounted in the spring of 1962. But the coming of coated stainless-steel blades had riveted attention on the shaving market.

From his spot on the firing line, Ziegler was convinced that Gillette's only immediate salvation was to counter with a coated stainless blade of its own, even though sales of Wilkinson blades were so scant that they failed even to register on the comprehensive market-share studies routinely conducted by Gillette staffers. But the British concern's runaway success with its first all-out advertising blitz, staged in Litchfield County, Connecticut, in April, 1962, convinced Ziegler beyond doubt that shavers were ready to make a wholesale switch from carbon-steel to stainless blades. With Wilkinson already first in the market, it behooved Gillette as the longtime industry leader to rush in and be at least second, rather than tarry and lag behind still other competitors.

Such, at least, was Ziegler's conclusion, but for reasons that could seem equally cogent at the time, his assessment was not fully shared at the highest corporate level. The Super Blue Blade, after all, continued its successful and profitable career, leading the company to ever new highs in sales and earnings. A mammoth defection to a stainless blade costing about twice as much, but lasting some three to four times as long, would have an obviously unpleasant impact on profits. To men accustomed to leadership in their field, it seemed beyond the realm of possibility — not to mention probability — that a virtually unknown upstart could sweep in and upset Gillette's best-laid plans. It was tempting to hope that the stainless-steel blade was a nine-day wonder, a fad that would pass when the initial novelty paled — and fond hope is easily transformed into firm belief, any questioning of which can be resented by the believer. Even super-salesman Boone Gross, by no means unpersuaded that the stainless-steel blade's time had come, was echoing a hopeful corporate position just months before Gillette's own stainless entry finally went to market. "There's a magic to stainless as long as we're not on the market," he told *Fortune* magazine. "But when the glamour wears off, the man most interested in the stainless blade may be the one who is now using our Thin — the economy-minded customer who wants to shave for about a penny a day."

From the start of Wilkinson's stainless-steel incursion into Gillette territory, Vincent Ziegler had suspected otherwise, and with little or no encouragement from his superiors had ordered work to proceed on a Gillette stainless-steel blade that would bear the code name EB-6. Then on July 9, 1962, on a balcony of the Skyline Hotel in Montreal, Ziegler presented his case to Boone Gross.

The two men had left Boston at nine o'clock that morning aboard Gillette's twin-engine Grumman Gulfstream I, ostensibly to visit with officials of the Canadian subsidiary. In fact, Ziegler explained later, he had asked Gross to join him on the trip to ensure a strictly private session, a quiet meeting of minds undistracted by the hustle and bustle of South Boston's eighth-floor executive row. On the hotel balcony, away from constant interruption — and distant, too, from the commanding presence of a still-doubting chairman, Carl Gilbert — Ziegler detailed his view of the stainless-steel blade situation. Public acceptance of the Wilkinson blade, he said, was overwhelming, and was not likely to lessen. Indeed, there was an ever mounting demand for stainless blades, a demand that would in time be met both by inevitably greater output from Wilkinson and by stainless entries from other manufacturers capitalizing on the coating technology first introduced by Gillette. The Pandora's box that Ziegler had augured a few years before had now opened dangerously wide, with obvious consequences for a laggard Gillette. Already, Ziegler disclosed, research was under way to develop a stainless blade to spearhead Gillette's counterattack; what was needed now was a full-scale commitment to make and market the blade.

Too shrewd a salesman not to see the relentless logic of Ziegler's argument, Gross agreed to his plan, and the two executives flew back to Boston that evening. The following day, Ziegler gave the signal to begin what he would describe years afterward as "a crash program to get this thing on the road." A little more than four months later, Chairman Gilbert issued a cautiously worded announcement disclosing that "our work in the development of manufacturing techniques for the mass production of a high-quality stainless-steel razor blade has been progressing at a satisfactory rate. We expect to be in a position before many months to introduce a remarkable new stainless blade."

The months, however, dragged on for nearly a year, as Wilkinson continued to ship its blades to the United States, and both Schick and American Safety Razor jumped merrily into the stainless race with their Krona-Plus and Personna blades. Not since the dark days when Henry Gaisman challenged Gillette with his Probak blade had the company found itself seemingly outpaced in the field that it had virtually owned. It was a far from pleasant situation, and Gilbert was moved at the time to complain that "some of the competition sounds like the guy in the seventy-five-cent bleacher seat who finally gets a chance to yell 'You're a bum' at a man who makes a hundred thousand a year." And much later, he would muse philosophically, "Some things have to be evolved. If you try to do them faster, you set back your cause."

"To plan for and implement The Gillette Company's future growth"

Both during and since what many observers have been pleased to characterize as Gillette's stainless-steel "fiasco" or "debacle," the company has been faulted for its apparent sluggishness in getting out its own stainless blade. Some criticism may be justified, and it is easy enough, with the benefit of penetrating hindsight, to say that Gillette should have known beyond doubt that a competitor would apply blade-coating technology to a long-lived stainless blade that would quickly decimate the market for traditional carbon-steel blades. But businessmen, like statesmen, journalists, and military leaders, are not gifted with unerring foreknowledge of what the future will bring. They make decisions based on their best information and insight at the time; thus committed to a course of action, they must accept responsibility for whatever consequences may come. And being fallible humans, they are not immune to an occasional misstep.

Having first committed itself to the carbon-steel Super Blue Blade, however, Gillette may have moved to stainless with almost as much dispatch as could be expected. It is one thing, for example, to hear a rival shout "You're a bum," but it is quite another when the same cry is taken up by the public. And this is precisely what would have happened if Gillette, after years of setting the highest quality standards for razor blades, had hurtled to market with a hastily conceived product that did not measure up to consumer expectations. Unlike other companies with relatively small shares of the blade business to begin with, Gillette could not hazard its good name and hard-won franchise — shades of 1930! — by launching a mediocre stainless-steel blade. Similarly, the company could not dribble a new blade to market — as the industry leader, Gillette had to be prepared to satisfy fully and in short order a huge, nationwide demand. And as Vincent Ziegler noted at the time, "It is not hard to make a comparatively small quantity of good razor blades. The trick is in making them by the million and to absolutely rigid standards of quality."

To turn this trick, Gillette researchers and production men worked with deliberate speed, fine-tuning the sharpening process and refining the application of the critical chemical coating. (Ironically enough, Gillette had patented the basic coated stainless-steel blade before Wilkinson did, and the British company later agreed to pay Gillette a royalty on Super Sword-Edge blades.) Stalled for a time by Eversharp-Schick's virtual corner on the high-grade European steel required for stainless blades, mass production got under way in August, 1963, in a recently completed $8 million addition to the South Boston factory. The new plant was longer than three football fields and billed as "the world's largest and most efficient razor and blade manufacturing facility." Its capacity: twelve million razor blades a day.

Gillette's stainless-steel blade was put on retail shelves in Philadelphia and New York early in September. By October, the blades were being sold in nearly all of the more than 500,000 outlets dealing in Gillette goods, and the company was well into a $4 million advertising and promotion program that included a mailing of free sample blades to 7.5 million American households. Being the last to emerge from the stainless-steel starting gate, Gillette was unable to claim in its advertising that its blades were startlingly new, but it did the next best thing: the Gillette blade was guaranteed to provide more shaves than any other stainless blade. Heavily advertised on the old standby "Cavalcade of Sports," it forged quickly ahead in the marketplace; early in 1964, sales of Gillette stainless blades were outpacing the combined totals of Wilkinson, Schick, and Personna.

There was, however, a somewhat pyrrhic undertone to Gillette's impressive performance. Although nearly all shavers who made the switch to stainless steel were abandoning Gillette Thin, Blue, or Super Blue blades, not all of them were changing over to Gillette stainless-steel blades. From a hefty 90 percent share of the double-edge market, Gillette's portion was relentlessly nibbled down to a low of about 70 percent. Never again would the company enjoy quite the same dominance in the shaving field, though it would in the future reassume its accustomed role as pioneer in razor and blade advances.

In the aftermath of what was to be an overwhelming consumer switch from carbon-steel to stainless-steel blades, Gillette officials frequently maintained that their company's failure to be first with stainless blades was more embarrassing than hurtful. There is no objective way to gauge embarrassment, but it is easy enough to measure corporate pain. In 1962, the last of the halcyon pre-stainless years, Gillette — led as always by the safety-razor division — posted record highs in sales and earnings. Flushed with understandable pride and unsuspecting of the toll that stainless-steel competitors were about to exact, Chairman Gilbert confidently predicted "another good year in 1963." Instead, while the 1963 sales were up (from $276.2 million to $295.7 million), profits declined by nearly $4 million (from $45.3 million to $41.5 million), pounded down by the rising cost of holding the company's own in a rapidly changing market. To the extent that corporate batting averages are computed on Wall Street, Gillette was clearly in a slump: from their 1962 high of 55, the company's shares dipped to a low of 28 in 1963. Clearly, the time had come for what the late John Foster Dulles had called an "agonizing reappraisal," a hard and fresh look at what kind of a company Gillette was, and where that company was bound.

It came, appropriately enough, from the chief of the safety-razor division, Vincent Ziegler, in a pointed and unbidden memorandum to Gilbert. "Under conditions which exist and under conditions which we foresee," Ziegler wrote in February, 1964, "Gillette ought no longer to be considered a growth company, if we think of that term as applying to one which can be expected to produce about 5 percent annual growth." For Gillette to retain its status as a growth company, he said, "it must reach certain definite sales and profit objectives, which as we analyze the changes occurring in the company's basic razor and blade business, seem questionable." This being the case, the supremely self-confident Ziegler continued, Gillette must embark on a broad and studied program of diversification and revamp its organization chart to ensure orderly progress toward its new corporate goals.

Many a top executive might have bristled at a subordinate's blunt call for such sweeping corporate alteration. But Gilbert, schooled in the law's complex precisions, was trained to assess cold facts — and events were proving Ziegler's facts to be all but unassailable. If Gilbert was proud, he was also a realist, and could see that Ziegler had drawn up more than a manual for mere change. In the final analysis, he had offered nothing less than a blueprint for corporate survival.

Implementation was not long in coming. Within months, the whole Gillette organization was restructured. Ziegler, the architect of the coming new order, was advanced to a newly created post of executive vice-president, charged with worldwide responsibility for all Gillette-branded grooming products. Joining him on the same executive vice-presidential plane was Toni's Stuart Hensley, whose purview was widened to include Paper Mate and two smallish disposable hospital-goods operations, one in the United States, one in Britain. The domestic concern, the Sterilon Corporation of Buffalo, had been purchased in 1962, not long after Gillette had jettisoned its profitless proprietary drug venture. Gillette Surgical (U.K.) had stemmed from an interest in medical matters on the part of Sir Ernest Cooper, chairman of Gillette Industries, Limited.

Aligned now on the basis of products rather than on the geographical lines of old, the company was in far better shape for the concerted competitive drives that would be necessary to regain the momentum lost during the stainless-steel setback. As President Gross and Chairman Gilbert had observed in their joint announcement of the radical corporate facelift, the new organization was a reflection of the changing nature of Gillette's business, "a sound framework within which to plan for and implement The Gillette Company's future growth." Recent events had stripped most of the mystery from the path that Gillette's future would take, and had also left little doubt about who, in due course, would be charting the way.

10

Sustained Profitable Growth

"Nothing touches you but the spray itself"

DRAPED IN A TERRY-CLOTH wraparound, an attractive teen-age girl stood in a bathroom doorway. In his adjoining room, her brother was carefully adjusting his necktie. "Jimmy," the girl called out, "where does Mother keep her deodorant? I left mine at school. All I see here is Right Guard."

"That's it, Sis," said Jimmy. "The whole family uses it now."

"But I thought it was a man's deodorant," Sis replied.

"Right Guard *is* a man's deodorant," said Jimmy, slipping into his jacket and striding down the hall. "But Mom and Betty found out how great it is. Give it a try." And lest anyone doubt the recommendation of an adolescent boy, a more mature voice chimed in from off camera to observe that "Gillette Right Guard power spray is just right for the whole family."

It was hardly high drama — few television commercials pretend to be — but this 1964 production helped mark a decisive turning point in Gillette's fortunes. It signaled, too, an important victory for

Vincent Ziegler. Over his much-used conference-room blackboard was a tastefully imprinted quotation borrowed from Dr. Samuel Johnson: "Nothing will ever be attempted if all possible objections must be first overcome." Along with Ziegler's insistent calls for a broadening of the Gillette product base, these would be corporate watchwords for more than a decade.

A Michigan native who began his business career in 1927 as a youthful assistant to the sales director at Chrysler Corporation, Ziegler had moved in 1935 to Hiram Walker, where he first met Boone Gross. Both men served in army ordnance during the war, Gross as a colonel, Ziegler as a major, and when Gross moved over to Gillette in 1946 he asked the younger man to join him as his executive assistant. While mulling over the offer, Ziegler toured the South Boston factory; he recalled later that while watching the tens of thousands of Blue Blades spinning off the production line, he imagined them all as freshly minted nickels. He took the job, and began his steady rise in corporate rank.

Intensely competitive, certain of his competence, Ziegler was not one to leave things as he found them. Even before the coming of rival stainless-steel blades had challenged Gillette's traditional ways, he had begun to show what sort of change he had in mind.

Gillette had been selling tubes of brushless and lather shaving cream since before World War II, and had introduced its Foamy aerosol lather in 1953. Proffered almost casually as mere frothy adjuncts to Gillette razor blades, none of these preparations had ever held a really substantial share of the market: by the late 1950's, in the midst of a wide-scale switch from traditional products to the newer and more convenient aerosols, Gillette's Foamy was running a poor fourth in its field. Under Ziegler, Foamy was pushed more heavily as a distinct item, and sales quickened at a steady pace. In 1962, the product was offered along with a new adjustable razor as the specially promoted World Series combination feature; by 1964, Foamy had overtaken its rivals and had moved to the premier position among aerosol shave creams. In the meantime, though, its performance had been upstaged by a still newer product that proved the power of Gillette's name and marketing expertise in the general toiletries market.

Toni's early failure, Hush deodorant, may have soured Gillette on women's underarm deodorants, but there were still men to be considered. And by the late 1950's it was clear that this rapidly growing market could be expanded still further by imaginative new products. Mennen, with its squeeze-spray plastic bottle and inspired advertising query — "Are you *sure* you don't need a man's deodorant?" — had pioneered in the field and run away with more than half the trade, but there were still millions of men who had not yet been won over to deodorants or who could conceivably be wooed away from their usual brand by a newcomer promising something different. Surveying the wide range of squeeze sprays, roll-ons, sticks, and other types of available products, Gillette hit on the still-novel aerosol method of application, then featured in only about 1 percent of the deodorants on the market.

Not everyone in the Gillette organization agreed that the razor and blade company had any business dipping its toes into something so seemingly far afield as deodorants, much less getting involved in the relatively untried aerosol-spray field. Nonetheless, Gillette researchers pressed on, developing suitable fragrances and working with experts at Aerosol Techniques, Incorporated, who were ironing out the technical problems that had plagued other spray products. And by January, 1959, a consumer test panel had concluded that the Gillette deodorant entry was as good as or better than all the competitive brands it was preparing to challenge.

The product was christened Right Guard by the veteran Boston advertising man John C. Dowd, who is widely credited with pioneering the singing radio commercial in the 1920's. (The Dowd agency did not land the Right Guard advertising account, however, and Dowd, a dapper and gentlemanly Harvard man, graciously declined to accept any payment for dreaming up the name.) Though chosen for its masculine connotations, the name Right Guard was shown by consumer tests to have good associations for both men and women, and a panel of females had judged the product a worthy match for all women's deodorants but one. But this last bit of information was filed away for possible future reference.

Sold on a pilot basis during the last half of 1959, Right Guard wound up with a smashing 20 percent of the men's deodorant market in four test cities, and was introduced nationally in mid-1960. Heavily promoted during the Gillette-sponsored World Series broadcasts and over other "Cavalcade of Sports" presentations, it grabbed an almost instant 11 percent of its market, and increased advertising dollars boosted that share to 27 percent in 1963. But Right Guard was still competing only in the men's deodorant field, which accounted at that time for about $35 million in sales; all told, the combined men's and women's market came to $130 million, of which Gillette had only a 7 percent slice. For shrewd marketers, expansion was becoming almost irresistible.

Gillette's studied advertising strategy had been to position Right Guard unequivocally as a men's product, an aim that was accomplished primarily by television commercials featuring sweating athletes and deep-voiced announcers who spoke of "Right Guard, the convenient deodorant made especially for men." The company's marketing men had noted the product's potential as a deodorant for other family members as well, but made the deliberate decision to concentrate first on capturing the male market that they knew best; as for widespread usage by women, in early 1961 a staffer advised the vice-president in charge of advertising, Craig Smith, "Perhaps we will try to encourage it at some point in the future."

That point came in 1963, with an equally deliberate decision to invade the women's deodorant market — though Gillette was at pains not to lose sight of its bread-and-butter male customers. "The advertising," in the words of one carefully drafted memo, "should avoid leaving the impression with men that the Right Guard formula has been changed and that it is now a 'female' product. . . . It is not considered prudent to recast this product as one designed for women and by so doing jeopardize the present business." Good marketing men, like able generals, do not change their strategy without first weighing the possible consequences, even when all objections cannot be overcome.

And there were objections to turning Right Guard into a family product. The attempt would, after all, require substantial advertising outlays at a time when Gillette was attempting to trim its budgets in response to the decline in profits following the move toward stainless-steel blades; worse, there was the risk of costly failure. But the strong-willed Ziegler persisted, and if he did not overcome the objections, he overrode the objectors. The new approach was tried with singular success in several test cities, and by mid-1964 television viewers throughout the nation were hearing Jimmy advising Sis to give

Right Guard a try even if it *is* a man's deodorant, and watching an irate father do a slow burn as he discovers that his wife, daughter, and son have all been using his Right Guard. The advertising sponsorship shifted from strictly sports programs to more family-oriented fare, and through it all sounded the tagline that was to be the secret of the product's success: "Gillette Right Guard is just right for the whole family . . . because nothing touches you but the spray itself."

It was an appealing idea to millions of Americans to whom using another's stick, roll-on, or cream deodorant was almost as abhorrent as using someone else's toothbrush, and Right Guard sales rose accordingly. The market share of 7 percent at the end of 1963 nearly doubled within a year, and Right Guard closed 1965 with more than 20 percent of a market that had in the meantime grown to some $200 million. It was a market, too, that had never before been so heavily dominated by a single brand; if Gillette can be faulted for stumbling at the stainless-steel starting line, it can surely take high marks for getting the jump on competitors — among them the giants of the toiletries industry — in the aerosol field. And while Right Guard was by far the most successful, keeping a brake on otherwise falling profits, it had not been Gillette's only departure from traditional products in the early 1960's.

"If we did not diversify, we'd go downhill"

Skweek. Head-in-the-Clouds. Squab. Duck 'n Splash. Top Job. White Froth. Cool Head. These were a few of the happy or unhappy brand names proposed as possibilities for a Gillette men's shampoo as early as 1958, when the company began assaying the prospects for a number of grooming products. Even the shoe-polish market was examined, but rejected as a bit too far afield. Mainly because of firmly entrenched competition, the shampoo idea was shelved, too, but after-shave lotion was another story. As Right Guard was nearing the test-panel stage, Gillette market researchers were also recommending that "serious consideration be given" to adding an after-shave lotion to the Gillette line. By early 1960 work was well along on a lotion that some had suggested calling Blue Balm, to go with Blue Blade, but which had later been dubbed Drive — a name that a report from the new-products department characterized as "short, memorable, youthful and masculine." There were others in the company, however, who doubted whether Drive was sensible as a name for an after-shave lotion, and by the time it reached the marketplace in 1963 the product was called Sun Up, its label blazoned with an early-rising rooster.

The rooster motif caused considerable problems for Gillette's advertising men. When they decided to feature a crowing rooster in the Sun Up television commercials, the ad chief, Craig Smith, refused to authorize the use of stock film footage of a crowing barnyard bird; instead, he insisted on starting from scratch with a live rooster. Gillette's ad-agency staffers dutifully constructed a rustic background in a New York studio, and on the day of filming they played it safe by bringing in several roosters, each in a specially built, black-covered box. Their plan was to uncover the birds quickly, in hopes that sudden exposure to the bright lights would produce a passable cock-a-doodle-doo from at least one of them. Whether from stage fright or surprise, none of the birds performed.

When Smith heard of the failure, he ordered a rerun, and arranged to be on the scene himself to make sure that everything went as scheduled. This time, too, despite all his urging, the roosters merely stood on the studio fence rail and blinked silently at the camera. A short time later, the scene was shot on a farm, where the selected rooster crowed almost on cue.

Two years after the debut of Sun Up, the after-shave lotion was joined by Heads Up, a men's hair-grooming preparation whose name was appropriated from the dormant shampoo list. And while neither product was fated to reach the same heights of market strength that Right Guard did, the trio of toiletries helped offset some of the shrinkage in razor and blade sales during the long aftershock of the stainless-steel imbroglio. By 1965, toiletries sales in the safety-razor division were 60 percent as great as razor and blade volume, up from just 6 percent in 1960. But if every cloud has a silver lining, the converse can also be true: because of higher production and selling costs, the return on toiletries fell far short of the profit on blades, and

Gillette would never regain the heady margins that had stamped the years of unchallenged Blue Blades and Super Blue Blades.

The safey-razor division was not alone in branching into new fields. As long ago as 1954, in fact, Toni had ventured below the hairline with a facial cleanser called Deep Magic, and if Hush deodorant had been a flop, Adorn hair spray continued to hold its top position. Even more important, Toni had come to terms with the inevitable erosion of its home-permanent kit business, though not before indulging in some wishful thinking. "For a while," then-president Stuart Hensley recalled, "we lived in hope that curly styles would come back. But it was clear that if we did not diversify, we'd go downhill."

To ensure continued upward movement in an age of more casual hair styles, Toni had taken on the sponsorship of the Miss America pageant in 1958, and used this annual extravaganza of femininity as a platform to promote a variety of new women's grooming products — among them additions to the Deep Magic line, variations on the hair-spray theme, and the highly successful Dippity-do setting gel. By 1965, Toni products other than permanent preparations accounted for three-quarters of the division's annual volume.

Not all of Toni's new product entries were as upwardly mobile as Dippity-do, however. In 1964, Toni launched Sofstyle (a name that was soon changed to Epic) hair straightener, geared for the Negro market; it came just as cries of "black is beautiful" were heard in the land, and most black women deserted straight hair in favor of more natural Afro styles. Like segregated lunch counters and classrooms, Sofstyle-Epic fell to the civil rights movement of the 1960's.

Even at Paper Mate, whose writing-instrument field is not exactly given to frequent revolution, change was under way, stimulated largely by sharply increasing competition from low-priced throw-away pens. (There had been a change in the division's management, too, with the resignation in early 1959 of Neison Harris. To fulfill Paper Mate's promise had proved harder than he had originally thought, and he decided to leave and concentrate on other interests.) Taking a hint from the safety-razor division, Paper Mate came out in 1964 with slim, regular, and husky versions of its ball-point pens, an idea whose novelty value was greater than its contribution to sales and profits — much of the public continued to favor completely disposable pens over the refillable Paper Mate variety. But high hopes were held for the porous-point Flair pen introduced in the summer of 1966.

There could be no question that Gillette's vital signs were rallying. After two years of slow-paced sales growth and declining profits, 1965 saw a substantial increase in both. The toiletries business was humming along at a respectable pace, and Gillette had also recovered its fumbled momentum as the foremost innovator in razors and blades. Improved alloys and chemical coatings had combined to make possible the introduction in the fall of 1965 of the so-called Super Stainless Steel Blade, which Gillette proudly claimed was better than any other existing blade — including its own. Rival manufacturers soon followed suit, but this time it was Gillette that had been indisputably first to the marketplace. At the same time, Gillette announced the new Techmatic band razor, whose edge was laid on a thin strip of flexible steel. Coiled within a disposable plastic cartridge and advanced as needed by the simple turn of a lever, the band completely eliminated conventional blade changing. Imitations appeared soon enough, but again, Gillette had been the pioneer.

While new products and new marketing approaches were the most publicly visible changes at Gillette, change was afoot in the executive suite as well, and it was soon apparent that the elevation of Stuart Hensley and Vincent Ziegler to their tandem executive vice-presidencies had been merely a first step in the reshaping of the company's upper echelon. To many of the directors it seemed obvious that Gillette's unsettling experience with stainless-steel blades called for a different type of leadership at the very top of the company. More than a decade before, when Joseph Spang had tapped the lawyer-coordinator Carl Gilbert as his successor, Gillette had sorely needed a skilled administrator at its helm, an able executive who could pull disparate divisions into a unified whole. It had seemed a time for consolidation, not for rapid-fire growth and hotshot merchandising. Now, Gillette's business environment had undergone fundamental alteration, and it was questionable whether the qualities in the chief executive that had been suitable in the past would stand the company in as good stead in the future. In the new world in which Gillette found itself in the mid-1960's, an able and aggressive salesman seemed the best candidate for the top corporate job. And Gilbert, aggressive and able as he was in so many other ways, could concede that he was no salesman — though he would observe years later that "lawyers are so arrogant that they think they can do anything."

Boone Gross, of course, was a salesman's salesman; there were those both within and without the company who believed that he was one of the best sales managers in all of American industry. His decisive reorganization of the Gillette sales force in the postwar years had produced enviable results, locking the company into a market position that battering rams of competition could shake but not shatter; from within this snug bastion Gillette had been able to marshal its forces in preparation for meeting the stainless-steel blade challenge. But it is a truism that great sales managers do not necessarily make the best top corporate executives, and in any case, Gross had to share with Gilbert much of the responsibility for Gillette's uncertain posture in the early 1960's.

A part of Gillette's top-management dilemma was resolved in July, 1965, when Boone Gross, at the age of sixty and after twenty years of company service, retired from the presidency. His operational duties were assumed for a time by Chairman Gilbert, but when the directors next met in September they elected Vincent Ziegler president and promoted Stuart Hensley from *an* executive vice-presidency to *the* executive vice-presidency. And it was obvious that further change was still to come: at the same board meeting the directors authorized the highly respected management-consulting firm of Booz, Allen & Hamilton to conduct a survey of Gillette's future and of its top-management needs and resources. It was generally understood by all concerned that the consultant's recommendations, barring some patently outlandish turn, would be virtually binding.

Management consultants are sometimes maligned for allegedly telling corporate clients what they already know or suspect — what they want to hear, in other words. In some instances this may indeed be true, though it is not necessarily a bad thing. A given course of action can be relatively — almost perfectly — clear, yet difficult to execute because of an understandable reluctance to bruise feelings or arouse personal animosities. Coming into an organization from without, a team of consultants can take a dispassionate look at its affairs and make recommendations based on presumably objective judgments. And if those recommendations happen to coincide with a con-

Consuelo O'Connor, the twin on the left, had the Toni in this December, 1947, ad. By the next month, Gillette had acquired the Toni Company.

Sharpie, the animated parrot introduced during the 1952 World Series telecast, became one of Gillette's most familiar pitchmen.

Can A Blade Be As Good As We Believe This To Be?

O UR belief in the new Gillette *Super* Blue Blade is so great that we guarantee to refund your money without question if you do not get the finest shaves you ever experienced—*no matter what shaving method you used in the past!*

The new *Super* Blue Blade is delivering a degree of shaving ease and comfort that user after user says is "almost unbelievable."

Originally intended for men with unusually tough beards or extremely tender skin, the new Gillette *Super* Blue Blade is bringing a new kind of shaving luxury to all types of shavers.

When you try this new *Super* Blue Blade you will discover shaving is so effortless that it actually feels as if you are shaving without a blade in your razor.

The Gillette *Super* Blue Blade has a radically new kind of shaving edge that requires extra processing. And this new blade is precision engineered to fit exactly all Gillette Razors. *Because production is slower, the distribution of the new Super Blue Blade will be somewhat limited in the immediate future.*

The new Gillette *Super* Blue Blade is priced at 69¢ for a dispenser of 10. It is also available in the Gillette Adjustable Razor set at $1.95.

No words can tell you how fine this new Gillette *Super* Blue Blade is. You'll have to use it to believe it. So if your retailer is out of stock, write The Gillette Co., P.O. Box No. 830, Boston, Mass., and we will send you two trial blades without charge.

The coated Super Blue Blade was launched in early 1960, ushering in a new era of shaving comfort. It also set the stage for the introduction of Wilkinson's stainless Super Sword-Edge.

Gillette's own stainless blades, produced in a huge new addition to the South Boston factory, went to market in 1963. Several years earlier, announcing plans for their expanded facilities, Vincent C. Ziegler, Boone Gross, and Carl J. Gilbert (standing, left to right) showed the architect's drawing to John Collins, mayor of Boston.

For nearly a decade as chairman and president, Vincent Ziegler was guided
by his favorite quotation from Dr. Samuel Johnson.

The drive for worldwide growth and diversification began in earnest when Gillette purchased Braun AG in 1967. The West German company is most famous for its electric shavers, and for designing prizewinning appliances such as this kitchen machine, on display at the Museum of Modern Art in New York.

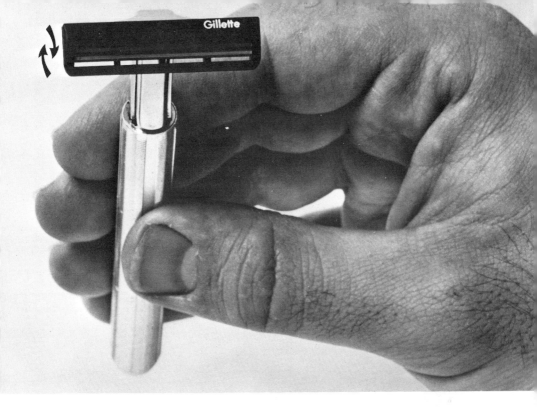

As always, Gillette's most profitable products were razors and blades, and while the Atra "shaving system" (above) introduced in 1977 was a great advance over the original 1903 razor, the basic principle remained the same.

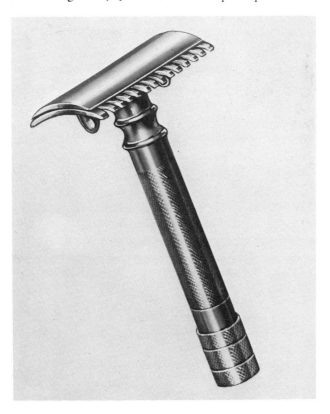

Chairman Colman M. Mockler, Jr. (left), and President Stephen J. Griffin seek "balanced long-term growth in sales and profits" as Gillette moves into the 1980's.

sensus within the client organization, so much the better — they can then be carried out as the wise and studied counsel of a disinterested observer. Thus it was that Booz, Allen, largely at the urging of Ralph Lazarus — president of the giant Federated Department Stores, Incorporated, and a Gillette director since 1961 — was called in to take a long look at the Gillette situation. In a report dated May 10, 1966, the firm submitted its conclusions to the board. Among them: Vincent Ziegler should be made chairman and chief executive officer; Stuart Hensley should be made president and chief operating officer; Carl Gilbert should become chairman of a newly formed executive committee of the board. Nine days later, it was done.

Gross and Gilbert remained for several more years on the board of the company they had done so much to help build, but by the end of the decade they were both gone from the directorate — Gross because of "pressure of travel and other business activities," and Gilbert to accept a high federal post as special representative for trade negotiations. By then, too, many more changes had been engineered at Gillette, not the least of which was an emblematic move of corporate headquarters from the South Boston razor and blade factory, where executive office windows offered a vista of decrepit wharves and disused railroad yards, to the sleek, uptown Prudential Tower, a symbol of the new spirit that was animating the old city of Boston after years of neglect and stagnation. Just blocks away, on Westland Avenue, was the four-story brick and brownstone apartment building — it was a cheap roominghouse now — where King C. Gillette had conceived his disposable razor blade more than seventy years before. Several miles distant, but clearly visible from the company's new thirty-ninth-floor offices, was Logan International Airport, a symbol of the jet age that had changed the company almost past recognition since the founder's day.

"We're no longer just the razor-blade people"

When Gillette opened its new South Boston razor blade factory in 1963, the low-slung red-brick building was crowned with brightly lighted letters proclaiming it to be "World Shaving Headquarters."

But in some parts of the world this proud boast was less true than in others, and in the fall of 1967 the parent company's vice-president for business development, Robert S. Perry, stood before the executive committee and reminded its members of some hard facts. Most painful of all, perhaps, was his blunt assessment of Gillette's position in Europe. For years, he said, the company had been powerless to control or even influence the European shaving market. And prospects for the future were no better.

Putting what he called this "gloomy picture" in perspective, Perry noted that the company was attempting to make up for its apparent impotence in Europe by developing Paper Mate and men's toiletries business there. And he recalled almost wistfully that an ambitious move into the international market for women's toiletries and cosmetics had been blocked just months before with the failure of negotiations to acquire a large French company. But in Europe, as in the rest of the world, shaving products remained the bread and butter of Gillette's business, and Europeans had opted in overwhelming numbers for the dry shaver over the safety razor. Only about 25 percent of the men in the United States regularly used electric shavers; in Europe, the figure was 44 percent and rising. Italians, with the lowest incidence of electric-shaver usage, topped the United States by a percentage point; Danes, with the highest, chose electric shavers by a margin of nearly three to one.

A primary reason given for this somewhat curious circumstance — one might expect, after all, that the technology-mad Americans would be more likely than Europeans to shave themselves with an electrical appliance — was that in much of Europe, low-cost household current was more common than bathrooms served with hot running water. Then too, a lower relative humidity made dry-shaving in northern Europe much more comfortable on a summer morning than in steamy New York or Kansas City. But if Gillette had no control over climate or the comparative pace of plumbing facilities and electrification, it had only itself to blame on another count. The largely autonomous British operation, charged with responsibility for the company's affairs throughout the Eastern Hemisphere, had not adopted the same aggressive sales and marketing policies that were pursued in the United States. Indeed, in seeking to maintain a high profit level, Gillette Industries, Limited, had become accustomed to scrimping on advertising and promotion budgets, an expedient that made for a short-term gain at great eventual cost to long-term business growth. And into this vacuum rushed a host of competitors whose success was told by two sets of doleful figures: in 1957, Gillette could claim nearly 40 percent of the European shaving market, while electric shavers accounted for only about 23 percent; by 1964, Gillette's share had slipped to little more than 30 percent, and electric shavers had risen to almost 40 percent.

Coincident with Vincent Ziegler's ascension in that same year to a Gillette executive vice-presidency, the European picture began slowly to change, and when Ziegler was named president a year later, one of his first priorities was still "to do something about Europe."

The task had been made much easier by the relatively recent advent of regular commercial jet flights across the Atlantic. Nearly twenty years before, Joseph Spang had marveled at the changes that commercial aviation seemed bound to effect in the conduct of international business. But these high hopes had been largely mirage. Propeller-driven aircraft were much faster than passenger ships, but transoceanic trips were still grueling experiences that only the hardiest traveler would choose to undergo on a really regular basis. It had been tempting to leave the conduct of overseas business largely in the hands of presumably competent managers, and for top executives from the home office to show up only for an occasional goodwill or ceremonial appearance. By halving flight times, the jet plane radically altered the nature of international management, and Gillette officials were soon winging their way across oceans almost as routinely as they might once have boarded trains for Detroit or Chicago.

In their luggage, they carried carefully worked out plans to reshape European operations after the American model, as well as new organization charts that put American executives in many key positions overseas. Proven sales techniques were instituted, new advertising approaches were adopted. "We went back to the fundamentals," Ziegler recalled later, "and did the same things that Boone Gross had done in the United States right after the war." European plants were also taken more firmly in hand, their processes and equipment brought in line with those in South Boston, and any improvements they developed incorporated into the company's worldwide production system. Now it would take only months, not years, for the introduction in

Europe of new razors and blades developed first for American consumption.

But standardized manufacturing and sharpened sales determination were not enough to loosen the electric shaver's hold on the European market, nor could even the most massive introduction of less-profitable men's and women's toiletries compensate for the steady sapping of Gillette's strength in its primary field. And as Robert Perry faced the executive committee that September day in 1967, he came to a forthright conclusion. "It is obvious," he said, "that if we are to retain or improve our true position in the shaving products business in Europe we must enter the electric shaver market in that area." One way to do so, he observed, would be to start at the very beginning and develop a competitive product, a course that would take at least four years. But there was another, more practical means, and after more than two years of diligent spadework it was now within Gillette's grasp.

A Prussian by birth and by temperament, Max Braun was afflicted for much of his life with digestive problems, a weakness that was passed on to his two sons. And while Braun's initial business was making radio and phonograph equipment of high quality, his interest in special diets led him eventually to develop kitchen blenders and other home equipment to simplify the preparation of healthful, easily digestible foods. Braun died in 1951, but the company that he had founded thirty years before continued under the management of his sons, both of whom had a strong sense of style and design. By the late 1950's a selection of their wares was on display at the Museum of Modern Art in New York; at the 1958 Brussels World's Fair, sixteen Braun products were exhibited in the German pavilion as examples of that country's postwar industrial rebirth.

The best-known items in the Braun line — and the most profitable, too — were electric shavers, introduced in 1950 but under development since before the war. By the mid-1960's, Braun's stylish and close-cutting shavers accounted for as much as two-thirds of the market in Germany, and for about 16 percent of total European electric-shaver sales. Acquisition of Braun AG (for Aktiengesellschaft, or Incorporated) would give Gillette an instant foothold in this strong and growing segment of the shaving market, and with a product that

Gillette's evaluation had shown to be superior to any competitive electric shaver.

Happily for Gillette, the brothers Braun were running short of capital, and had become interested in forming some sort of association with a larger concern — though Gillette was hardly the sole possibility. Impressed by Braun AG's quality products and rising sales curve, a number of European as well as American companies — among them Philips', Siemens, Westinghouse, General Electric, IBM, and IT&T — were approaching Braun with various offers. But Gillette negotiators, after making their first official contacts with the German company in the summer of 1965, pressed on even as other suitors seemed poised to capture the prize. Then in early 1967, in what Ziegler termed a "shock offer," Gillette proposed an outright purchase of Braun for $50 million. By the end of the year the deal was closed, and Gillette's influence in the European shaving market seemed assured.

Europe was not the only overseas area in which Gillette was showing a newly aggressive spirit. In Latin America, where razors and blades had once been the company's only product entries, toiletries were introduced for the first time in 1965, with Right Guard going to the Spanish-speaking market as Valet, and Sun Up as Le Mans. Brazil, Mexico, and Argentina proved to be particularly lucrative markets, but neither blades nor toiletries found their way to blockaded Cuba, where all of Gillette's assets had been seized not long after Fidel Castro's triumphant arrival in Havana. But even the bearded Cuban dictator harbored fond memories of the Boston-made blades, and in 1977 he told Barbara Walters in a television interview that the reason he had first grown his beard while waging guerrilla warfare from the Sierra Maestra was that his supply of Gillette blades had been cut off.

In those countries of the world where consumers could get their hands on Gillette goods, the company mounted a concerted drive to put more and different items on retail shelves, and in the first six months of 1968 forty new products or package variations were introduced overseas. And though most of them had first been launched in the United States, Gillette would later market abroad many other products that for reasons of deeply entrenched competition it wouldn't bother with at home. From sunglasses in Australia to mouthwash in

Argentina, the company was ever ready to pounce on likely market opportunities.

By 1968, overseas sales of razors and blades had more than doubled from a decade before; toiletries volume had increased fivefold. By 1970, 43 percent of Gillette's record $672.7 million in sales volume came from outside the United States and Canada. More telling, fully half of the $66 million net profit that year came from foreign sources, some of them countries where Gillette's onetime rigid insistence on total ownership of overseas plants would previously have kept its goods off the market. Bowing to changing political and economic realities — chief among them trade barriers that blocked imported blades and the insistence in some countries on a degree of local owner-ship — Gillette scrapped its old all-or-nothing policy and adopted a more flexible course. A small blademaking plant with a 40 percent native financial participation kept Gillette in the Malaysian market in 1968, and two years later the company accepted a minority 49 per-cent interest in an Iranian blade company. By 1972, significant local financing had also made possible blade factories in Jamaica and Indonesia.

If there had been any room for doubt before, there was no question by the late 1960's that Gillette was deeply committed to multinational, highly diversified enterprise. Along with pushing for a bigger share of the overseas market in both traditional and nontraditional goods, the company continued a vigorous program of new product introduction, going far beyond such things as Foamy, Right Guard, Sun Up, and Heads Up products. As Chairman Vincent Ziegler explained to stock-holders at their 1969 annual meeting, Gillette's general sphere of in-terest when it came to diversification was in products bought for individual or family use, products with clear competitive advantages, and products costing relatively little.

Not all of Gillette's new products seemed to fit all these criteria, however. Among them was a premium-priced men's cologne dubbed Nine Flags. First introduced in 1966, this distinctively bottled line con-sisted of fragrances said to be representative of nine nations, and was seen as an opening wedge for Gillette products in prestige retail outlets such as specialty shops and department-store fragrance counters, places where the company had not been represented before. Nine Flags marked still another departure for Gillette — it was handled by a newly formed separate division, the Colton Company, to avoid the Gillette image as a mass marketer of popular-priced goods. (Once, "Colton" had been used for an opposite purpose. The name of a South Boston street long since swallowed up by Gillette's expanding factory complex, it had also been the name of a subsidiary company that put out cheap blades such as Ring.)

Nine Flags was developed within the company; Gillette got into other fields through acquisition. In 1967, the Eve of Roma high-fashion cosmetics line was acquired, and Gillette moved into still another new arena with the purchase in 1970 of a New York wig manufacturer. It was a long way from razor blades, but the world had changed and Gillette was changing along with it. By 1970 nearly half of the company's total sales volume — which had nearly doubled in five years — was generated by products outside the traditional areas of shaving equipment, home permanents, and writing instruments. "This is a new company," Ziegler would tell a reporter for *Forbes* magazine in 1972. "We're no longer just the razor-blade people."

Gillette was no longer the same company in terms of organization and structure, either, not the least of the changes having begun on a late-spring Saturday morning in 1967, when President Hensley telephoned Ziegler at his Wellesley home and asked if he could come by for a talk.

Known familiarly to associates as "Vin" and "Stu," Gillette's chairman and president had much in common, having respectively worked their way to the top of the safety-razor and Toni divisions and then to the two uppermost corporate posts. But they had their temperamental differences, too. Schooled in the relatively quiet atmosphere that had come to characterize the Boston operation — Boston is Boston, after all — Ziegler was not given to issuing blunt orders, preferring instead to lay out corporate objectives and then ask his executives for their help in achieving them. Above all, perhaps, he prized harmony. Hensley, having won his managerial spurs in the more free-wheeling environment of Toni's Chicago headquarters, was a rougher sort who could be cold and direct in making his wishes known.

Given their equally strong wills and instincts for leadership — and given the fact that only one of them could be chief executive officer — a certain amount of friction between the two men was almost inevitable, and Ziegler was perhaps more relieved than surprised when Hensley appeared at his house that day to announce that he was leaving Gillette for what he called a better opportunity as chief of the Warner-Lambert Pharmaceutical Company, a corporate descendant of onetime Gillette president Gerard Lambert's old pharmaceutical concern. On June 15, Ziegler was elected Hensley's successor. He retained the chairmanship and assumed a position of power and influence unknown at Gillette since the Joseph Spang era. From the start, he was seen as an agent of great change. "Vin is going to turn this company upside down," a Boston executive remarked to a London colleague not long afterward. "Yes, I'm sure he will," the Britisher replied.

Ziegler quickly began recasting the organization chart, putting it in trim to face the altered nature of the company's business. By the end of 1967 responsibility for overseas operations was centralized under a single group vice-president, as were United States and Canadian activities in the company's traditional men's and women's grooming products. A diversified products group was formed to oversee Paper Mate, Sterilon, and Colton. Then in 1968, a separate division was set up to handle Gillette's expanding activities in the popular-priced toiletries business, which had grown so large that by the following year the company was opening up a new $11 million toiletries manufacturing and distribution center to the north of Boston in Andover, Massachusetts. Still more structural adjustment took place in 1971, along with a name change that found Toni restyled as the personal care division. All of Gillette's operations in the United States and Canada, from blades and pens to hair sprays — including The Dry Look, a highly successful hair spray for men — and underarm deodorants, were put under the wing of the newly formed Gillette North America. Gillette International became the new name for the division charged with responsibility for the overseas market for the more traditional Gillette wares.

If Gillette had outgrown a corporate structure more suitable for simpler times, it had put aside old symbols, too. In the United States, at least, the familiar portrait and signature of King C. Gillette were largely phased out of the company's packaging and advertising with the introduction of stainless-steel blades, though these durable trademarks still appear in parts of Europe and in quarters of the globe where illiterate shavers are accustomed to asking shopkeepers for a package of "man's face" blades. Even the universal diamond-and-arrow sign, chosen with such care by King Gillette more than half a century before, was seen less and less (on products other than blades) after the middle 1960's, and in 1970 Gillette adopted a new corporate symbol designed by Braun's Dr. Fritz Eichler. Consisting of a circle enclosing three bars, it looked to some like an impressionistic initial G, and to others like an abstraction of global diversity and strength; it was a considerable departure from what had gone before.

Some things remained more constant, however, among them the heated competition for the bulwark razor-blade market. The Techmatic band razor and the Super Stainless blade continued their dominion even as rivals promoted similar products, and when competitors sought in 1969 to gain an advantage over Gillette by launching smoother and longer-lasting stainless blades with chromium-plated edges, the Boston company accelerated the already-planned program to introduce the Platinum-Plus blade with a platinum-chromium alloy on its edges. It quickly became a leading brand, in the process providing singular evidence of the longevity of Gillette razors. To give the new blade a truly distinctive appearance, the traditional shape of the perforation was streamlined, a move that produced howls of outrage from diehard shavers who discovered that Platinum-Plus blades would not fit their old three-piece razors, some dating to World War I and even before. Though the complaints were relatively few — they did, however, outnumber the letters praising the blade's shaving characteristics — the product manager who had authorized the change was quickly nicknamed "Dogbone," after the general shape of the redesigned slot. It wasn't long before Gillette bowed to tradition and quietly reverted to the standard configuration, unaltered since the early 1930's.

Restoration of the old curlicue pattern may have been a tactical retreat of sorts, but Gillette was still preparing broad advances on the shaving front. By the close of 1970, the company was ready with two more products, either one of which might well have put considerably more distance between Gillette and its rivals.

"Each one of us came back to the office in great excitement"

Disguised as white-jacketed men's room attendants, an advertising agency copywriter and an art director handed soap and towels to groups of ten unshaven men who had signed up to evaluate a new razor. As the test panelists lathered and began stroking their cheeks and chins, the ad men stood unobtrusively by and eavesdropped on their spontaneous conversation. Almost to a man, the experimental shavers commented that the razor and blade were the best they had ever used; subsequent tests, conducted more scientifically and on a broader scale, confirmed that a majority of American men felt the same way, and the new product would soon rank as one of the most successful ever to come out of the Gillette factory. It was, however, considerably different from anything that most Gillette officials had had in mind just months before, and the change had come with almost lightning speed.

At any given time, Gillette researchers are tinkering with several new concepts in shaving equipment, any of which might conceivably be moved into the marketplace with great fanfare and high hopes for sales success. Cheered by initial consumer infatuation with the Techmatic band razor idea, the company pursued variations on the same theme, developing a battery-operated, oscillating version and a self-contained plastic unit designed to be wholly discarded after all coiled edges had been advanced and dulled. The disposable model, called the Sure Touch and tentatively slated for a massive, $5 million advertising push in 1971, was viewed as a premier Gillette shaving product of the immediate future, and marketing plans were well under way by the fall of 1970. In one stroke, many Gillette marketers believed, the Sure Touch razor (or "shaver" as it was to be called) would rout the competitors who had entered the Techmatic refill cartridge market and "reinforce Gillette's position as the creative leader in the shaving industry."

Others, however, were not quite so enthusiastic. Hill & Knowlton, Gillette's longtime New York public relations counsel, observing that the shaver's one truly novel feature was its disposability, concluded that this was "the one feature, unhappily, that must not be underscored in this time of ecological sensitivity." Within the company itself, a seasoned advertising executive noted the striking similarity between Sure Touch and the five-year-old Techmatic, and added drily that it seemed to be "a bit incongruous to try to sell a new idea by pointing out it incorporates a blade that has already set a selling record." Such misgivings aside, the introductory engines were stoked up and Sure Touch went quietly into the test market stage in early 1971. Meanwhile, the joint efforts of Gillette's British and American research laboratories had come up with what promised to be a far better idea.

Basically, the whole notion was simple enough: if a man can get a good shave with one blade, he should be able to get an even better shave with two blades. Indeed, some men had been putting this belief into practice for years, clamping two blades in their double-edge razors and claiming satisfactory results. Such makeshift methods seemed a bit crude to Gillette's more precision-minded researchers, and in the early 1960's work had begun in the company's Reading, England, laboratories to see if some refinements might be possible. One alternative, which Ziegler dubbed "the Emperor razor project," consisted of a pair of wire-narrow blades strung side by side in a harplike holder. Elegant in theory but not carried further because of difficulties in maintaining the edges in a rigid position, the Emperor scheme was in time melded with another project, in which two conventional blades were spaced in tandem array. Merged, the two efforts were given the equally royal designation of Rex.

Meanwhile, off on still another track, the ingenious Britishers came up with a razor whose narrow blades faced one another much like the cutting edges of a potato peeler. Wielding this model, a shaver could adopt a scrubbing motion and shear off his whiskers on both the up and down strokes.

As almost simultaneous work proceeded on the Rex and opposing-blade projects, it grew apparent that the twin-bladed Rex razor presented some problems: among them was the tendency of whiskers and shaving cream to clog the space between the two blades, rendering them less efficient. The facing blades proved more immediately promising, however, and by 1967 such a razor was consumer-tested in Australia. It was called Contra at the time, but was later named Atra, an acronym for Autralian test razor. Results were encouraging, and

Gillette prepared to launch the new product in the United States sometime in 1972 — a timetable that was advanced by a year when Wilkinson introduced its new bonded-edge blade in 1970.

Such a move, of course, would mean virtual abandonment of the push that had been planned for the disposable, Techmatic-like Sure Touch razor, and if many Gillette executives believed that this would prove to be a good riddance — the razor was not performing particularly well in test markets — they also nursed nagging doubts about the Atra and cursed the problems that had blocked advances in the tandem-bladed Rex project. Said William G. Salatich, president of Gillette North America: "From the marketing standpoint, there was no question in my mind that the tandem system would be easier to sell and would have far more appeal to consumers. Forcing a shaver to stroke upward or let the other blade edge lie dormant would, I was afraid, be a strong negative factor to some shavers." Then came a stroke of inspired good luck that made all such misgivings academic.

While the Atra project had moved along with few really major difficulties, work proceeded also on the more technically different Rex program. Highly sophisticated photographic studies of the shaving process had convinced Gillette's British researchers that tandem blades indeed had much to recommend them. They found that the first blade not only cut the whiskers in its path, but also pulled whiskers partway out of their hair follicles. Properly spaced, a second blade moved in and cut these exposed whiskers before they retreated back to their normal positions. The result was a far closer and smoother shave than was possible with even the keenest single edge. But clogging between the two blades still occurred for some men, and stood in the way of perfecting a twin-bladed shaving implement.

To bring more minds and resources to bear on finding the elusive solution to this problem, Gillette designers in South Boston were called upon in the fall of 1970, even though they were busily preparing final plans for production of the soon-to-be-launched Atra. One of them, a young mechanical engineer named Frank Dorion, found extra time to devote to the tandem blades, and by November he had come up with a way to virtually eliminate clogging: he perforated the narrow blades to allow shaving cream and sheared-off whiskers to flow through, and designed a comblike metal spacer to hold the flexible blades in rigid alignment. Like King C. Gillette's original idea for a disposable blade, the Dorion solution seemed painfully simple once it had been accomplished, but it was in reality the final breakthrough culminating an international research and development team effort in which succeeding steps made the technical achievement a reality. (Dorion's obviously bright future at Gillette was cut short by his untimely death in 1975.)

Company executives who tried out razors based on the new design were as flabbergasted by its performance as they were by the technical achievement that had made it possible. "Each one of us came back to the office in great excitement," said Salatich, "because we had just shaved with the most superior shaving system we had ever used." More testing followed, with equally satisfactory results, and by mid-February of 1971 the Atra razor was shelved in favor of the twin-bladed model developed by the British and American researchers.

From then on, final development work proceeded at a dizzying pace, with staffers working overtime to iron out the many problems that still stood in the way of the new razor's scheduled introduction during the World Series in the fall. Putting an edge on the narrow, perforated ribbons of steel — one engineer likened it to "trying to sharpen lace" — proved to be difficult, but processes developed in connection with the Techmatic band razor had laid the groundwork for a timely solution to that problem. Happily, the handle of the Atra razor was compatible with the tandem design, but the blade assembly was an entirely different matter. New machinery was needed for assembling with high precision the five elements of the shaving cartridge — the two blades and a spacer, and the plastic platform and cap. Within weeks, production men engineered the necessary equipment, and Gillette was ready by July to start mass-producing a product that not long before had been little more than a speculative idea. With its two single-edged blades — made of the same material as the highly successful Platinum-Plus double-edged blade — gripped in parallel by a plastic cartridge, it was unlike anything that shavers had ever seen before.

Meanwhile, as manufacturing techniques were being worked out, Gillette grappled with choosing a suitable name for the new shaving instrument. The ideal choice seemed at first to be something that incorporated "tandem" as an operative word, but some legal staffers doubted that tandem could be registered as a trademark, and feared that the inevitable competitive cartridge systems would also be able to use the word. (Later, it *was* registered.) Double Track, Dimension II, and Face Saver were among some of the possibilities suggested, but Gillette decided in late March on an acronym for "Twin-blade razor and cartridge." The new product would go to market as Trac II.

Highlighted by the advertising slogan "It's one blade better than whatever you're using now" — a notion suggested at least in part by the conversations overheard by those inquisitive advertising men playing the part of washroom attendants — the Trac II went public as planned during the World Series, and quickly became the most frequently advertised shaving product in America. In addition to appearing on standby sporting events, Trac II commercials were aired on top-rated evening entertainment shows; early risers heard sales pitches for the new razor on the "Today" show; night owls got the message during the "Tonight" show. In October alone, Gillette estimated that Trac II commercials were beamed into seven out of ten American homes at least once a week, and print advertising appeared in *Sports Illustrated*, *Life*, and other leading consumer magazines.

The Trac II quickly regained for Gillette whatever initiative it may have lost previously. Backed in its first full year on the market by a $10 million advertising and promotion push and sample mailings to twelve million American consumers, the Trac II became the nation's best-selling razor, and its refill cartridges captured some 10 percent of the blade market. In another year, this share would nearly double, giving Gillette a stronger grip than ever on some 60 percent of the total razor-blade market. Introduced overseas under the more universally pronounceable name G II, the new razor with twin-bladed cartridges was soon on its way to becoming an international standard as well. The facing-blade razor, meanwhile, was set aside — quite possibly forever — and the disposable band-type razor made a relatively quiet market debut as the Lady Sure Touch, available in several hues.

Perfection of the twin-bladed Trac II, major accomplishment that it was, represented only a part of Gillette's research and development activities, all of which had been considerably broadened since the days when razor and blade quality seemed to be the company's paramount technical concern. Carl Gilbert, beginning in the middle 1950's, had been largely responsible for expanding the Gillette research horizon. A studious man who frequently passed the time in airport waiting rooms by examining technical and industrial displays, Gilbert could glimpse the role that new technologies were to play in Gillette's future; it was at his urging that the company in 1956 named the highly respected Dr. Milton Harris (a longtime consultant to both the Toni and safety-razor divisions) to head all Gillette research, and acquired his Washington-based Harris Research Laboratories. From then on, the company's research efforts expanded rapidly and were devoted more and more to long-range programs. By 1959 four of the five research laboratories were moving into new and enlarged quarters, and the company was spending a total of $4 million on research — up five times from a decade before. By 1969 the outlay had risen to nearly $16 million. Meanwhile, the Harris Research Laboratories had become the nucleus of the Gillette Research Institute of Rockville, Maryland, whose staffers are widely recognized as authorities on skin, hair, and textile fibers.

Out of Gillette's various divisional research facilities came the explosion of new products and product variations that characterized the company's growth pattern in the late 1960's and early 1970's, but Gillette also found time along the way to take on research projects for outside clients, too. Expertise gained in the development of new writing instruments led to a government contract to devise fuel-feed systems for space-bound rocket engines that must operate in the absence of gravity; other work was conducted for the Department of the Interior to help develop phosphate-free detergents. And in 1971, the company undertook — largely at its own expense — an Environmental Protection Agency project to study the recycling of paper, cardboard, and similar waste products.

If Gillette could seek research projects beyond its normal commercial orbits, it could also continue to look for promising acquisitions outside its laboratories — even as the once-bright prospects of several previous new ventures dimmed and finally died. In 1971, for example, the company discontinued the Colton and Eve of Roma lines, both of which had become serious drains on corporate profits. Colton's Nine Flags brand products had just never been able to penetrate the premium-price market where so many powerful competitors were already deeply entrenched, and the sudden death in April, 1969, of Eve of Roma's colorful founder and namesake, Eve Zoltan Elmes, left that subsidiary without its all-important figurehead personality. (On promotional tours, Madame Eve had arrived at each city on her itinerary by private propjet, and was accompanied by fifty pieces of luggage, eight blond wigs, and a Yorkshire terrier. It was a tough act to follow.) At the same time, Gillette disposed of Sterilon, whose disposable hospital-supplies business had never lived up to expectations.

Meanwhile, in the same year that saw the foundering of these three subsidiaries, Gillette was adding a like number of other enterprises. In the summer, the company bought Welcome Wagon International, Incorporated, the well-known community-service organization, for $7.65 million, a figure just slightly in excess of the final year's losses of Sterilon and Eve of Roma. Later in 1971, the directors approved the $9.1 million purchase of Buxton, Incorporated, a maker of fine leather goods. And by the end of the year, the company had concluded a deal to buy a minority interest in a French-based concern whose luxurious cigarette lighters were so highly priced ($180 and up) that the well-paid Gillette chairman, Vincent Ziegler, once quipped that even he could not afford to own one. But the French company had something else in its stable, too, something far more within the means of the Gillette chairman and tens of millions of other consumers. And despite its almost imperial antecedents, the product bore striking kinship to the disposable-razor-blade idea that had made the whole Gillette enterprise possible.

"A worldwide sales potential of 10 to 25 million dollars"

The Franco-Prussian War was a critical juncture for the future of Europe, and also for the fortunes of young François Tissot-Dupont, who had come from his Alpine village to become court photographer to the Emperor Napoleon III. With the fall of the last French empire, Tissot-Dupont was left without a job and wound up making briefcases and other leather goods for the Paris carriage trade. The firm's name became S. T. Dupont when Simon, a nephew, took over. By 1923 Simon's sons André and Lucien had moved their operations back to the family's ancestral village of Faverges, in the Haute-Savoie region between Lake Annecy and the Mont Blanc chain. They also expanded their product line to include artfully lacquered compacts—Maurice de Rothschild bought them by the dozen—and luxurious, custom-made travel cases fitted with containers for the multitude of creams, lotions, and other toilet articles required for journeys by ship and train. (Many of the cases were equipped with Gillette razors and blades.) S. T. Dupont went on crafting travel cases for a super-wealthy clientele untouched by such petty occurrences as global economic collapse, and the company's customers continued to include movie queens, maharajas, and the likes of corpulent King Farouk and the Count of Paris, as well as commoners with such household names as Renault, Dubonnet, Rockefeller, and Cinzano.

World War II cut Dupont off from both patrons and raw materials, and the company turned as a stopgap to manufacturing high-priced pocket cigarette lighters fashioned of aluminum, the only metal available in sufficient supply. With the coming of peace, Dupont switched to weightier brass, and also returned to the travel-case business. But the age of regal travel had all but vanished with the war, and lighters soon became Dupont's primary product. The last and possibly most beautiful of the fitted cases was given by the French president, Vincent Auriol, to Princess Elizabeth of Britain at her marriage in 1948, though André Dupont — who had taken personal charge of the painstaking work — did not live to see the presentation. Late on the night he died, he returned to his home, picked up a newspaper, and eased into his favorite chair. "The Princess's case is finished at last," he announced to his wife. They were his final words.

Europe's rising postwar middle class fastened on the costly and distinctive Dupont lighter as a symbol of economic and social status. Few products ever achieved such symbolism. In restaurants, trains, airplanes and other social settings, people in Italy and France, Spain and Germany, as well as Japan, would display their Duponts as if they were a membership badge of an international club. And then one day while examining one of the replacement cartridges, Bernard Dupont was struck with a notion that would have quickened the spirit of King Camp Gillette. Capped with a simple striking mechanism, he thought, the refills could be transformed into cigarette lighters so inexpensive that they could simply be discarded and replaced when they ran out of fuel.

Other Duponts, worried that the family company's image might be tarnished by association with a cheap throwaway item, did not fully share their kinsman's enthusiasm, but in 1961 the world's first disposable cigarette lighter went on sale in France. Made and marketed by a separate Dupont subsidiary, it was called Cricket – in French, though meaningless, the word rhymes happily with *briquet*, or lighter – and many buyers assumed that it was a product of American ingenuity.

Despite a design problem that led to frequent fuel leakage, the Cricket caught the public fancy. Unfortunately, S. T. Dupont lacked both the resources and the will to capitalize on the disposable lighter's initial success; a rival French product vigorously attacked the Cricket on its home ground and captured much of the market, and by the time the Cricket tried to crack the United States market in 1963 a competitor had already arrived on the scene; barely able to establish an American beachhead, the Cricket was withdrawn across the Atlantic.

Dupont's disposable lighter had come to Gillette's attention almost from the start. Both companies, after all, had major facilities near Lake Annecy. But for all of the Cricket's conceptual similarities to disposable razor blades, most Gillette executives had little interest in the product. For one thing, it still had that pesky fuel-leakage problem; once, attempting to demonstrate the Cricket to an associate, a red-faced Gillette official discovered that all the butane had drained away, leaving him with a flameless lighter and a weak argument. For another thing, it was difficult to see much market potential for the Cricket in the United States, where matches are freely available at no charge. As late as the summer of 1969, a Gillette feasibility study could find no justification for the company's entry into the disposable-lighter field. But two years later this assessment had changed considerably, and Gillette was preparing to buy a sizable interest in S. T. Dupont.

The Gillette-Dupont courtship had begun in earnest on a beach along Lake Annecy in the summer of 1970, when Michel Grinberg, general manager of Gillette's French subsidiary, chanced upon his old friend Michel Dupont. When the conversation got around to business, Dupont complained that Cricket sales were growing so rapidly that the company could not keep pace in either production or distribution. It was clear to Grinberg that S. T. Dupont was in desperate need of capital and the kind of manufacturing and marketing expertise that a company like Gillette was eminently suited to provide. It was becoming clear, too, that disposable lighters were no mere passing fad: before a year was out, the head of Gillette's diversified companies division was urging the Dupont purchase on Chairman Ziegler, observing with what proved to be great underestimation that "we see a worldwide sales potential of 10 to 25 million dollars by 1975."

Following many months of complicated negotiations — Grinberg resigned as head of Gillette France to devote all his time to the Dupont affair — the deal was finally closed in December, 1971. At the insistence of the French government, always leery of company takeovers by large foreign corporations, Gillette was limited initially to purchasing 48 percent of S. T. Dupont. And while Gillette's major interest had been in the Cricket disposable lighter, the company acquired the luxury line as well — after first giving assurances that the tradition of handcrafted quality would be respected and maintained.

The Cricket was something else again. By necessity rather than by choice, many assembly operations on this inexpensive disposable product were done by hand, largely on the kitchen tables of the workers (it was not unheard of for irate customers to return defective lighters that were found to be clogged with bread crumbs or bits of marmalade). As rapidly as possible, Gillette began mechanizing manufacture to bring output up to the growing demand. New plants were opened in Puerto Rico, Mexico, and Brazil, and by 1973 the lighters had been launched in the United States. Dupont was selling a worldwide total of more than forty million Crickets, up fivefold from the last pre-Gillette year. In 1973, too, Gillette upped its holdings in S. T. Dupont to 80 percent, and the French company introduced a line of luxurious writing instruments highlighted by the radiant, hand-applied natural lacquers that had come to signify the prestigious Dupont pocket and table lighters.

Gillette had also been busy with the affairs of its German subsidiary, Braun AG, which had not been running along quite as smoothly as had been anticipated in the first hopeful flush of acquisition in 1967. Not the least of the parent company's problems with Braun was a drawn-out suit by the United States Department of Justice, filed on Saint Valentine's Day of 1968, less than two months after the purchase of the German company. Charging that the acquisition would eliminate Braun as a potential competitor in the domestic shaving market — though a licensing agreement with Ronson barred Braun from selling shavers in the United States until 1975 — the complaint asked that

Gillette be ordered to divest itself of all interest in the company. Gillette attorneys were relatively confident that things would never come to quite so dire a conclusion, but in addition to this continuing legal threat, the Gillette-Braun union also faced difficulties of a more fundamental kind.

The German reputation for relentless efficiency is frequently well deserved, but at Braun it proved to be something of an illusion. By American standards, at least, management practices were somewhat lax, providing no clearly defined chains of command or responsibility. As the company had expanded into new areas, considerable duplication of effort and function had cropped up, and while Braun had rightly earned its name as a maker of stylish products, not all of its wares were designed with an eye to economic production. All in all, Braun seemed ripe for a swift infusion of American textbook business-management techniques.

The solution was not to be quite so simple as that, however. Braun had become almost a national institution in Germany, and a suspicious German press kept close watch on Gillette's behavior toward its acquisition. Any rapid moves to "Americanize" Braun would unleash withering rounds of public criticism of the sort that a seller of consumer goods could ill afford. Then, too, there was within Braun itself an undercurrent of resentment against the large American corporation, and precipitate action on Gillette's part could damage all-important morale. So change came slowly at Braun. Not for three years was Gillette able to convince the German company that it would be good business to calculate the actual cost and sales contribution of each of its products, and it took even longer to combine overlapping divisions and to streamline marketing practices. But through it all, Braun's volume continued to rise — largely as a result of new product introductions — though profits failed to keep pace with sales gains. And the German company was becoming truly international in scope: by 1973 Braun was doing more than half its volume outside of its homeland, versus a little more than a third in pre-Gillette days.

If Gillette was throwing much overseas effort into the Braun operation, it was hardly neglecting the more traditional sides of its own business. By the close of 1973 the G II twin-bladed razor was on sale in fifty nations, and in the same year the company strengthened its foreign position still further with purchase of a Spanish blademaker and with minority participation in a blade plant in Yugoslavia. There was action on the home front, too — not all of it to Gillette's liking. Two new antiperspirant products, after passing all customary medical evaluation tests, were found after further study to cause slight lung inflammation in laboratory monkeys. Robert P. Giovacchini, who as head of the Gillette Medical Evaluation Laboratories had been given extraordinary powers of decision, concluded almost immediately that the company should stop manufacturing the products. Some Gillette officials argued that the tests were inconclusive and had in any case far exceeded normal usage, but Giovacchini stood firm. Then rumors of the problem leaked out, and it appeared that the entire Right Guard line was in danger of market damage by association.

At a stormy session with twenty-two Gillette executives — it was, in Chairman Vincent Ziegler's recollection, "a long, sweaty meeting where we listened very sympathetically while people blew off all their steam" — the almost inescapable conclusion was reached. The antiperspirants were withdrawn from the market, at an eventual cost to Gillette of about $1.5 million in cash. And while consumer advocates hailed the company's move, other deodorant manufacturers continued to market products containing the same ingredient, zirconium, that Giovacchini had deemed unsafe. (It is a measure of Gillette's commitment to consumer protection, and of its respect for Giovacchini's judgment, that he was promoted some months later to the unusual post of vice-president for corporate product integrity, with full and unquestioned responsibility for product quality and safety.) In time, the Gillette position was ratified by the federal Food and Drug Administration, which banned the use of zirconium as an ingredient in aerosol antiperspirants. Gillette's action was surely a rare instance of a manufacturer's withdrawing a product before being told to do so by the government agency.

On a more commercially happy note, 1973 also saw the formation of a separate appliance division to handle the company's burgeoning family of hand-held, portable hair dryers. The first such Gillette appliance, called simply the Max hair dryer, had been launched just two years before by the personal care division, and by 1972 had spawned Super Max, Max for Men, and Max Plus. Two more dryers, Mighty Max and Max Hatter, were added to the line in 1973.

Two more Gillette subsidiaries were added, too. In February, the company acquired Jafra Cosmetics, Incorporated, a California-based company whose wares were sold by independent saleswomen–beauty consultants who staged classes and product demonstrations in consumers' homes. In August, Gillette bought the Hydroponic Chemical Company, Incorporated, a maker of household plant-care products, among them Hyponex plant food. Later, this would become the nucleus of Gillette's new plant care division, augmented the following year with the purchase of a producer of potting soils.

Nineteen seventy-three also brought Gillette to a significant sales milestone: for the first time, total volume exceeded a billion dollars, reaching a level of $1,064,427,000. And in that same year, the directors moved to provide for Gillette's future top management, though in doing so they neglected to ponder a forgotten voice from their company's distant past.

"It just hasn't worked out"

In November of 1928, in one of his regular reports to John Aldred, Frank Fahey had described in some detail the international scope of the Gillette enterprise at that time. Noting that sales and advertising executives must be "familiar through long experience and training with trade conditions in every country," he added that financial executives must have "a thorough knowledge of foreign exchange that is equally comprehensive." He was calling all this to the chairman's attention, Fahey explained, "in order that you may realize why Gillette management feels that external selection of executives is, in general, out of the question, and it is so necessary to build for internal selection."

The corporate housecleaning that followed the landmark 1930 "merger" with AutoStrop had effectively demolished such notions, and the upper echelons at Gillette were for a number of years filled by men who had first made their marks with other companies and in other industries. By the late 1960's, however, after more than a quarter of a century of corporate growth and stability, there was within the company a cadre of seasoned executives who had spent a goodly part — if not all — of their working lives at Gillette or its various divisions.

It seemed reasonable enough to expect that the company's future top officers would be selected from that pool of talent.

Chief among the contenders was Paul M. Cuenin, who had lost a leg in a German minefield and signed on with Gillette in 1949 after earning a master's degree in business administration from Boston University. Within ten years he had become director of marketing research in the safety-razor division, and by 1969, after moving through a succession of more and more responsible positions, he was the third-ranking man in the Gillette hierarchy, holding down the key post of executive vice-president in charge of international operations. Neither within nor without the company was there much doubt that this dynamic and able executive was first in line to scale the remaining rungs in Gillette's corporate ladder, nor did his fellows begrudge him his hard-earned success. Then on January 26, 1970, at the age of forty-seven, Paul Cuenin died of a heart attack while on a business trip in West Germany.

If Cuenin's untimely death had opened a sudden gap in the path of smooth succession to the Gillette presidency and eventual chairmanship, many of his contemporaries within the company were confident that the breach could and would be closed by internal selection — just as the company veteran Stephen J. Griffin was named to succeed Cuenin as head of the all-important international operations. Griffin had joined Gillette in 1941, not long before beginning his World War II military service. As a master sergeant in the army, he entered Berlin in the summer of 1945, gaining for himself the distinction of becoming the first Gillette staffer to make a postwar inspection of the company's German subsidiary. The windows were shattered and much of the machinery was gone, he reported back to South Boston, but the building itself was still standing — as President Joseph Spang would see for himself a full year later. Returning to civilian life and the job he had left behind, Griffin had worked closely with Vincent Ziegler in the safety-razor sales department, moving up in 1967 to the post of corporate vice-president for administration. The bulk of his experience had been in domestic sales, but he quickly proved to be an able executive in the international arena as well — and at a time when wildly fluctuating foreign currencies made extraordinary demands on the managers of multinational enterprises. His ready adaptability to new challenges had only helped strengthen the assumption among senior officers that Gillette's very top posts would in due time be filled from within their own ranks.

But Chairman-President Ziegler, planning ahead for his inevitable retirement in 1975, favored a more open process. After careful assessment of Gillette's current position and future management needs, he determined that the company needed at its helm a highly imaginative and creative marketing man. Not finding among his own subordinates a candidate who fully satisfied him on all counts, Ziegler opted for external selection. His choice: Edward Gelsthorpe, a tall, pipe-puffing marketing whiz whose promotion of a cranberry–apple juice combination had rejuvenated Ocean Spray Cranberries, Incorporated, in the early 1960's and had saddled Gelsthorpe with the unshakable nickname of Cranapple Ed. More recently, as head of Hunt-Wesson Foods, he had launched such new products as the Snack Pack single servings of puddings and salads put up in pull-tab cans, and Manwich Sandwich Sauce, a canned mix for Sloppy Joe hamburgers. With his vaunted intuitive sense of consumer desires, Gelsthorpe seemed an ideal executive to lead Gillette through still more diversification.

Gelsthorpe came to the company in three stages, having first been elected to the board of directors in May, 1972, while still president of Hunt-Wesson. An ingratiating man, he proceeded to introduce himself to each secretary stationed along executive row; it was the first time in memory that a freshly elected director had made such a gesture. A few months later Gelsthorpe joined Gillette full time, assuming the newly created post of vice-chairman, marketing. And in April, 1973, this time to no one's surprise, he was voted in as president and chief operating officer. It was, perhaps, a portent of things to come that the Boston *Globe* managed in its extensive story on Gelsthorpe's elevation to spell his name correctly only in the picture caption.

Even more than Gerard Lambert long before him, Gelsthorpe arrived at Gillette with a reputation for uncanny marketing skill. Unlike Lambert, however, Gelsthorpe did not come to a company demoralized by scandal and reeling from sales setbacks. While Wall Street analysts — a breed notoriously hard to satisfy — frequently carped that Gillette lacked the marketing razzle-dazzle so fashionable at the time, the company had closed 1972 with a 19 percent sales increase and a boost of 20 percent in net income. Led by the highly successful Trac II razor, Gillette had regained considerable momentum. Now came Cranapple Ed Gelsthorpe, an "outsider" hailed in a glowing New York *Times* profile as "Gillette's Legendary Marketeer," to imply by his very presence that those who had helped to rally Gillette's considerable strength in the recent past were not really equal to major-league marketing standards. And much to the chagrin of those around him, this was a judgment that the self-assured and sometimes impulsive Gelsthorpe did not always leave to subtle implication.

All institutions develop their own distinctive personalities and styles — frequently based on cues provided by the top leadership — and Gillette was no exception. The chairman and chief executive officer, Vincent Ziegler, disliked discord in his management ranks, and during his years in office, harmony had become a keynote of the Gillette executive style. Open controversy was studiously avoided; disagreements between company officials were talked out and resolved in private. There was no executive dress code, but long usage and the chairman's precedent practically dictated a certain buttoned-up, suit-jacketed formality that had become almost second nature to Gillette veterans. They were, after all, in the grooming business, and it behooved them to set a good example, even among themselves. Asked once about his company's conservative image, Ziegler replied proudly: "If it's conservative to put every last ounce of effort into product development and quality assurance, then we're conservative. From every conceivable angle, to talk to as many consumers as you can reach, to test-market in the most effective ways known, to do everything possible to avoid a pitfall, we're conservative."

Gelsthorpe, given to rolled-up shirt sleeves and rakishly loosened ties, came from a somewhat different school — in California with Hunt-Wesson, he had commuted the four miles to his office on a decidedly undignified bicycle. His reputation was for quick-fire launching of new products in the hope that some would succeed, and if this was not exactly the traditional Gillette style, the new president made plain his belief that he knew more about marketing than nearly anyone at Gillette. To some, he came as a breath of fresh air, but there were others who saw him as a chill wind, whose withering comments were devastating and disruptive. To Gelsthorpe's mind, of course, he was merely dealing with an old guard that didn't want him to rock the boat.

In some ways aloof from the tension that was building in the Gillette ranks, Ziegler was by no means unaware of it. Nor was he unaware of the consequences that could follow from continued friction between company officials. Only a band of saints could fail to resent and react to such an increasingly uncomfortable situation, and sainthood is seldom sought — much less achieved — in the executive suite of any corporation.

As discreetly as he could under the circumstances, Ziegler began to inquire into the causes of the contention that had embroiled much of his company's upper echelon. With mounting concern, he learned that while Gelsthorpe's talents as a marketer were generally unquestioned, his skills at human relations sometimes left something to be desired. Too often, it seemed, Gelsthorpe made snappish remarks that humiliated executives in the presence of peers and underlings alike. Worse, perhaps, in a large and highly structured corporation, the president seldom communicated his specific aims in writing — and oral instructions are notoriously subject to forgetfulness and misinterpretation.

Ziegler informed Gelsthorpe of his findings and of his growing unease, hoping that the situation might still be salvaged. But it was soon apparent — to Ziegler, at least — that Gelsthorpe's position was growing untenable.

Subsequently, Ziegler would say of the Gillette-Gelsthorpe match that "it just hasn't worked out," a painful assessment he confided to Gelsthorpe himself shortly before he had to announce it in the public press. And then one day in late June, 1974, over lunch at the Algonquin Club in Boston, Gelsthorpe informed his chairman that he would be leaving the company to become a senior vice-president of United Brands Company. Less than two years later, when Eli Black, the chairman of United Brands, committed suicide by jumping from the Pan Am Building in New York, Gelsthorpe was caught quite innocently in the backwash and was passed over for promotion to chief executive officer. He then left United Brands to become president of H. P. Hood, Incorporated, a large, Boston-based dairy products concern.

Gelsthorpe's successor, chosen this time by internal selection, was forty-four-year-old Colman M. Mockler, Jr., Class of 1954 at the Harvard Graduate School of Business Administration and a onetime research associate at the school. Joining Gillette in 1957 when the Blue

Blade was still king, Mockler had started as an assistant to the controller, and in 1965 he was named treasurer of the corporation; in 1971, following the unexpected death of Malcolm Stewart, his immediate superior and vice-chairman of the board for administration and finance, Mockler was elevated to that key position.

He was hardly a hotshot marketing man, but with Gillette's sales nearly tripled since 1966, and with its business more and more influenced by external factors, such as foreign exchange rates, international politics, and materials supply, someone of Mockler's quiet competence and even temperament — he had remained steadfastly uninvolved in the management cliques that had formed during the rocky times of Gelsthorpe's presidency — seemed to be the proverbial right man in the right place at the right time.

And for all that, Mockler had displayed an unerring marketing insight at a critical time in Gillette's fortunes: while still a relatively junior staffer, he had helped produce some of the figures used to back the arguments in favor of an early Gillette stainless-steel blade to counter the Wilkinson entry, and had been among those urging such a course on top management. As one of the American executives dispatched to London for seasoning at Gillette Industries, he had even stepped out of his accustomed financial function to aid in the development of a marketing plan for the British version of the coated stainless blade. Had Gelsthorpe remained as president and chief operating officer, in fact, it is not unlikely that the broad-gauged Mockler would have been vaulted to the chairmanship upon Ziegler's retirement. As it happened, he now stood just that much closer to the very top.

"Substantial opportunity for sustained profitable growth"

Standing at a lectern beneath a sky-blue canopy masking the businesslike girders of a spacious storage area, Colman Mockler faced the Gillette stockholders gathered at the Andover plant in the spring of 1977 for the annual meeting. It was the second such session to be presided over by Mockler, who had succeeded the retiring Vincent Ziegler in the dual posts of chairman and president on the first day of 1976. By the end of that year, however, Mockler had relinquished some of his responsibilities to Stephen J. Griffin, who was named president and chief operating officer. Together, the two executives would be guiding their company into the 1980's.

At the very first annual meeting of the old Gillette Safety Razor Company in 1902, a handful of desperate shareholders had ratified the last-ditch financing scheme that saved a faltering company from looming ruin. They were presented with no sales figures, because there had been no sales; at that pioneering point, there was not even a product to sell. Now, after seventy-five years of sometimes fitful progress, the situation had changed considerably. Something like 850 Gillette products were being marketed in more than two hundred countries throughout the world, and Colman Mockler could inform the company's 47,883 stockholders of 1976 sales that had reached a record $1.5 billion, more than double the level of just five years before. It was true, of course, that a decade of explosive sales growth, fueled as it was by the addition of product lines generating nowhere near the return on razor blades, had failed to yield a corresponding rise in profit. (Razors and blades accounted for just 29 percent of Gillette's sales in 1976, but contributed a heavy 73 percent of corporate profits.) But even the company's severest critics, who maintained that there had been errors in the execution of the Gillette diversification program, could hardly claim that diversification itself had been a mistake. As *Forbes* magazine — seldom given to patting corporations on the head — had observed at the close of 1972, Gillette's program of rapid, wide-ranging expansion had saved the company "from being permanently locked into the narrow, static razor market — and freed it from the risks a one-product company always faces."

Gillette had faced a variety of risks and challenges in its long journey from one-room experimental enterprise to highly diversified international corporation, and the mid-1970's had been no exception. Continuing public concern over possible damage to the earth's protective ozone layer by the fluorocarbon propellant used in many aerosol products had depressed sales of the company's hair sprays, deodorants, and antiperspirants. The reclusive Frenchman Marcel L. Bich — coincidentally enough, a former suitor for the hand of Gillette's S. T. Dupont subsidiary — had stepped up the competitive pressure from his throwaway Bic ball-point pens and cigarette lighters, and had engaged

Gillette in its mainline business with a one-bladed, disposable razor. And in nearly all of Gillette's product areas, inflation and energy problems were taking their inexorable tolls.

Troubles of a different kind had surfaced in the fall of 1976, when Gillette, as scores of other large American corporations were doing, made public the results of an internal investigation into possible questionable payments made out of corporate funds. In Gillette's case, the tally came to $400,000 over a four-year period, all of the payments having been made in foreign countries. In disclosing the findings of its year-long probe, Gillette also announced the reaffirmation of a stiff policy against any illegal or questionable expenditures in the future, and the whole affair was more embarrassing than anything else.

As it had when faced with expiration of its original patent in 1921, as it had when harried by cut-rate, low-grade rivals in the 1930's and by Wilkinson's Super Sword-Edge blade in the 1960's, Gillette was responding to new problems, though it was still too early to judge with what long-term effect. Aerosol products were converted to pump sprays or charged with propellants other than fluorocarbon, and some deodorants were offered in stick or roll-on form. Early in 1977, the somewhat redundant toiletries and personal care divisions had been merged into a single, more efficient unit bolstered by old standby products like Right Guard deodorants and Foamy shave creams, and by such relative newcomers as the highly successful Earth Born shampoos.

If Bic had captured much of the market for throwaway ball-points (stick pens, they are called in the trade), hard and imaginative marketing had retained the Paper Mate division's lead in refillable models and in the porous point (Flair pens) field. The Cricket was gamely holding its own against the flicking Bic, though profits for both contenders were eroded by price-cutting and high advertising and promotion expenses. And Bic's disposable razor challenge had been strongly countered with Gillette's own Good News model, incorporating the same twin blades that had made the Trac II–G II razor a worldwide leader.

One of the top performers on the Gillette stage was the company's Braun subsidiary. The long-pending antitrust suit had at last been resolved, with Gillette agreeing to establish a separate subsidiary to market Braun-made electric shavers in the United States. Under terms of the settlement, Gillette was to divest itself of this unit, called Cambridge Shaver Imports, Incorporated, by early 1980. And certainly as important as the conclusion of a knotty legal problem, the careful reshaping of the German subsidiary had at last paid off, making Braun one of the leading profit-producers among Gillette divisions. Since 1974, nearly two hundred marginal items had been pruned from the unit's product line, and the American-led management had considerably streamlined the company's operations. The result: Braun in 1976 accounted for 21 percent of total Gillette sales, and 10 percent of its profits. New products, such as improved electric shavers, pocket electronic calculators, and hair-care appliances, all gave promise of a brighter future; even the German press, once critical of alleged "Americanization" at Braun, had changed its tune. The company had not only recuperated, said *Die Welt* in the spring of 1977, but was showing "a sound, lasting upward trend as well."

Division by division, subsidiary by subsidiary, the whole worldwide Gillette organization was striving for the same sort of showing. And as he stood beneath the canopy on annual meeting day Colman Mockler could speak with well-grounded conviction of "substantial opportunity for sustained profitable growth," as he laid out for stockholders his prescription for "balanced long-term growth in sales and profits." To build on the past decade's rapid expansion, he said, the company must continue its aggressive marketing, research, and development in order to maintain the market shares of such major products as razor blades, lighters, writing instruments, and toiletries.

At the same time, the chairman added, Gillette would go on with a program of selective diversification (with hard emphasis on selectivity), from both within and by acquisition. Recently, the appliance division had launched a line of home smoke detectors; in Italy, Gillette was marketing a children's game involving transferring characters onto a background scene by rubbing with a ball-point pen or pencil. Gillette was also looking for acquisitions with selling methods similar to Jafra Cosmetics in order to expand the home-party merchandising business. But both new and existing product lines, Mockler stressed, would be subject to rigorous cost controls, and to swift elimination if growth was slow or if they showed only limited potential for long-term profits. Already, in 1974, Gillette had dropped its profitless wig business, and a year later the company abandoned a prospective entry in the popular-price pocket-calculator field after a brief market test indicated that returns would not justify a costly national introduction. Similarly, in early 1977, a line of digital watches was aborted in the test market stage, and before the summer was out arrangements would be made to sell Buxton, whose leather-goods line had never measured up to expectations. From past experience, Gillette had learned the value of cutting its losses early in the game, and had come to terms with the fact that not all it touched would turn to gold.

Foremost among Mockler's carefully stated objectives for the future had been research and development, coupled with resolute marketing drives, to hold the Gillette lead in major products. And those who might have wondered what sorts of things he had in mind did not have to wonder for long: a high point of the shareholders meeting that year came with the unveiling of a new razor intended in time to supersede the best-selling Trac II as Gillette's premier shaving product. Designed so that its twin-bladed cartridge would pivot to adjust to the contours of a shaver's face, thus keeping the blades always at the best cutting angle, the razor had been shown in extensive consumer tests to provide significant advantages in comfort and closeness over other shaving instruments, including even the Trac II.

Like its predecessor in the twin-blade field, the new razor had been hatched at Gillette's Reading, England, research laboratories, then refined and readied for mass production at the main South Boston plant. The whole process had taken about five years, and as with Trac II, much time and thought had gone into the selection of a brand name. Among the possibilities considered were Face Hugger, Contour, and just plain Hugger, but in the end it was dubbed Atra. This was, of course, the name once given to the experimental Australian test razor that had been developed six years before into Trac II; now, by happy coincidence, Gillette had found that it could also be an acronym for automatic tracking razor action.

With its hefty aluminum handle, push-button loading system, and movable blade cartridge, the Atra razor was separated by many technical generations from the rudimentary razor and blade envisioned by King Camp Gillette late in the previous century. But a fundamental resemblance still remained, and if the trim plastic cartridge with its pair of durable platinum- and chemical-coated stainless-steel blade edges was far removed in time and sophistication from King Gillette's first handmade blade, the two also had much in common. As Gillette had written long ago in his original patent application, "My blades are made of uniform size and are detachably combined with the holders, so that a purchaser need buy but one holder and can then readily substitute a sharp blade for a dull one whenever necessary." There are, indeed, few things that are totally new under the sun.

By August, Atra would be launched nationally, backed in its first year on the market by a $7.7 million advertising campaign that would reach something like 90 percent of American shavers between the ages of eighteen and forty-nine. In due time, it would be introduced overseas as well, though it seemed likely that shavers in many parts of the world would continue to favor more traditional Gillette blades, some of them still packaged in wrappers imprinted with the founder's portrait and boldly scribed signature.

Once, these had been the lone trademarks of a struggling company whose only wares were razors and blades turned out laboriously in a small factory on the Boston waterfront. By later standards, the company's advertising was somewhat primitive at best, and Gillette salesmen called with considerable trepidation on dealers and distributors not wholly convinced that the disposable razor blade was an idea whose time was coming.

Now, the company that had grown from these meager beginnings had scores of trademarks, many identifying products undreamed of in those earliest days. Gillette factories and research facilities — among them some of the most sophisticated in all industry — dotted the globe, their output moving out to consumers through a smoothly running worldwide distribution network. And once launched, backed up as they were with powerful advertising and marketing support, Gillette's products were enviably equipped to succeed in the competitive marketplace.

The rise to such international eminence had not been easy, but if Gillette had sometimes stumbled along the way, the company still managed to learn from failure and build on its successes. Through the boom years of the 1920's and the dismal decade of the Depression, through the high-flying days of the "Cavalcade of Sports" and the sometimes-troubled 1960's, Gillette had always managed to keep strengthening its foundation. And as the new Atra razor joined the hundreds of other Gillette products that had sprung from that foundation, there could be little doubt that it was only the latest of many more to come.

More than eighty Augusts before, the enigmatic King C. Gillette had paced the sands of Nantasket Beach near his summer retreat at Kenberma, dreaming at the same time of razor blades and a colossal restructuring of human society. Mankind never listened to his social philosophy, but considering Gillette's dual nature, it might have given him no small measure of consolation to know that a company bearing his name and based firmly on his invention would still be flourishing in the closing decades of the twentieth century, its host of products used in nearly every nation of a world that he had hoped to lead to paradise.

Acknowledgments

IN THEIR VARIOUS WAYS, numerous people aided in the preparation of
this book. Foremost was Albert S. Leonard, retired public relations
manager of Gillette's safety-razor division, whose research, recollections, and comments were of invaluable assistance. He also conducted
useful interviews with G. Herbert Marcy, Raymond Reed, Paul R.
Burns, Milton Schenkein, John O'Connor, R. Neison Harris, Leonard
Zieve, Donald Nathanson, Del Torrens, and A. Craig Smith. Susan
Betz was an able researcher, and other past and present Gillette staffers
whose help is appreciated include Janice Marnell, Patricia Holland
Klarfeld, Gail Pomerantz, Elaine Regan, Dennis Donahue, Mandel
Slater, John J. Folan, Kenneth Gleason, Gloria Chun, Patricia Griffin,
Nancy Cox, and Dorothy Joyce, who was a tireless typist.

In Germany, France, and the United Kingdom, Bernard J. Rohner
was a gracious interpreter and guide, and among those giving valued
insights and information were Alistair R. M. Sedgwick, William C.
Smallman, Rodney S. Mills, John W. Runacres, George H. J. Robinson, Richard Cousens, John F. Garrett, Richard H. Burton, Peter
Tilbury, Michel Grinberg, Felix Mouton de Villaret, Georges Roca,

Robert Pinard, Maurice Mescam, Martin Gallusser, Michel Roux, Wlady Kapturkiewicz, Jean Malamoud, Maurice Guinot, Jean Fontaine, Lothar Wate, Ernst Stier, W. Bernhard, Olaf Ensrud, Werner Schmidt, Friedrich von Friedeburg, Dieter Hauenstein, H. Rohlf, Albrecht Schultz, Dr. Fritz Eichler, Dieter Rams, Alfred M. Zeien, and Dieter Schmitt. Their contributions may not always be specifically apparent, but they were appreciated nonetheless.

The Gillette Company's corporate secretary, Winifred E. Ellis, was gracious in providing access to materials kept in her care, and the late vice-chairman George O. Cutter gave generously of information and an irrepressible sense of humor and perspective.

The late George Gillette supplied photographs and family lore, as did Maurice J. Curran III. Olaf J. Nordland of Indio, California, former editor of the Indio *News*, provided valuable information about King Gillette's years in California.

Notes on Sources

Throughout, much use was made of personal interviews and unpublished company documents, including letters, miscellaneous reports, and the minutes of directors' and executive committee meetings. No studied effort was ever made to preserve papers from the company's earliest days, but many of them have survived. Unfortunately, the papers of King C. Gillette — they must surely have been voluminous — seem to have gone the way of the rest of his estate, though some of his business correspondence and personal letters to Frank J. Fahey and others are still in the company archives.

Chapters 1–5

One of the very few scholars to deal with King C. Gillette's utopian schemes is Kenneth M. Roemer, whose *Obsolete Necessity: American Utopian Writings, 1888–1900* (Kent State University Press, 1976) contains a chapter on Gillette the social philosopher. Roemer has also written a detailed introduction to a reprint of Gillette's first book, *The Human Drift* (Scholars' Facsimiles & Reprints, Inc., Delmar, N.Y., 1976). James Gilbert, in *Designing the Industrial State* (Quadrangle Books, 1972), devotes a chapter to Gillette's social theories and his relationship with Upton Sinclair.

The invention and early development of the Gillette safety razor and disposable blade are amply documented in memoirs prepared by King Gillette and William Nickerson for the company's house organ, the *Blade*. Relying largely on this material, George B. Baldwin of the Massachusetts Institute of Technology produced an excellent monograph, "The Invention of the Modern Safety Razor: A Case Study of Industrial Innovation," published in *Explorations in Entrepreneurial History*, December, 1951. Composed some two decades after the events they describe, the Gillette-Nickerson accounts frequently seem somewhat fanciful and self-serving. In court testimony and affidavits filed in connection with patent suits early in the century, details are often quite different from those published in the *Blade*. In instances of clear contradiction, precedence is given to sworn statements and other contemporary documents.

During the 1920's, the *Blade* chronicled the growth of the self-shaving habit, and is a treasure trove of anecdotes about the people and events figuring in Gillette's growth during that decade.

Chapter 6

Anticipating a possible legal problem, the production engineer Theodore L. Smith kept meticulous records of the development of the new razor and blade of 1929. Later, when preparing to defend themselves against Henry Gaisman's infringement suit, Gillette's top officials prepared detailed summaries of their contacts with Gaisman and their activities in connection with the new blade's introduction.

As one of Boston's greatest financial scandals, the 1931 suit against Gillette's directors was covered lavishly in the press. The most cogent and complete accounts appear in the Boston *News Bureau*, a respected business paper of the day, and in the October, 1931, issue of *Fortune*.

Chapter 7

Gerard Lambert's breezy autobiography, *All Out of Step* (Double-day, 1956), describes his experiences at Gillette as well as his personal background. The decline of King C. Gillette's estate was outlined by James E. Kelby in his 1938 letter requesting that the company pay a pension to its founder's widow.

Chapter 8

Detailed stories on the rebirth of Gillette under Joseph Spang's presidency appear in the June, 1952, issue of *Fortune,* and in *Forbes,* November 15, 1952. The Neison Harris–Toni saga followed an almost instant path into American folklore, and is chronicled in *Life,* April 4, 1949. Gillette's long involvement with sports broadcasting is the subject of an article by Albert S. Leonard in *Advertising Age,* October 22, 1973.

Chapter 9

Joseph Spang's description of his postwar European trip appears in the August, 1946, issue of *Industry* magazine, the official publication of the Associated Industries of Massachusetts. *Fortune,* in February, 1966, published a lengthy article, "The Frawley Phenomenon," in which Patrick Frawley's work with Paper Mate and Eversharp-Schick is discussed, as well as his recovery from alcoholism. A profile of Carl Gilbert appeared in the October, 1956, issue of *Fortune.* Gillette's advertising and marketing posture in the 1950's is covered in *Forbes,* January 15, 1957, and in the October, 1959, issue of *Television* magazine.

As a technical and marketing coup of the first order, the Super Blue Blade was widely examined in the business press, most notably by *Printers' Ink*, December 4, 1959, and *Business Week*, May 14, 1960.

The introduction of stainless-steel razor blades was one of the major business stories of the 1960's, and was reported in both the trade and general press. The following are among the best accounts: *Newsweek*, November 12, 1962; *Wall Street Journal*, November 19 and December 26, 1962; *Time*, November 23, 1962; New York *Times*, December 2, 1962; *Business Week*, December 22, 1962; *Barrons's*, January 28 and September 2, 1963; *Newsweek*, February 18, 1963; *Drug Trade News*, June 24, 1963; *Fortune*, July, 1963 (in an article aptly titled "Gillette Faces the Stainless-Steel Dragon"); New York *Times*, August 27, 1963; *Advertising Age*, September 2, 1963; *Financial Times* (London), September 5, 1963; *New York Times Magazine*, October 6, 1963; *Printers' Ink*, December 20, 1963. Denys Randolph, chairman of Wilkinson Sword, Limited, described the technical development of his company's stainless blade to the Royal Society of Arts in January, 1974, and his presentation is printed in the society's *Journal* for May of the same year.

Chapter 10

Gillette's diversification following the stainless-steel challenge is described in *Business Week*, April 1, 1967, in *Dun's Review*, April, 1967, and in *Forbes*, March 1, 1968, and December 1, 1972. Heated competition in the razor-blade business is analyzed in the *Wall Street Journal*, September 26, 1969. The story of the development of the Trac II is told in *Newsweek*, October 11, 1971, and, in considerably more detail, in a series of memoranda composed by Gillette researchers who worked on the project. William G. Salatich described some of the Trac II marketing problems in a 1971 speech to a group of Boston University graduate students in business administration.

The recasting of Gillette's foreign operations is scrutinized in *Fortune*, November, 1974. Edward Gelsthorpe's arrival at Gillette is discussed in *Business Week*, May 5, 1973, and in the New York *Times*, May 6, 1973. Robert P. Giovacchini's role as Gillette's "consumer advocate" is examined in the *Wall Street Journal*, November 5, 1973, and December 12, 1975.

As Gillette moved toward the late 1970's, a number of publications sought to assess the company's performance and prospects. Among them: the Boston *Sunday Globe*, December 5, 1976; *Forbes*, December 15, 1976; *Business Week*, January 31, February 28, and April 18, 1977; and the *Wall Street Journal*, June 28, 1977.

Index

Abbreviations: KCG = King Camp Gillette   GSR = Gillette Safety Razor Company
GCo = The Gillette Company (the parent company after 1952)

Adams, Cedric, 236
Adams, Charles Francis, 165
Adorn aerosol hair spray, 231, 254
advertising: of first GSR razor and blade, 44, 45; as key to rapid sales growth, 55, 109; early strategy, 56; allocation of funds for, 56, 190-191; use of testimonials, 79, 168-169, 178, 187, 217-218, 236; in 1905, 81-82; KCG's views on, 85-86; of products for feminine market, 92, 109, 211-212; directed to the military market in WWI, 101-104; in 1920, 105; of the New Improved razor (1921), 106; in 1930, 155; International Series of ads, 168-169; use of "social consciousness" ads, 169-170, 177-178; public confession ad, 171-173; use of test towns, 172-173; scare campaigns, 175-176; cartoon ads, 178, 216-217; use of radio for, 186-188; use of musical slogans and theme songs, 187, 201, 216; use of prizes in, 187; use of contests, 188, 193, 199; use of taglines, 192, 199; and sponsorship of sports events (*see* baseball; boxing; football; horse racing; "Gillette Cavalcade of Sports"); during WWII, 199-200; early use of television, 200-201, 213; costs of, 212, 225; of Toni products, 212, 254; use of TV commercials, 213, 217-218, 248; of Super Blue Blade, 235-237; of toiletry products, 248, 251-252, 253; and sponsorship of Miss America pageant, 254; for Trac II razor, 270. *See also* Batten, Barton, Durstine & Osborn; marketing; Maxon, Inc.; sales

aerosol products, and fluorocarbon propellant, 285
Aerosol Techniques, Inc., 250
after-shave lotion. *See* Sun Up
Aldred, John E., 180; and purchase of GSR, 94; as chairman of GSR board, 140, 142, 148, 153, 157, 167; and overstatement of GSR revenues and profits, 159, 160-161, 164; retirement, 192
Aldred & Co., 139, 148, 191; takes over GSR (1917), 94; as fiscal agent for GSR, 153, 157, 167
Allen, Mel, 218
American Saddle Co., 68-69
American Safety Razor Co., 79; founded